— THE SECRET LIVES OF —
Dragons
— AND OTHER —
Mythical
Creatures
AND HOW TO DRAW THEM

MICHAEL DOBRZYCKI
KYTHERA OF ANEVERN
JACOB GLASER
BRYNN METHENEY

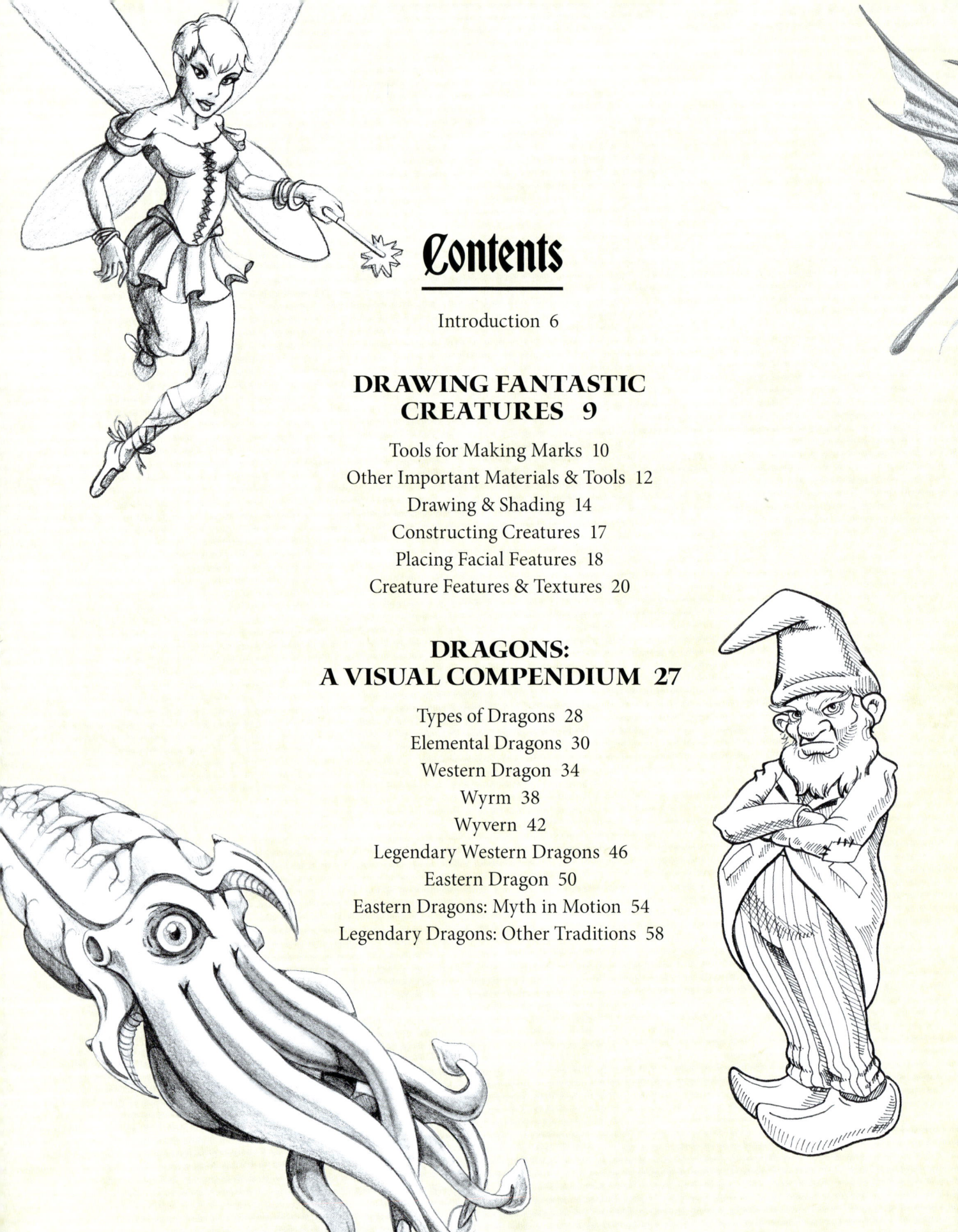

Contents

— THE SECRET LIVES OF —

Dragons

— AND OTHER —

Mythical Creatures

AND HOW TO DRAW THEM

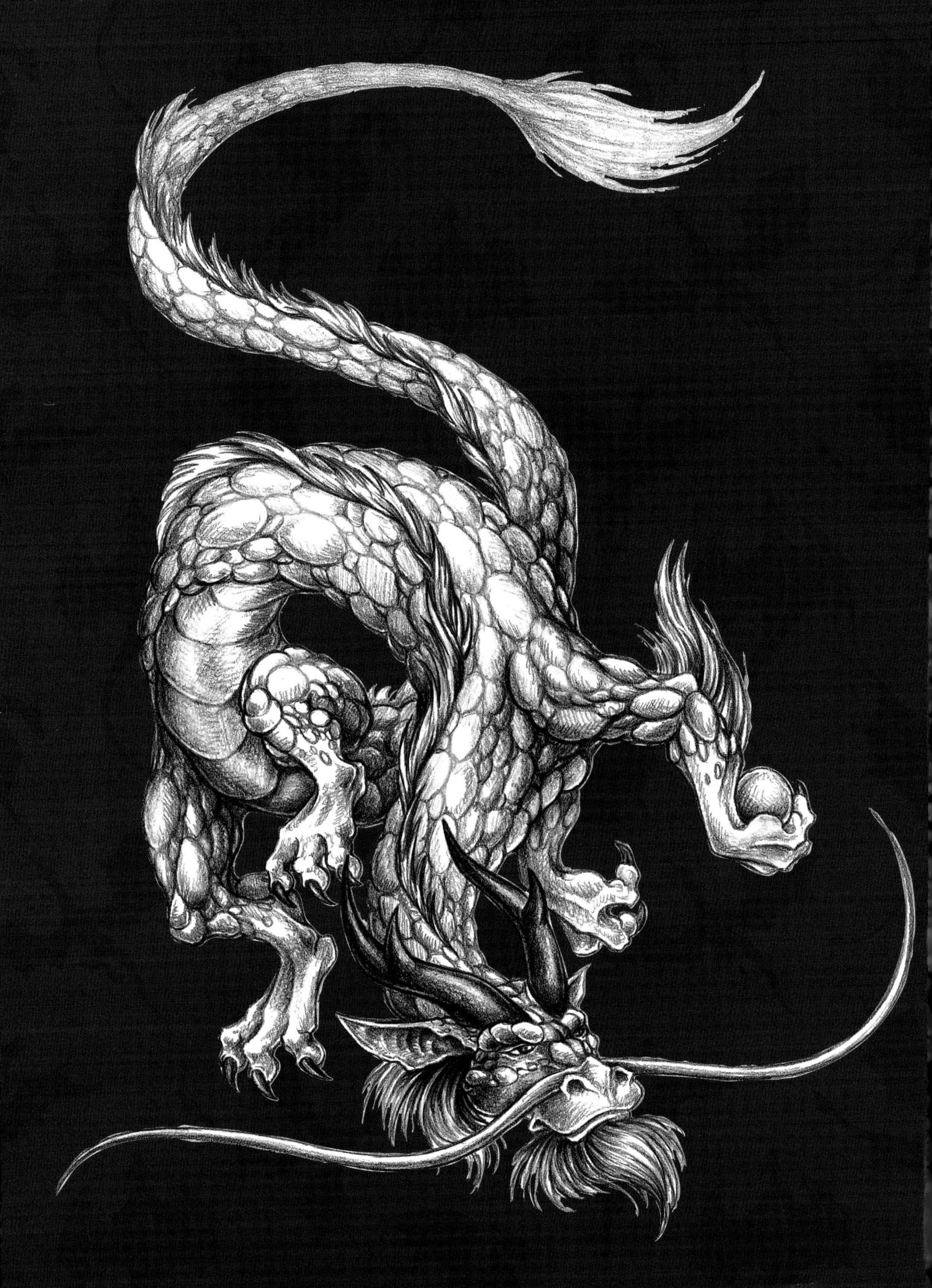

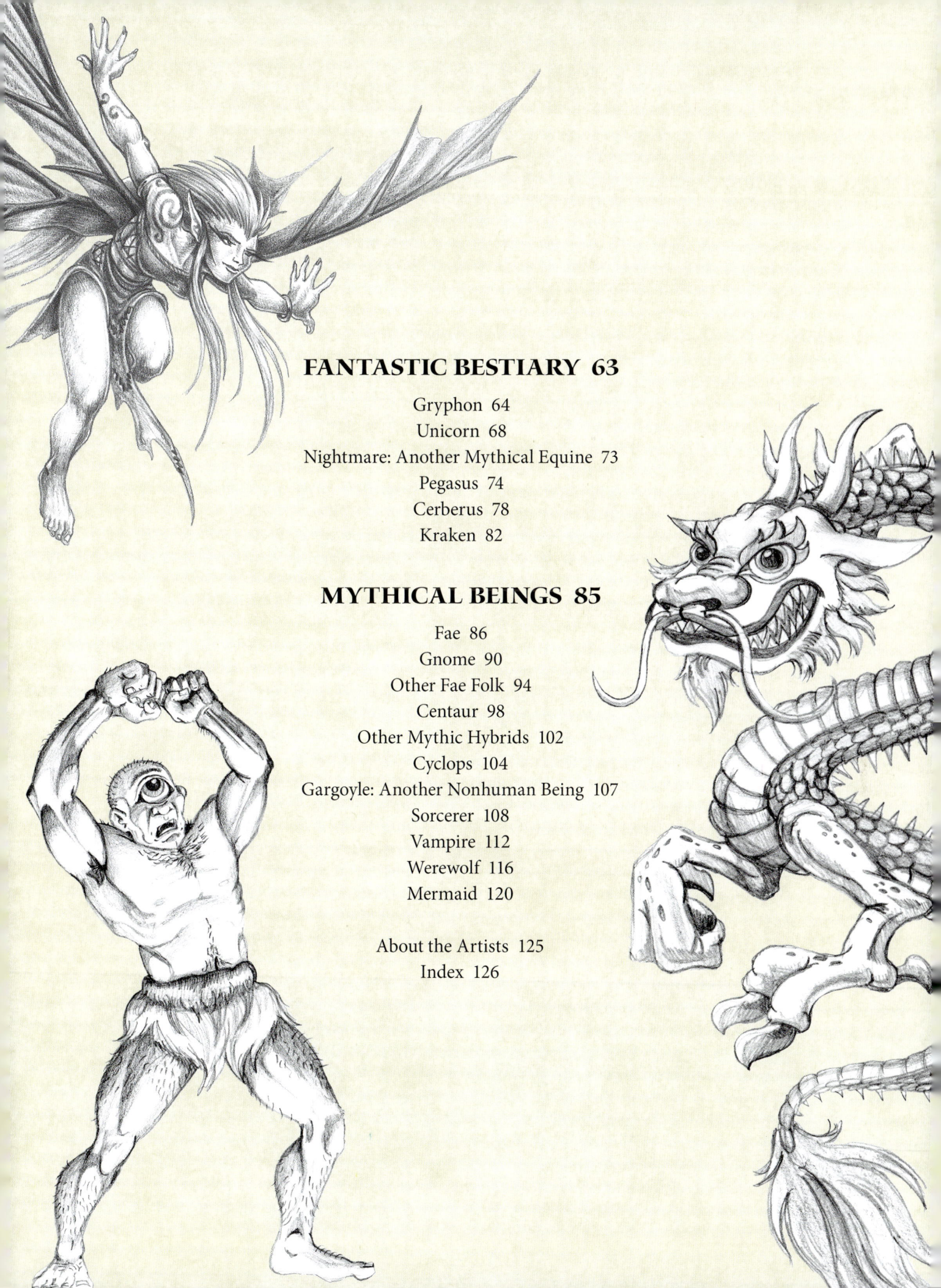

FANTASTIC BESTIARY 63

MYTHICAL BEINGS 85

Introduction

Across every culture and every age, humans have imagined creatures that soar, coil, stalk, shimmer, and shape-shift through the shadowy corners of our collective storytelling. Dragons twist through storm clouds, gryphons patrol ancient skies, mermaids drift between tides, and trickster fae lurk in moonlit paths. These beings are more than myths—they're mirrors, reflecting our fears, hopes, and the wildest edges of our imagination.

The Secret Lives of Dragons and Other Mythical Creatures invites you into that world—not as a passive observer, but as an artist-adventurer. Here, you'll uncover the origins, legends, and symbolic meanings behind dozens of fantastical beasts while learning exactly how to draw them with confidence. Each chapter blends mythology with practical instruction: step-by-step lessons show you how to build creatures from simple shapes; refine anatomy, texture, and expression; and bring movement, personality, and atmosphere to your drawings.

You'll explore the major dragon lineages—Western, Eastern, wyrm, wyvern, and elemental dragons—before venturing into a fully stocked bestiary of gryphons, unicorns, kraken, gnomes, centaurs, vampires, and more. You'll also learn how artists throughout history have interpreted these beings, and how contemporary illustrators use mark-making, shading, construction lines, and perspective to breathe life into creatures that have never walked our world . . . at least, not literally.

Whether you're new to drawing or already deep in creature design, this book gives you the tools, techniques, and imaginative spark you need to create convincing, charismatic fantasy beings. Sharpen your pencils—your menagerie awaits.

—The Walter Foster Creative Team

Mythic Lineage Map

This lineage map shows how the creatures in this book are grouped by type and tradition.

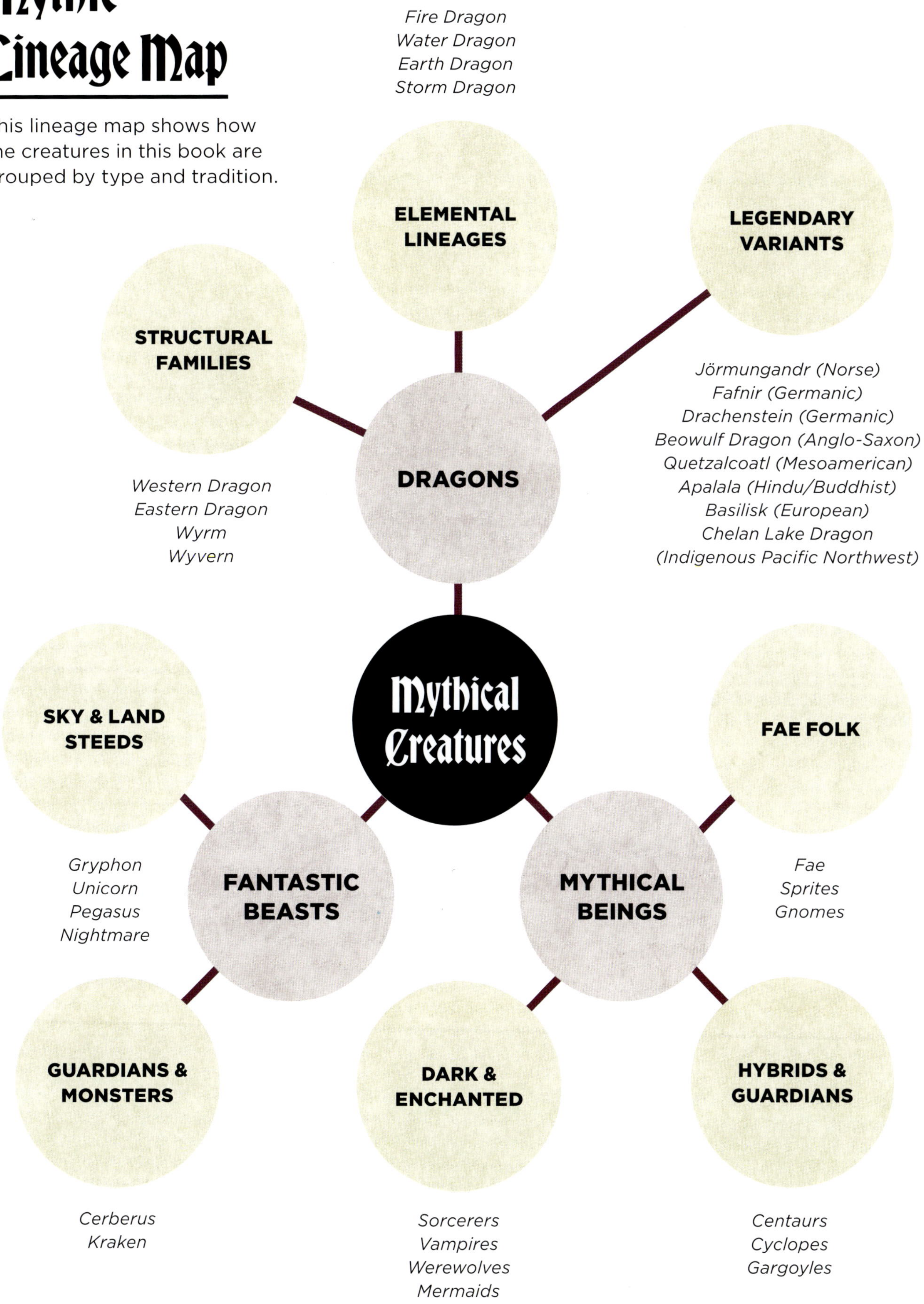

DRAGONS

ELEMENTAL LINEAGES

Fire Dragon
Water Dragon
Earth Dragon
Storm Dragon

LEGENDARY VARIANTS

Jörmungandr (Norse)
Fafnir (Germanic)
Drachenstein (Germanic)
Beowulf Dragon (Anglo-Saxon)
Quetzalcoatl (Mesoamerican)
Apalala (Hindu/Buddhist)
Basilisk (European)
Chelan Lake Dragon
(Indigenous Pacific Northwest)

STRUCTURAL FAMILIES

Western Dragon
Eastern Dragon
Wyrm
Wyvern

Mythical Creatures

FANTASTIC BEASTS

SKY & LAND STEEDS

Gryphon
Unicorn
Pegasus
Nightmare

GUARDIANS & MONSTERS

Cerberus
Kraken

MYTHICAL BEINGS

FAE FOLK

Fae
Sprites
Gnomes

DARK & ENCHANTED

Sorcerers
Vampires
Werewolves
Mermaids

HYBRIDS & GUARDIANS

Centaurs
Cyclopes
Gargoyles

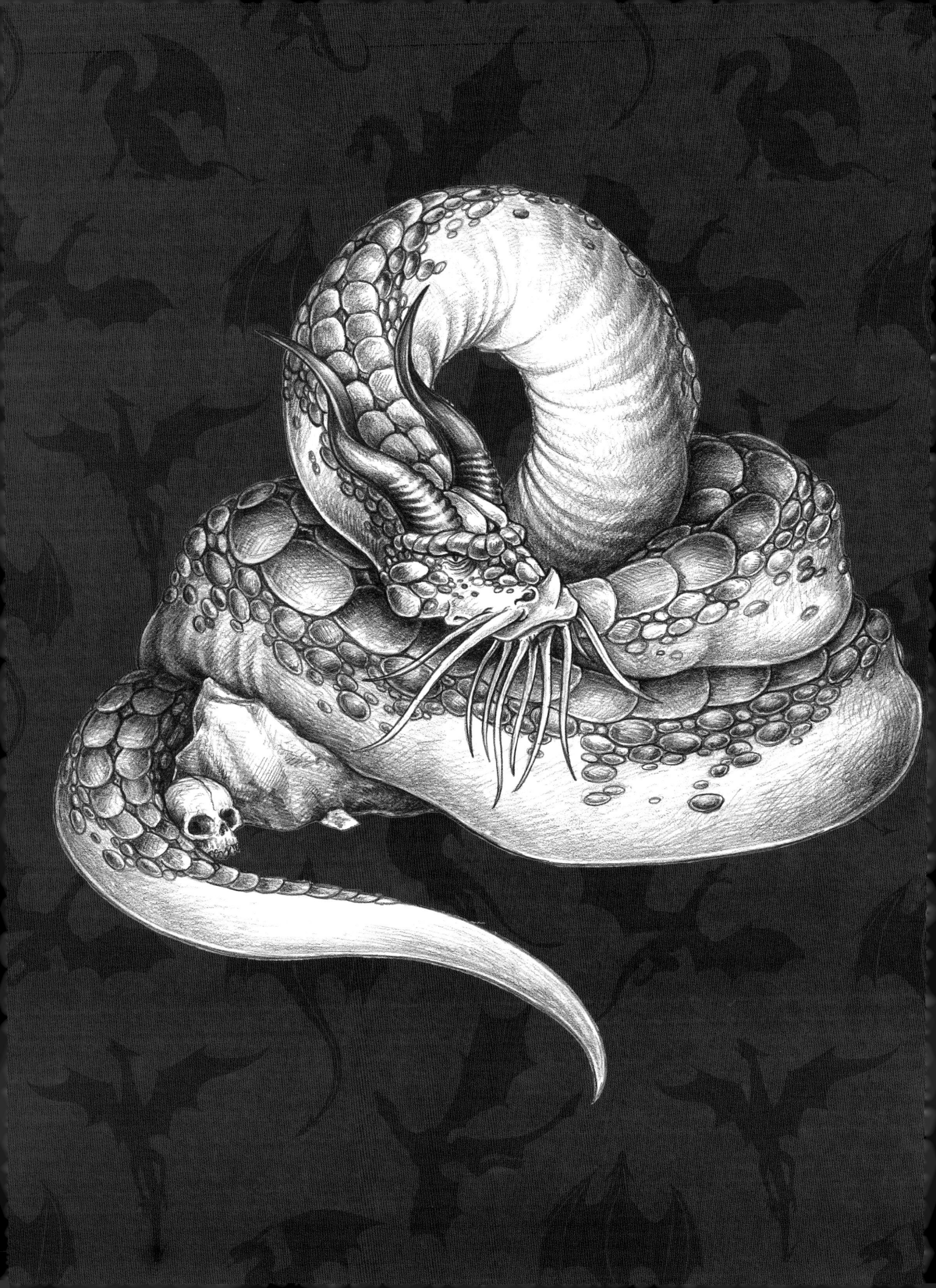

Drawing Fantastic Creatures

Tools for Making Marks

DRAWING PENCILS

Drawing pencils are classified by the hardness of the lead (graphite), indicated by a letter. The soft leads (labeled B for "black") make dense, black marks, and the hard leads (labeled H for "hard") produce very fine, light gray lines. An HB pencil is somewhere between soft and hard, making it an excellent tool for beginners. A number accompanies the letter to indicate the intensity of the lead—the higher the number, the harder or blacker the pencil. To start, purchase a minimum of three pencils: 2B, HB, and H. Any of the leads can be sharpened into points, but you'll get a different quality of line depending on the hardness of the lead and the texture of your paper. Make some practice strokes with various tips and leads to see the differences among them. Aside from graphite pencil, you also can use a charcoal pencil for very dark black marks or a colored pencil for softer black marks.

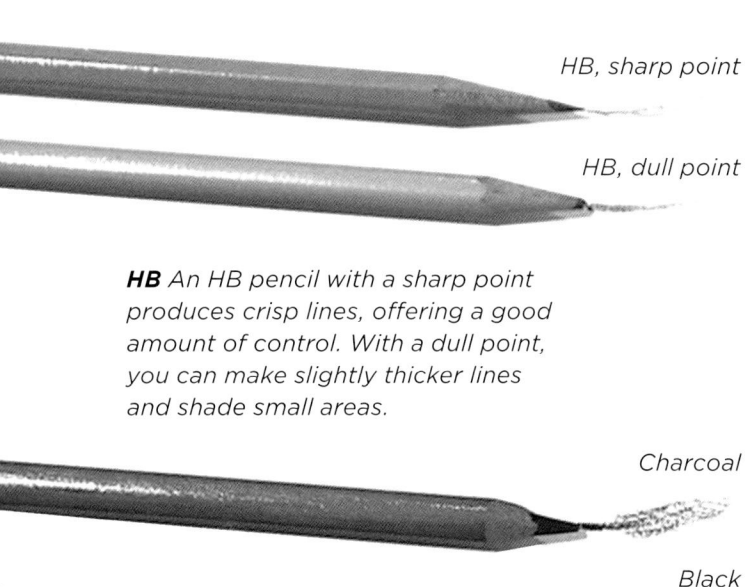

HB, sharp point

HB, dull point

HB *An HB pencil with a sharp point produces crisp lines, offering a good amount of control. With a dull point, you can make slightly thicker lines and shade small areas.*

Charcoal

Black colored pencil

Charcoal and Black Colored Pencil *Charcoal is very soft, so it smudges easily and makes a dark mark. A black colored pencil has a waxy binder that resists smudging, to a degree—as a result, colored pencil is rather difficult to erase.*

Artist's Erasers

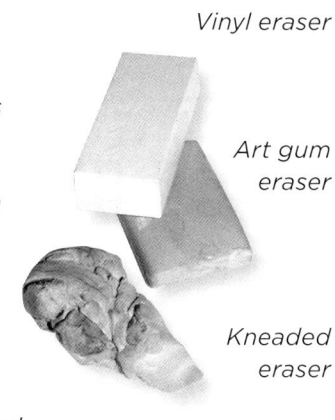

Vinyl eraser

Art gum eraser

Kneaded eraser

Different erasers serve different functions; you'll want a few different kinds on hand. You can form a kneaded eraser into small points to remove marks in tight areas. A vinyl eraser removes pencil marks thoroughly. An art gum eraser crumbles easily, so it is less likely to mar the paper's surface—use this when doing a lot of erasing!

INK PENS

To define pencil lines with ink but with more control, use waterproof ink pens. These pens are available in a variety of tip sizes, each with its own function. If you're looking for lighter, thinner lines, you even can use a regular ballpoint writing pen!

Waterproof Ink Pens

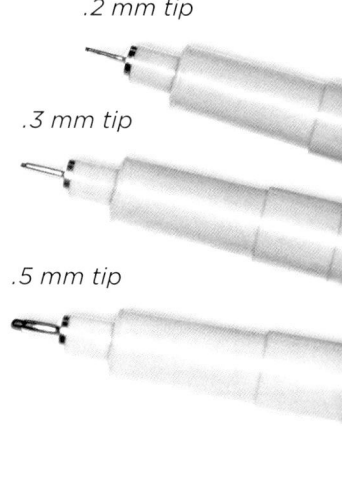

.2 mm tip

.3 mm tip

.5 mm tip

The thicker tips of waterproof ink pens (such as the .5 mm) are great for creating heavy lines, whereas the finer points (such as the .2 mm tip) are best for detail lines and small areas. Medium tips (such as .3 mm) offer more versatility, as you can use the side of the pen for thicker lines and the point of the pen for thinner ones.

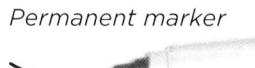

Permanent marker

Permanent Marker *The line produced by a permanent marker is bold, thick, and very easy to control. The ink of many "permanent" markers will fade over time, so you may want to spray your drawing with fixative.*

WORKING WITH LIQUID MEDIUMS

To add dynamism to artwork, you can incorporate **India ink**, which is available in bottles. For dark, permanent lines, apply pure (undiluted) India ink with a paintbrush. You can also dilute the ink with water to apply a thin, light gray tone (called a "wash"). These washes also help add depth to a drawing.

You can achieve the same wash effect (see "Ink" above) using **watercolor paint**. Watercolor paint comes in tubes or cakes; a tube is shown to the right.

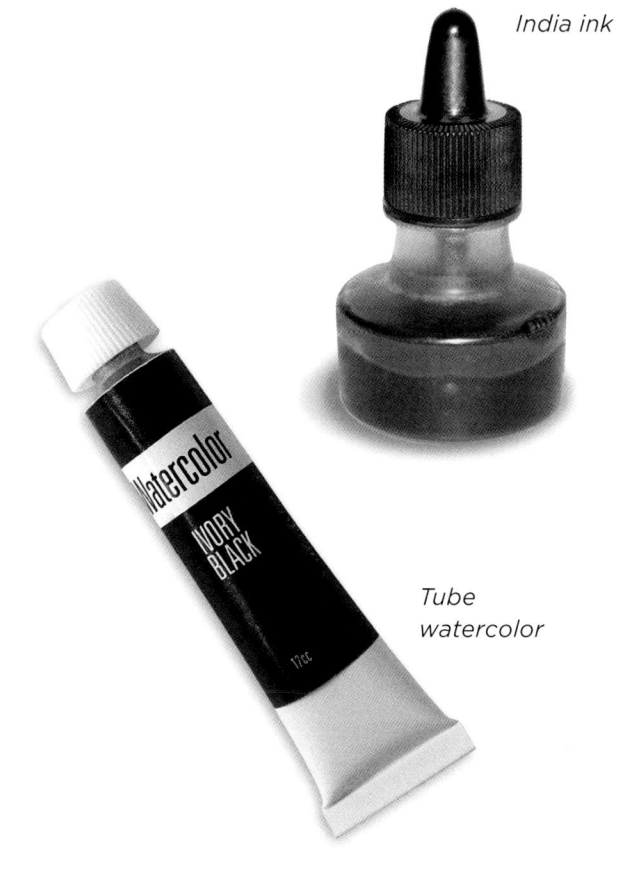

India ink

Tube watercolor

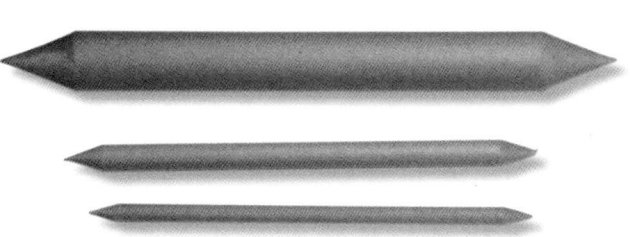

Blending Stumps *These are sticks of highly compressed paper pulp are used to help blend graphite on the page. Never use just your finger to blend, as the natural oils in your skin can damage the paper.*

Color Blender
A color blender is a soft, rubber-tipped tool that is designed to manipulate paint on canvas. In pencil drawing, it comes in handy for making deliberate, controlled smudges.

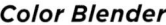

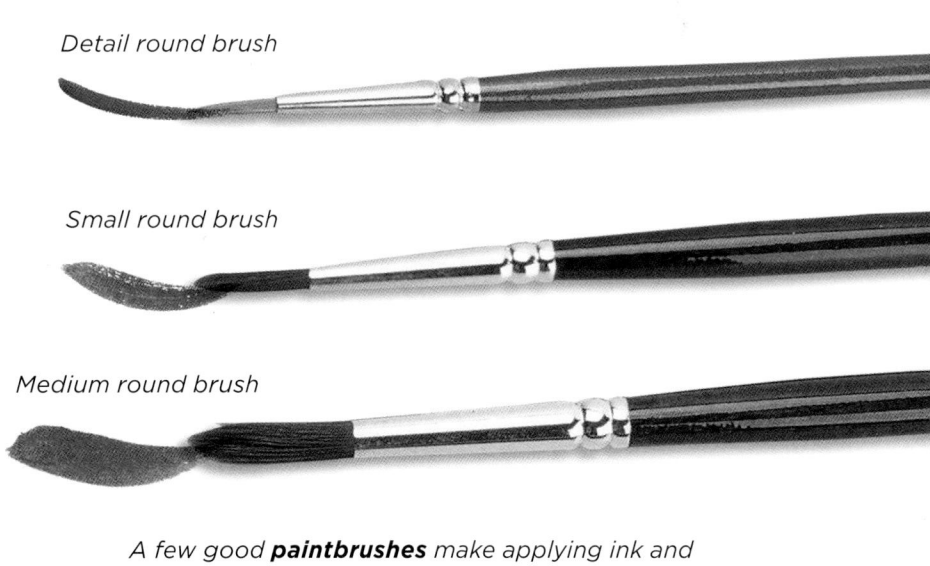

Detail round brush

Small round brush

Medium round brush

*A few good **paintbrushes** make applying ink and paint more enjoyable. Round brushes like these taper to a natural tip—purchase them in a variety of sizes, from very small for adding details to medium for filling in larger areas.*

Other Important Materials & Tools

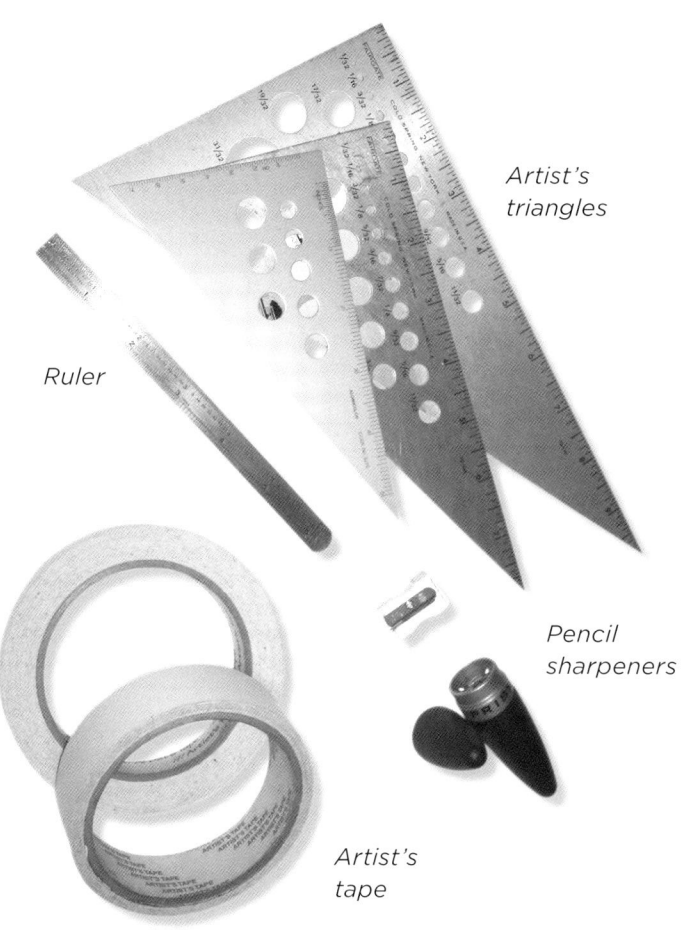

Artist's triangles

Ruler

Pencil sharpeners

Artist's tape

RELATED DRAWINGS TOOLS

Drawing isn't just about pencils, ink, and erasers. Use **artist's triangles** for measuring and drawing borders. Keep a small **ruler** on hand for drawing straight lines in smaller areas.

Pencil sharpeners are essential if you are using wood-cased or woodless pencils. You can purchase special sharpeners for mechanical leads. A traditional handheld sharpener is shown, along with a sharpener that has a reservoir to catch pencil shavings. Some sharpeners also have a cap that keeps smaller pencil shavings and graphite dust from escaping and making a mess.

You might also find it helpful to keep **artist's tape** on hand for securing your drawings to a surface or creating clean borders and edges. Artist's tape is easy to peel off and won't leave a sticky residue when you remove it like masking tape does.

SHARPENING YOUR DRAWING IMPLEMENTS

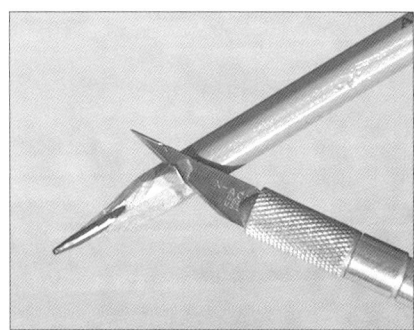

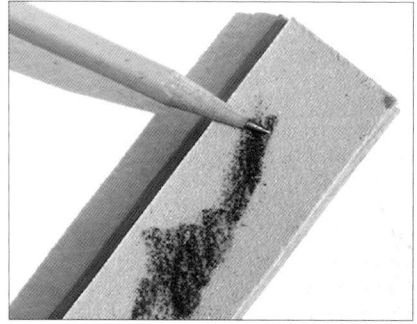

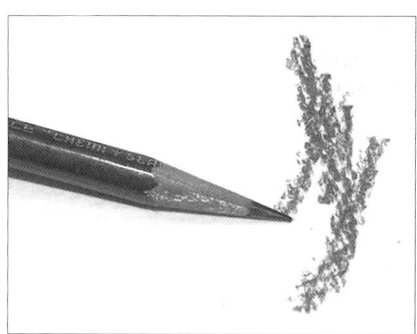

Utility Knife This tool can form more different points (chiseled, blunt, or flat) than an ordinary pencil sharpener can. Hold the knife at a slight angle to the pencil shaft; always sharpen away from you, taking off only a little wood and graphite at a time.

Sandpaper Block Sandpaper will quickly hone the lead into any shape you wish. It also will sand down some of the wood. The finer the grit of the paper, the more controllable the resulting point. Roll the pencil in your fingers when sharpening to keep the shape even.

Rough Paper The tooth of the paper is wonderful for smoothing a pencil point after it has been tapered with sandpaper. It also is a great way to create a very fine point for small details. Be sure to gently roll the pencil while honing it to sharpen the lead evenly.

PAPER

Drawing paper comes in different sizes and textures. Some textures are better suited to certain materials than others: When working in graphite, a paper that has some texture (tooth) is preferable, because the graphite adheres better; when working with pen and ink, smoother paper is usually better. Experiment with different kinds of paper to see how your drawing materials react. Just make sure your paper is acid free, as this paper will last for a long time and won't yellow with age.

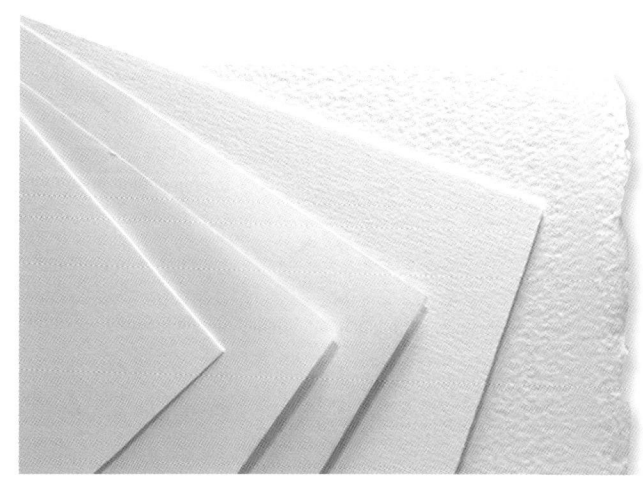

Paper

LIGHT TABLE

A light table (also called a "light box") is a great tool for transferring a messy sketch to good paper. Tape your sketch to the surface of the light table, cover the sketch with a clean sheet of drawing paper, and flip the switch—the fluorescent bulb illuminates your drawing and will help you accurately trace the lines of the sketch onto a nice sheet of drawing paper. You can get the same effect by taping your sketch and drawing paper to a bright window, but this will only work during the day.

Light table

WORK AREA

If you don't have the luxury of a large workspace, you can try a **small, adjustable tabletop easel**. The easel shown is about the size of a briefcase and has a carrying handle and wood brackets for holding paper in place. It also has a drawer incorporated into the base, which is great for storing tools.

You can also consider a **drawing board**, which can be used as a drawing surface for an easel. Any smooth, hard, flat surface can be used as a drawing board, but the one shown fits nicely on the easel and accommodates a smaller size of paper.

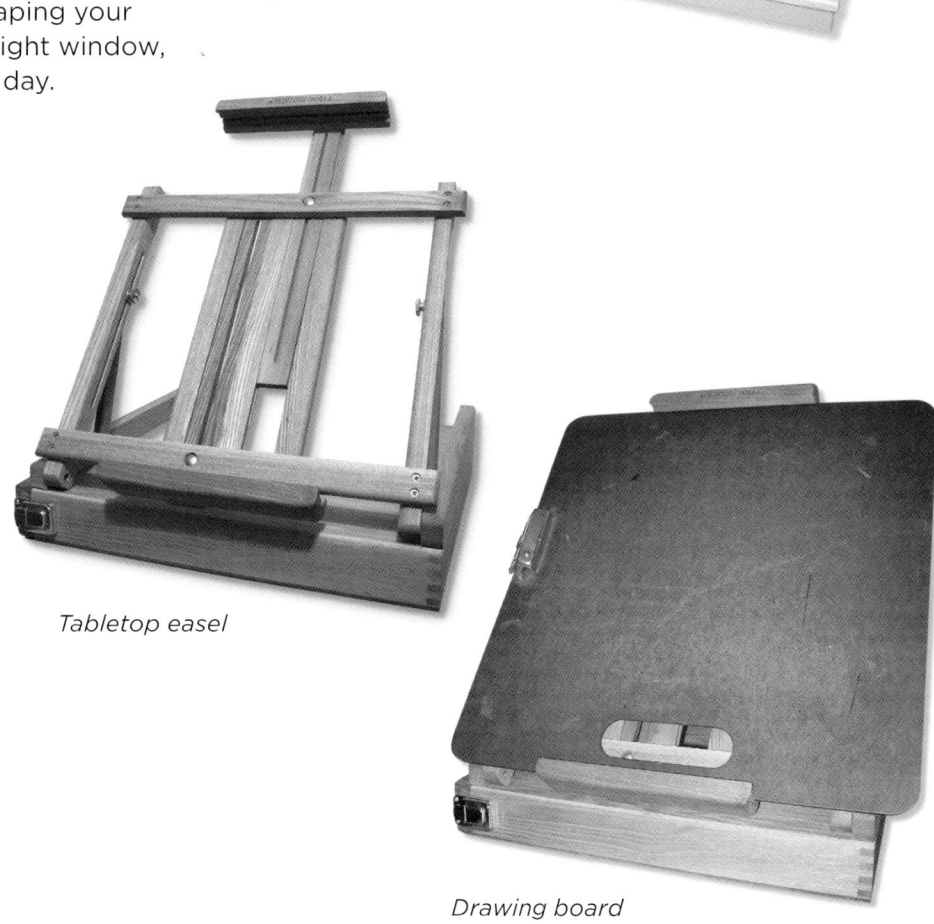

Tabletop easel

Drawing board

Drawing & Shading

To make something look convincing and three-dimensional on two-dimensional paper, you need to give the object form by adding highlights and shadows. If you aren't familiar with shading methods, here are some techniques to get you started. It's a good idea to practice some of these techniques to get the hang of them before you apply them to a drawing. Don't be afraid to experiment and be adventurous, though; these are just a few ideas to get you started. You might want to line up some household items (such as fruit, bowls, and bottles) on a tabletop and try to sketch them as they are. This is good practice for helping you learn how highlights and shadows fall on items of different shapes and sizes.

Hatching *This technique involves placing several lines parallel to one another. Lighter, widely spaced lines create lighter areas; darker, more dense lines create dark areas. While the lines in this example don't form identifiable rows, you can achieve a smoother look by mixing where each line starts and stops.*

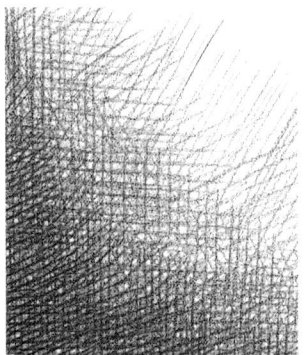

Crosshatching *The addition of another layer of hatching, placed at an angle, is called "crosshatching." As with hatching, lighter, widely spaced lines create light areas, whereas denser areas create darks. An advantage of crosshatching is that the direction of your lines can be used to define the shape of an object.*

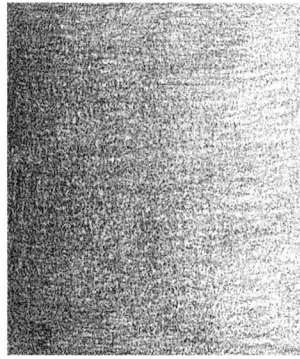

Gradating *This technique creates smooth, graduated values (from dark to light). Start with a soft pencil to lay down darker layers; then use harder pencils and less pressure for progressively lighter tones. Going back over the edges of your dark areas with a slightly harder pencil can help blend the shadows into the lighter areas.*

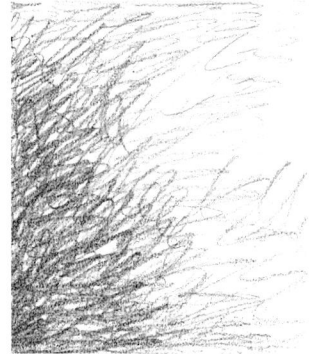

Scribbling *This is a fast, effective way to shade when sketching, and can also work effectively in finished drawings. Loose, light scribbles create lighter areas, whereas thicker, darker lines define darker areas. Switch between hard and soft pencils to keep your lights and darks distinct.*

Blending with a Stump *The bottom half of this gradated example has been blended using a blending stump. By rubbing the blending stump over the shaded areas, you can smooth the shading and create various looks.*

Blending with a Chamois *The bottom half of this example has been blended using a small piece of chamois leather, which is very soft. Chamois come in handy for blending large areas, such as expansive skies, or other elements that are built up with other marks and eraser techniques.*

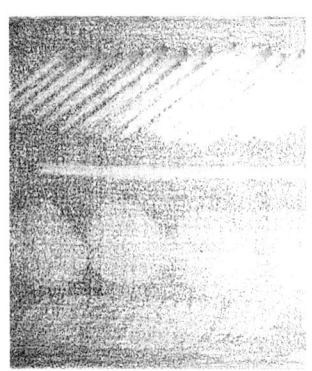

Erasing *Use a stick eraser to draw hatchmarks (shown at top), and a kneaded eraser to lift out blotches of graphite (bottom). Try using erasers to bring out details in shaded areas or to draw lighter shapes into dark areas. Just be mindful as to how much graphite the eraser can lift.*

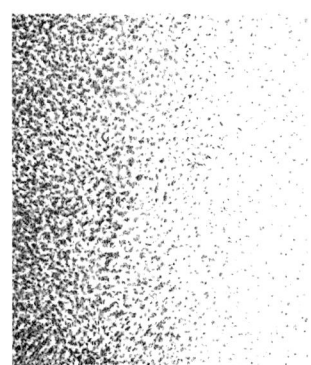

Stippling *This technique of using small dots to define shape and shadows can be very time-consuming. It is best done with softer pencils that aren't quite sharpened to a point, and without using a great deal of pressure. A point that is too sharp or applied with too much pressure can leave pockmarks in your paper.*

SHADING EXERCISE

Shading a sphere is a simple yet useful exercise for developing shading skills and techniques, and for locating the different types of highlights and shadows on an object. Variations of this exercise can be used to shade just about anything, allowing you to give your drawings form and volume. This example uses a combination of gradating and hatching with lines that follow the curve of the sphere to achieve a smooth texture that also shows the shape of the object.

First shade the sphere with a very light tone, leaving the white of the paper at a spot near the top of the sphere (though not quite at the edge). This white spot is the *highlight*—the area where the light shines brightest on the object. Next build up layers of darker tones as you reach the bottom of the sphere. Even though you are building up the shading in layers, it is important to try to blend each layer smoothly into the previous layer. Eventually, the darkest shadows should be in a thin band around the base of the object, leaving a range of *midtones* (middle values) between the highlight and the

darkest area, which is the *core shadow*. Note that the core shadow does not extend all the way to the base of the object. Rather, there is a lighter band just below the core shadow—this is the *reflected light*. Even if a surface is not shiny, it will still reflect a small amount of light back onto the object resting on it. Below the sphere is the *cast shadow*—this is the shadow cast by the object itself. Notice that the cast shadow is not a solid tone; rather, it gets lighter as it moves away from the object.

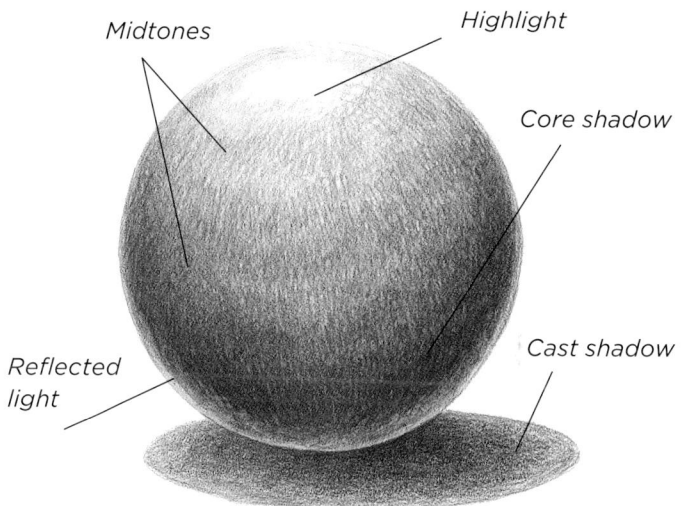

Midtones *Highlight* *Core shadow* *Reflected light* *Cast shadow*

USING ATMOSPHERIC PERSPECTIVE

Once you have mastered the basics of shading, there are other techniques you can use to make objects look closer or farther away. Notice that in this example, the tail of the dragon on the left gets lighter as it extends from its body (just like the cast shadow in the sphere example above). This is called "atmospheric perspective"—the tendency of objects that are farther away to become lighter as they recede into the distance. This is easily observed if you live in an area with mountains—the farther away the mountains are, the lighter they get, until they almost blend into the sky. Note that this rule applies only to daytime drawings. If your drawing is a nighttime scene, the opposite is true—objects that are farther away are darker, and objects that are closer are lighter and more clearly defined. Diminishing levels of detail also help show distance. Notice that the tail and the spikes of the dragon on the right get smaller and less distinct as they get farther away. You can still tell that the spikes extend all the way down the dragon's tail, but they become less and less defined, showing the distance and making the drawing more convincing.

UNDERSTANDING VALUE

Shading gives depth and form to your drawing because it creates contrasts in value (the relative lightness or darkness of black or a color). In pencil drawing, values range from black (the darkest value) through different shades of gray to white (the lightest value).

To make a two-dimensional object appear three-dimensional, you must pay attention to the values of the highlights and shadows (see page 15). When shading a subject, you must always consider the light source, as this is what determines where your highlights and shadows will be. Before you start drawing, look at a few objects around your home and study them in terms of their values. Squint your eyes, paying attention to all the lights and darks; look at the different values in the shadows cast by the objects. Then find the values you see in the value scales shown below.

Pencil Scale *As the scale to the right demonstrates, a range of values can be produced using different pencils. A 2H pencil creates a very light tone, whereas a charcoal pencil makes the softest, darkest tone.*

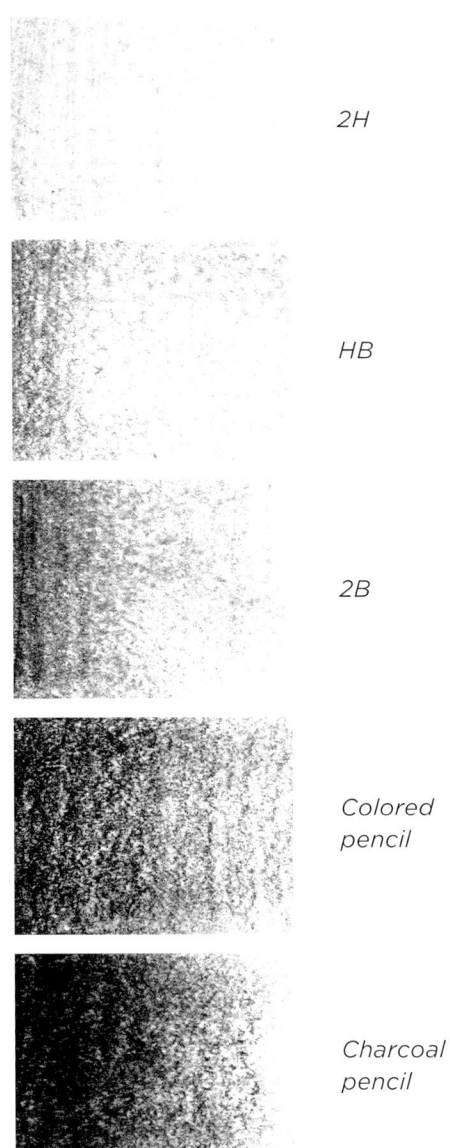

2H

HB

2B

Colored pencil

Charcoal pencil

VARYING VALUES WITH PAINT AND INK WASHES

The values and textures that can be created with pencil can also be created with inks and paints. Adjusting the amount of water you use in your ink or paint washes provides a range of values. When creating a wash, it is best to start with the lightest value and build up to a darker value, rather than adding water to a dark wash to lighten it. To learn how to mix various values, create a value chart like this one. Start with a very diluted wash, and gradually add more ink or paint for successively darker values.

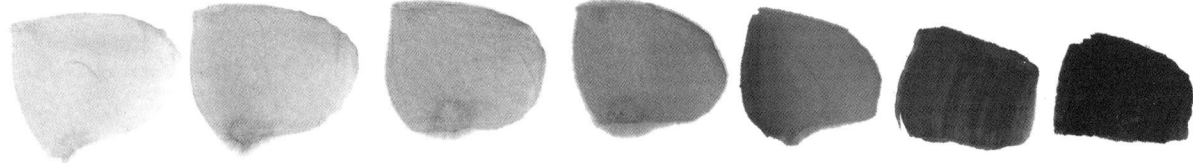

Constructing Creatures

Approaching a drawing becomes a much simpler process when you begin by breaking down the subject into basic forms, or three-dimensional shapes. And these simple shapes, with a little refinement, easily can become body parts of your creature. Cylinders often act as the underlying forms of legs, and cubes usually become feet. (See the example at right for a demonstration of this drawing method.) That's all there is to the first step of every drawing: sketching the shapes and developing the forms. After that, it's just a matter of connecting and refining the lines and adding details.

Transforming Shapes into Forms *These are drawings of the four basic shapes and their respective forms. The shapes are like flat frontal views of the forms; when tipped, they appear as three-dimensional forms. Use ellipses to show the backs of the circle, cylinder, and cone; draw a cube by connecting two squares with parallel lines.*

START WITH BASIC SHAPES

When you draw the outline of your subject, you are drawing its shape. But your subject also has depth and dimension, or form. The corresponding forms of the four basic shapes—circles, rectangles, squares, and triangles—are spheres, cylinders, cubes, and cones. Once you've learned to develop the forms of simple shapes, you'll be able to draw any subject!

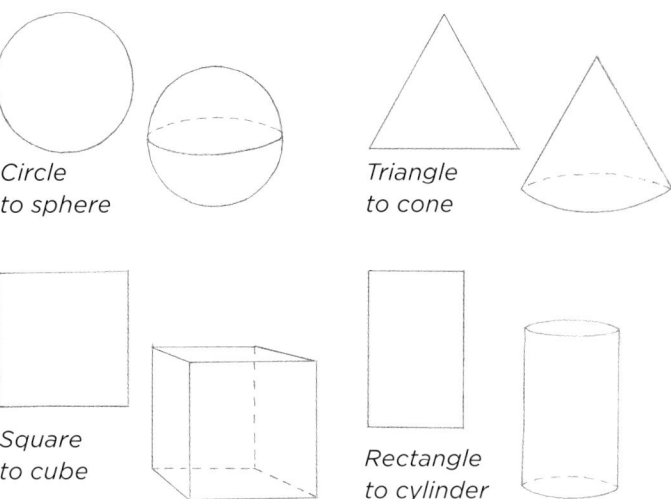

Circle to sphere

Triangle to cone

Square to cube

Rectangle to cylinder

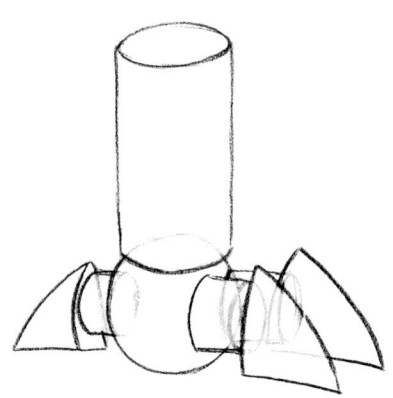

Starting with Shapes
This is what a dragon ankle would look like rendered entirely with geometric forms: cylinders for the leg, a circle for the ball of the foot, and triangle shapes for the claws.

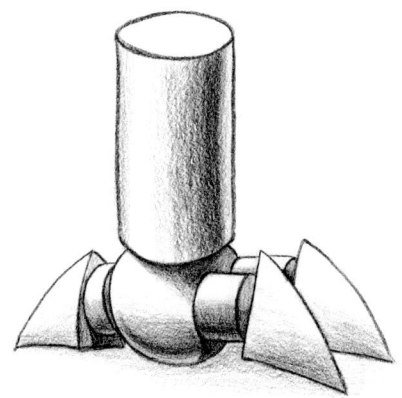

Shading for Depth
By adding variations of value (shading) to the basic shapes, you can give them form. Don't go this far when building up a real drawing, though; this is an intermediate step to demonstrate how shading produces dimension.

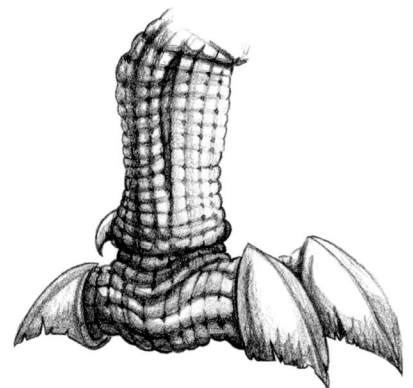

Final Drawing *Use basic shapes as a guide to develop the final drawing, adding details and more shading. Although my foundational shapes have changed, you still can imagine them underneath the shading.*

Placing Facial Features

Believe it or not, dragons and other fantasy creatures have the same general facial proportions (the comparative sizes and placement of parts to one another) as humans. Whether you are viewing the subject from the front, in profile, or from a three-quarter view, the basic proportions are the same.

FACIAL GUIDELINES

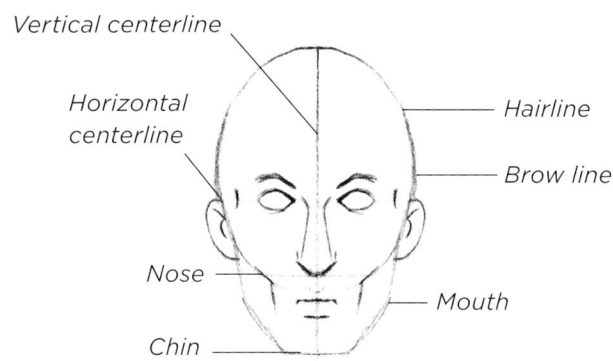

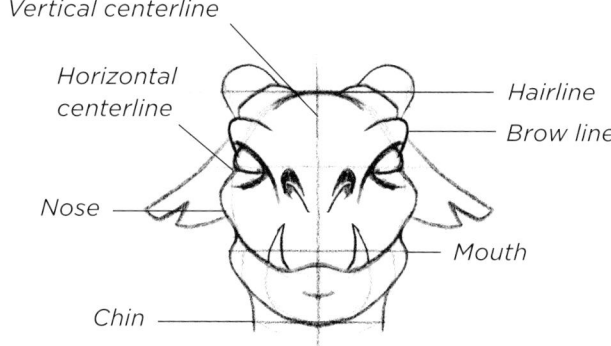

Human Facial Guidelines *Divide the face in half horizontally and vertically. Then divide the bottom portion in half again to show where the end of the nose will be. Divide once more to see where the bottom lip ends. The hairline is about one-third from the top of the head to the eyes, and the brow line is just above the ears. The eyes are centered between the vertical centerline and the sides of the head, with one eye width between them.*

Dragon Facial Guidelines *The dragon head follows the same general rules of proportion as the human head, although the guidelines (and the features) are spaced a little differently on the dragon. For example, the dragon's hairline is higher, and the space between the bottom of the nose and the horizontal centerline is much smaller than on the human.*

PROFILES

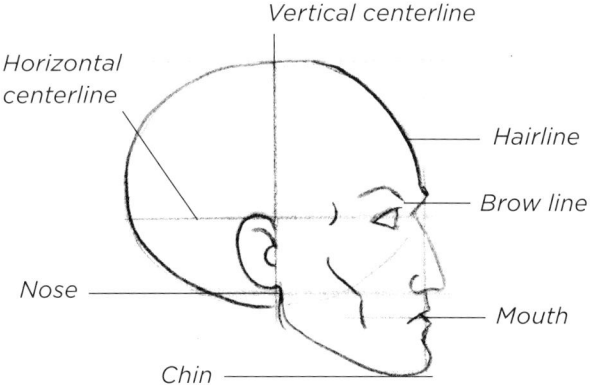

Human Profile *When drawing a human head in profile, use a large cranial circle as a guideline for placing the features. The nose, lips, and chin fall outside the circle, whereas the eye and ear remain inside the circle. When the head is turned in profile, the facial guidelines remain in the same positions as the frontal view.*

Dragon Profile *Use a smaller cranial circle for the head, as dragons don't have the large brains that humans do. The nose and mouth fall outside the circle, whereas the eye remains inside the circle. The ear begins inside the circle, but dragons' ears tend to be longer and larger than humans', so their ears extend farther.*

SHIFTING PROPORTIONS

Once you understand the basics of proper proportion, you can experiment with modifying the "average" proportions to fit the unique, individual characteristics of your subject. You'll notice that the sizes, placement, and even the number of features vary from creature to creature, so you'll sometimes need to tweak the "normal" proportions above to fit the individual subject. Study the examples below to see how the features undergo change as you approach different characters.

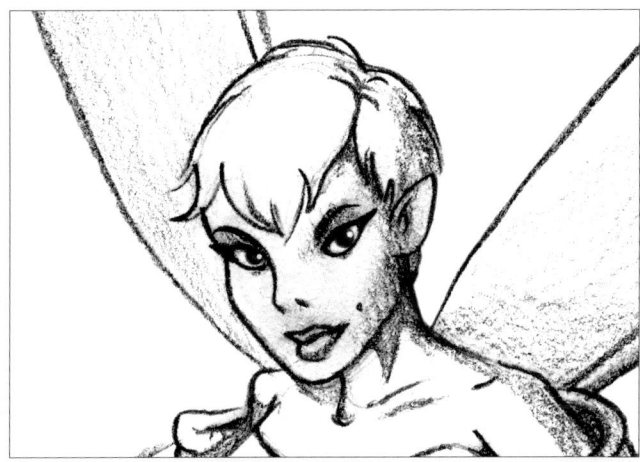

Normal Proportions The pixie's facial proportions are fairly average: There is about one eye width between the eyes, which lie on the horizontal centerline; the nose is positioned halfway between the brow line and the bottom of the chin; and the ears line up with the brows.

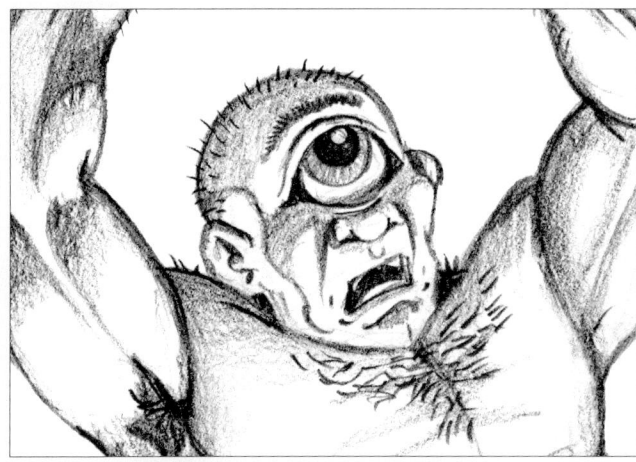

Abnormal Proportions The Cyclops differs vastly from the status quo, simply in that he has only one eye. The rest of the features line up in an average way, but the eye is nowhere near proportional to the ears, nose, and mouth, as it takes up the majority of the face.

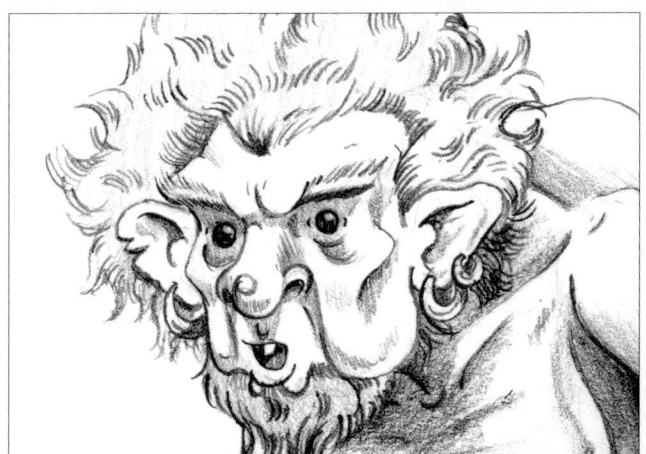

Less Normal Proportions This troll's eyes are much smaller than average, and there are about two eye widths between them. The nose is oversized compared with the tiny mouth, and the chin is very short and small. The ears also are oversized, and they are placed lower on the face.

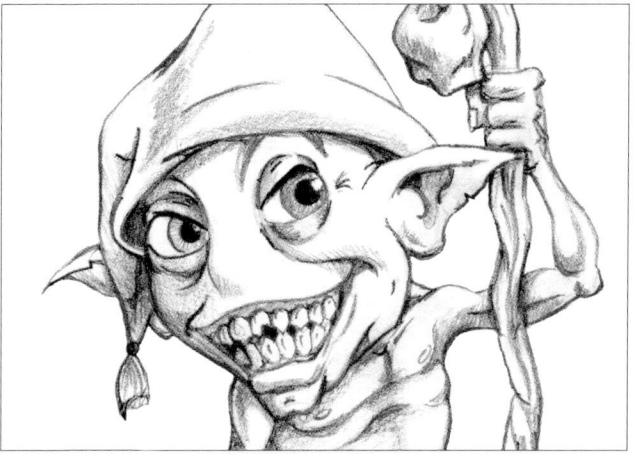

Exaggerated Proportions In this example of a gremlin, the eyes and ears are about twice as big as they should be, following standard guidelines. The nose is almost nonexistent, and the mouth nearly stretches across the entire face. These alterations provide more personality to the little gremlin.

Creature Features & Textures

Horns, wings, feathers, fur, claws: There are a lot of features and details to consider when designing your creatures. When drawing these features, keep in mind that it's often helpful to use photo references of animals or humans with features similar to those you want to add to your fantasy drawings.

This section will help you experiment with creating textures such as smooth scales and ridged horns, as well as with depicting elements such as wings and tails. And if you're almost finished with a drawing and can't shake the feeling that something is missing, consider some of these options to give your creature that last bit of oomph.

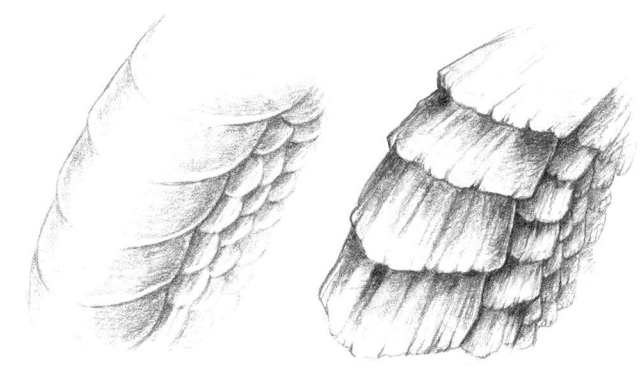

SCALES

Study real-life scaly creatures, such as snakes, crocodiles, and even fish to get inspiration for scales. The scales on the left are smooth and slick, like the belly of a snake. By keeping the shading light and blending away the edges of the scales where the lightest highlights are, the scales appear to be thin and flexible. The scales on the right, however, have very deep shading and are riddled with ridges, nicks, and cracks along the edges. These scales look very thick and hard—the sort that would make up the armor-like plates on an old, weathered dragon.

See below for additional scale textures.

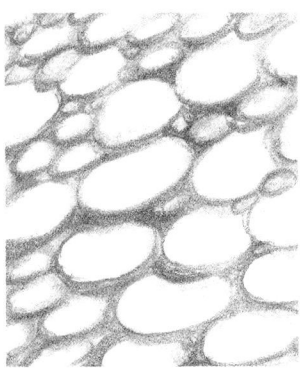

*For **smooth scales**, which can be found on the slick skin of sea-dwelling dragons, first draw irregularly shaped ovals, then shade between them.*

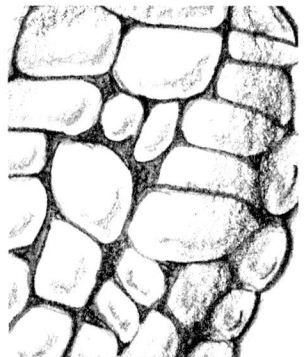

*To create **rough scales**, draw irregular shapes that follow a slightly curved alignment. Shade darkly between the shapes, then shade over them with light, parallel strokes.*

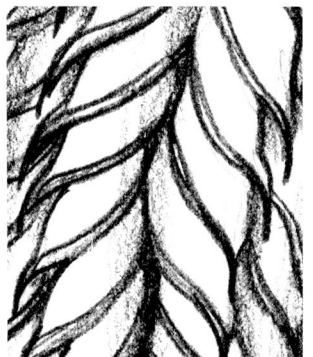

*For **sharp, spiny scales**, sketch the form with a 2H pencil, adding details with a black colored pencil. Lightly grip the pencil to create softly curving arcs for the differently shaped spines.*

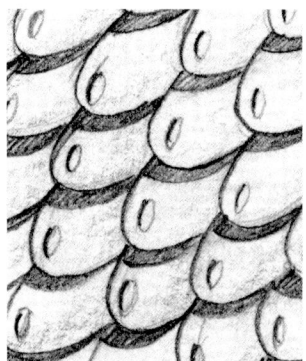

*To depict **fishlike scales** such as those found on most Asian dragons, draw arcs of various sizes. Partially cover each scale with the next layer and add a cast shadow below each to show overlap.*

FUR & HAIR

When drawing short hair, use medium-length strokes and avoid creating parallel rows, instead interspersing your lines and drawing them in the same general direction. Darker, denser lines can show stripes or other patterns and areas of shadow (left). Wiry, bristly hair (center) is drawn with short, quick pencil strokes. This is a good technique for drawing close-cropped hair or the stubble on an ogre's knuckles and toes. The long hair shown at right is good for manes and tails. Use long, smooth lines that follow the direction of hair growth. To make the hair look shiny, let some of the white paper show through in areas. Not all hair is the same length, so let some lines trail off into wisps or curls for a more natural look.

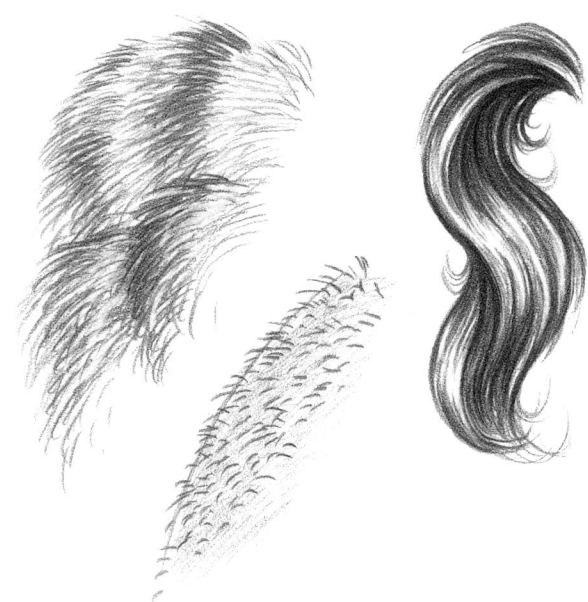

Short Hair *To create short hair, make quick, overlapping hatch marks with the broad side of the pencil. For subtle wrinkles and folds in the skin, vary the values by changing the pressure on the pencil.*

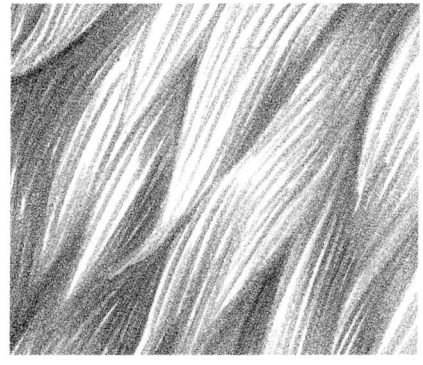

Long Hair *To render long hair— whether it's all over the body or just on the head or tail—use long, sweeping strokes that curve slightly, and taper the hairs to points on the ends.*

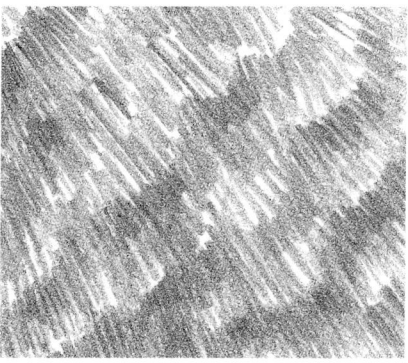

Rough Hair *For a subtle striped pattern, apply short strokes in the direction that the hair grows. Overlap some strokes to create darker values, and keep your strokes farther apart for light areas.*

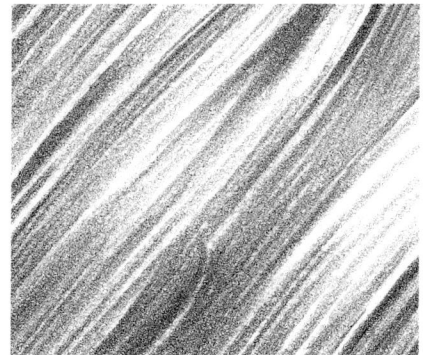

Smooth Hair *For smooth, silky hair, use sweeping parallel pencil strokes, leaving the highlighted areas free of graphite. Alternate between the pencil tip and the broad side for variation.*

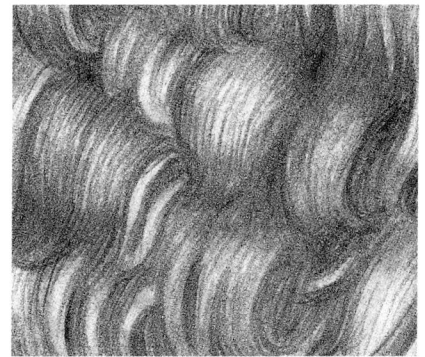

Curly Hair *Curly hair or fur can be drawn with overlapping circular strokes of varying values. For realism, draw curls of differing shapes and sizes, and blend your strokes to soften the look.*

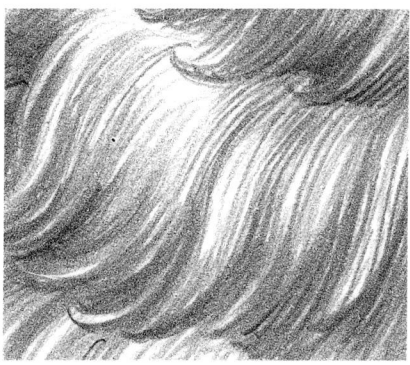

Wavy Hair *For layers of soft, wavy curls, stroke in S-shaped lines that end in tighter curves. Leave the highlights free of graphite and stroke with more pressure as you move to the shadows.*

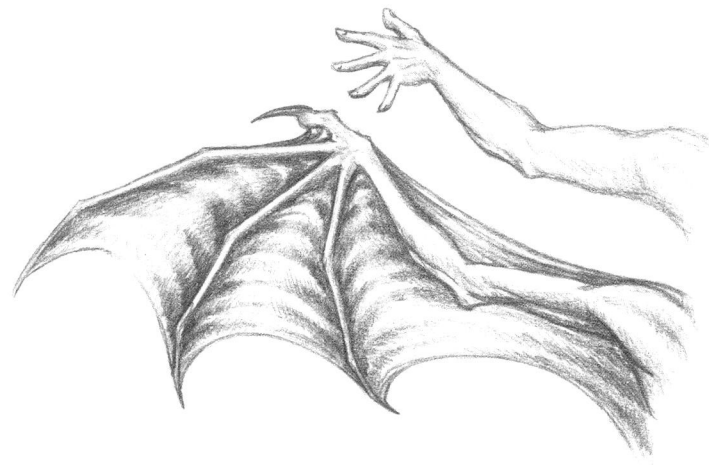

Leathery Wings Wings are, essentially, a second pair of arms and hands. The bones are thin and elongated, but the basic structure matches that of human hands and arms. Bats are the primary living example of this in that their forelimbs are their wings. In the example above, compare the "fingers" of the wing to the splayed fingers in the hand. Note that both limbs have a wrist, an elbow, a shoulder, and even a thumb. Keep this basic structure in mind, and then expand on it. Add more or reduce the number of wing fingers, or consider long spikes that protrude from the elbow.

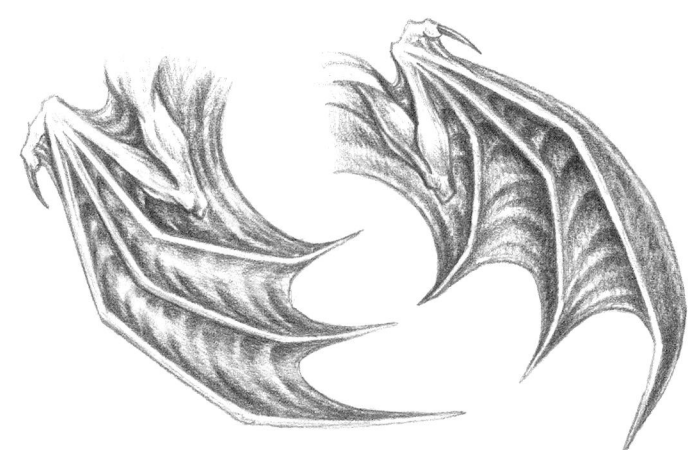

Folded Wings When not in flight, creatures usually fold their wings to keep them out of the way and to keep themselves safe. Folded wings can be held close to the body, or simply held low and relaxed. The membrane of wings—as with bats—is usually stretchy, even when relaxed. The examples above don't show too much slack, other than folds between the wing fingers; however, you can also draw wings with folds that run parallel to the wing fingers and hang a bit like drapes when relaxed.

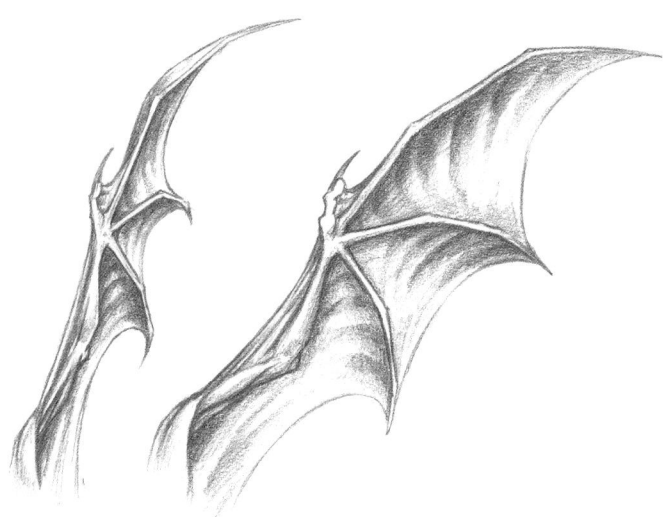

Open Wings When wings are open, the membrane between the wing fingers stretches and is pulled tight. Some folds are present, but not too many. Note that the edge of the membrane has a smoother arc where it stretches between the wing fingers, instead of the steep arc that occurs with folded wings. The example on the left shows an open wing that is tilted away from the viewer.

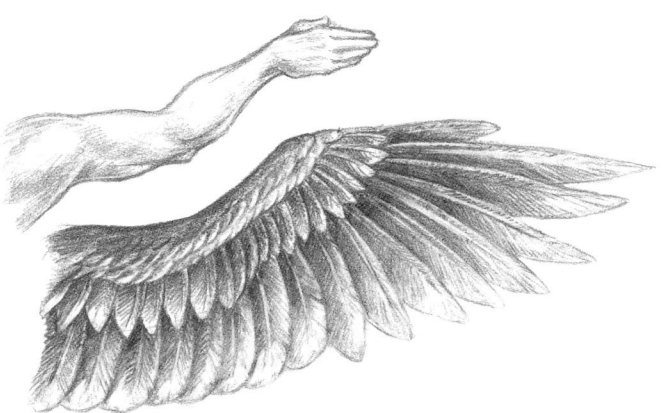

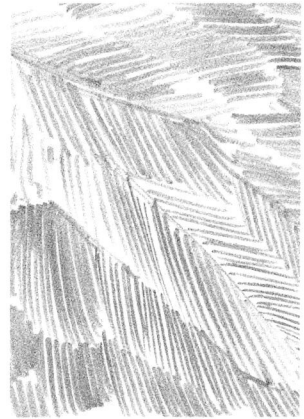

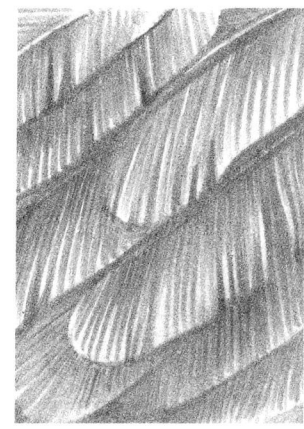

Feathered Wings Bird wings are also similar to human arms and hands. Unlike leathery wings, where the wing is supported by elongated fingers, the "fingers" of a feathered wing are fused together. The feathers make up the bulk of the wing and give it its shape. Though feathers can be intimidating, you don't need to draw every individual feather. Emphasize the primary feathers—the long feathers that look almost like fingers along the outer edge of the wing—and use less definition for the smallest feathers on the top layer (though you should emphasize the outer edges and perhaps show some markings).

Fine Feathers
For light, downy feathers, apply thin, parallel lines along the feather stems, forming a series of V shapes. Avoid crisp outlines, which would take away from the softness.

Heavy Feathers
To create thicker, more defined feathers, use heavier parallel strokes and blend with a tortillon. Apply the most graphite to the shadowed areas between the feathers.

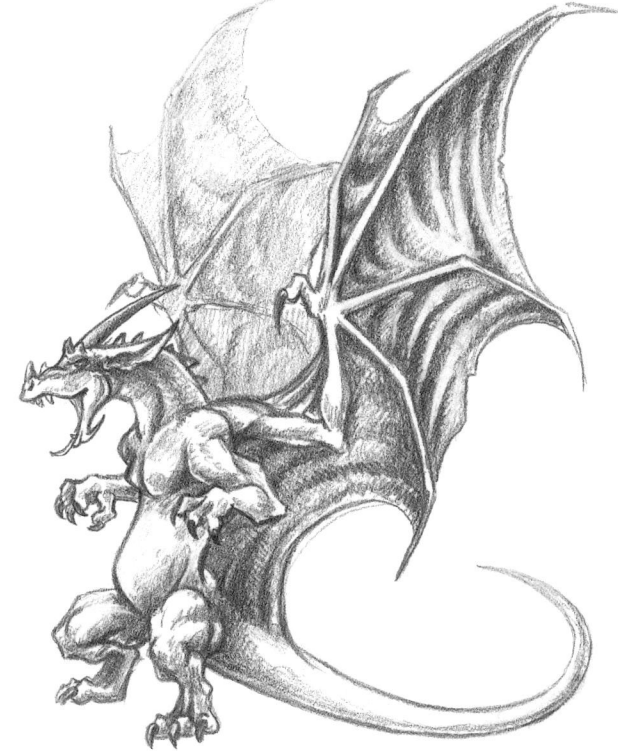

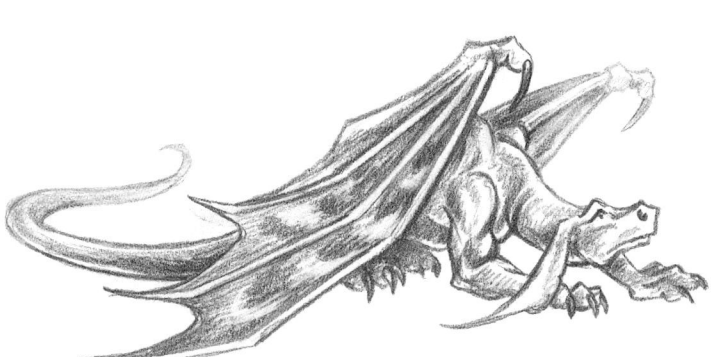

Expressive Wings Creatures are quite attached to their wings. When extra limbs are naturally part of a creature's anatomy, they will come into play as another means of expressing that creature's thoughts and feelings through body language. In this example, the dragon on the right is clearly agitated, spreading his wings to make himself look bigger and more intimidating. The dragon on the left is cowed by the other dragon's display of aggression and is tucking his wings in close, as if to cower behind them in a submissive, nonthreatening pose.

HORNS

As with the other examples in this book, you can find ideas for your creature's horns by modifying what you see in nature. Many animals have horns that are fantastically exotic, but something standard, like the curled ram horns on the left, also works nicely for a range of fantasy creatures. Adding twists to smooth horns, as in the middle example, creates a refined look. In the example on the right, growth ridges can blend into smooth horn tips, creating a look that is both rough and dignified.

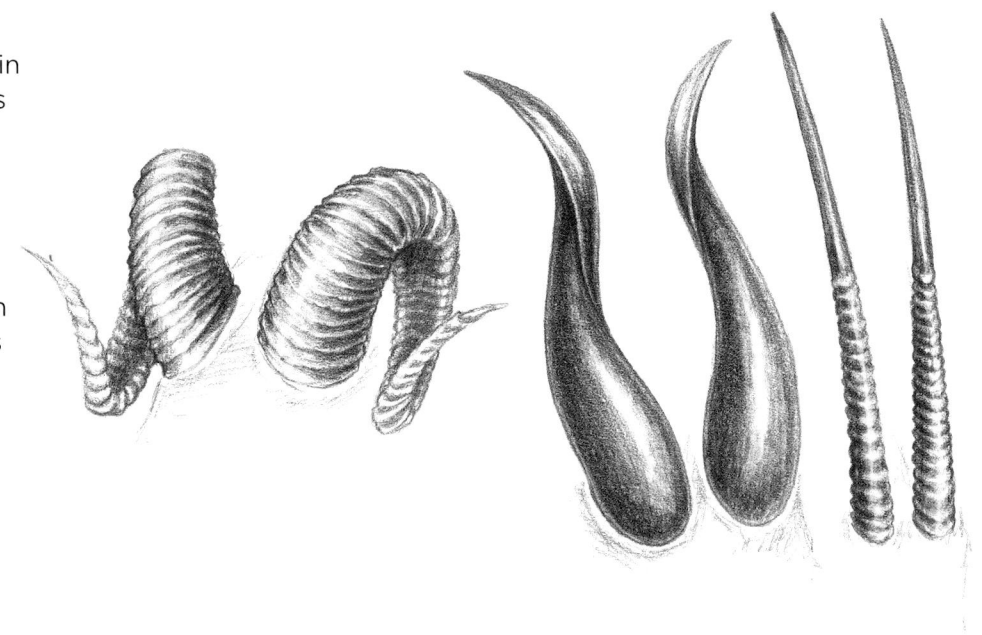

CLAWS

Claws come in a wonderful variety of shapes and sizes and have many functions. Take a look at the examples in nature, such as tigers, eagles, lizards, and even dogs. Then think about the type of creature you are drawing and what purpose it might use its claws for.

The example right, top, shows how long, thick talons might look on a gargoyle's hand—useful for attacking, defending, and climbing. The example right, center, could be found on the toes of a dragon or harpy. Based on an eagle's talon, this claw is good for hooking and grasping. The example right, bottom, is a good all-purpose claw with ridges.

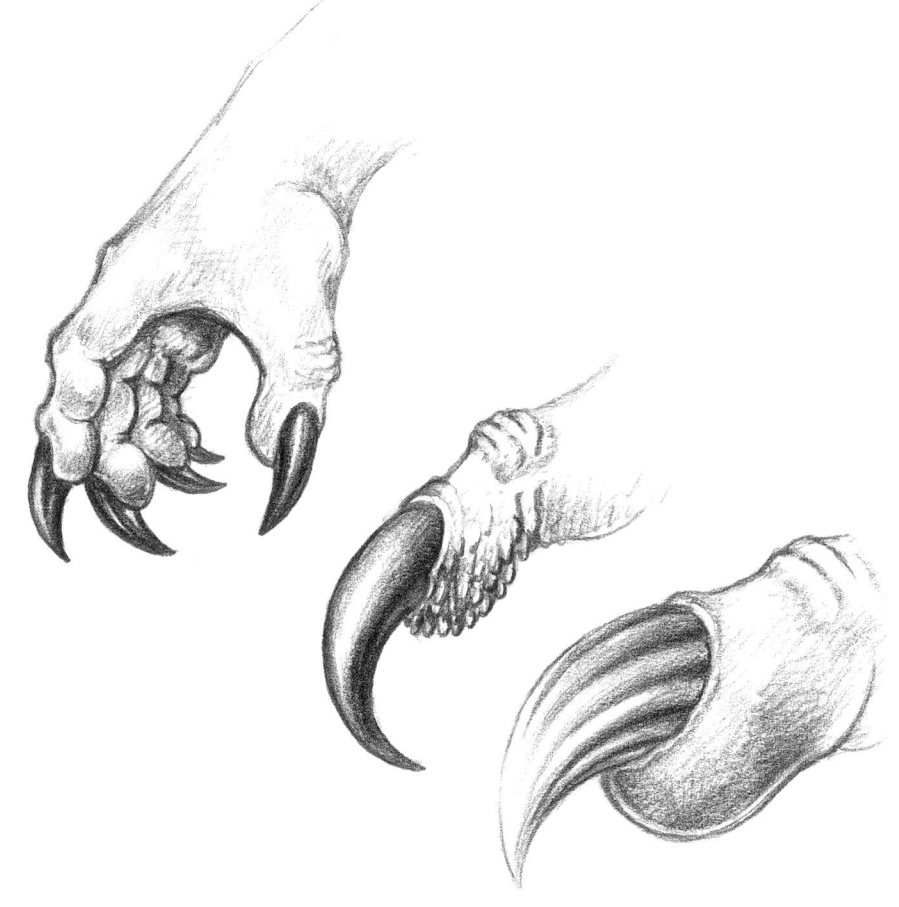

SHIFTING HANDS

Here we combine a human hand with an iguana claw to create a dragon claw. The dragon claw has many of the same structural elements as the human hand, but the textural elements are more iguana-like.
In many instances, using the iguana claw on the dragon would be perfectly acceptable. However, if your dragon needs to be emotive, humanlike features (such as the nails shown here) can be beneficial.

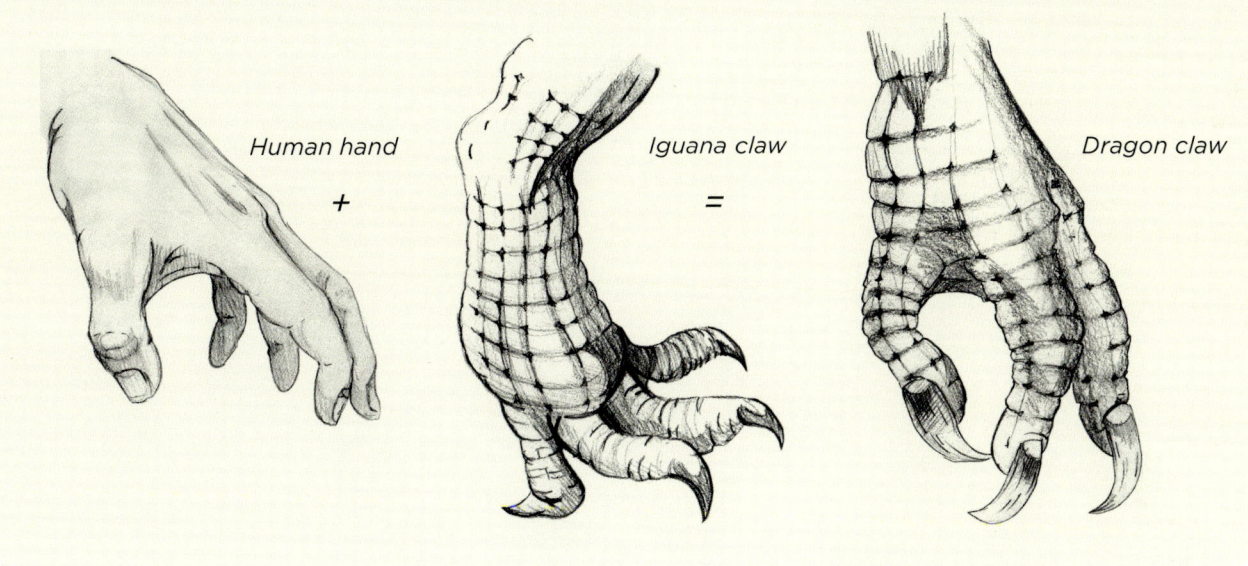

Human hand + *Iguana claw* = *Dragon claw*

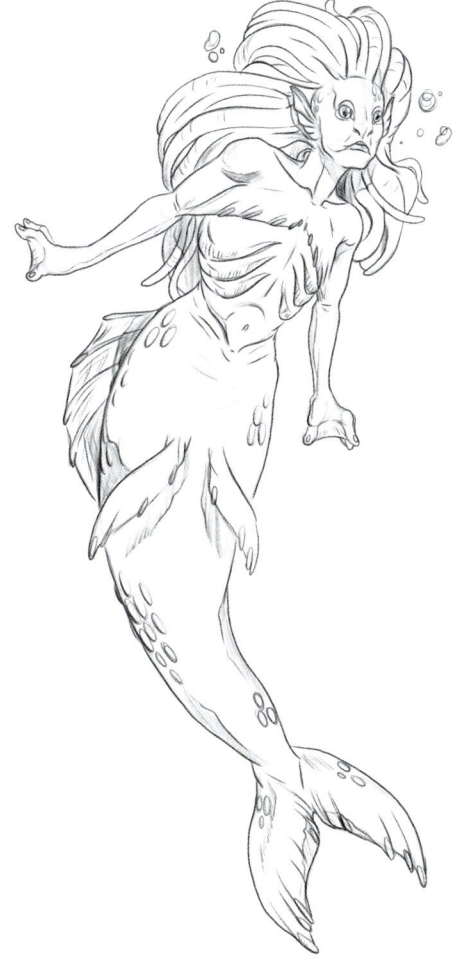

This menacing mermaid sports shimmering scales as well as luxuriant hair buoyed by water.

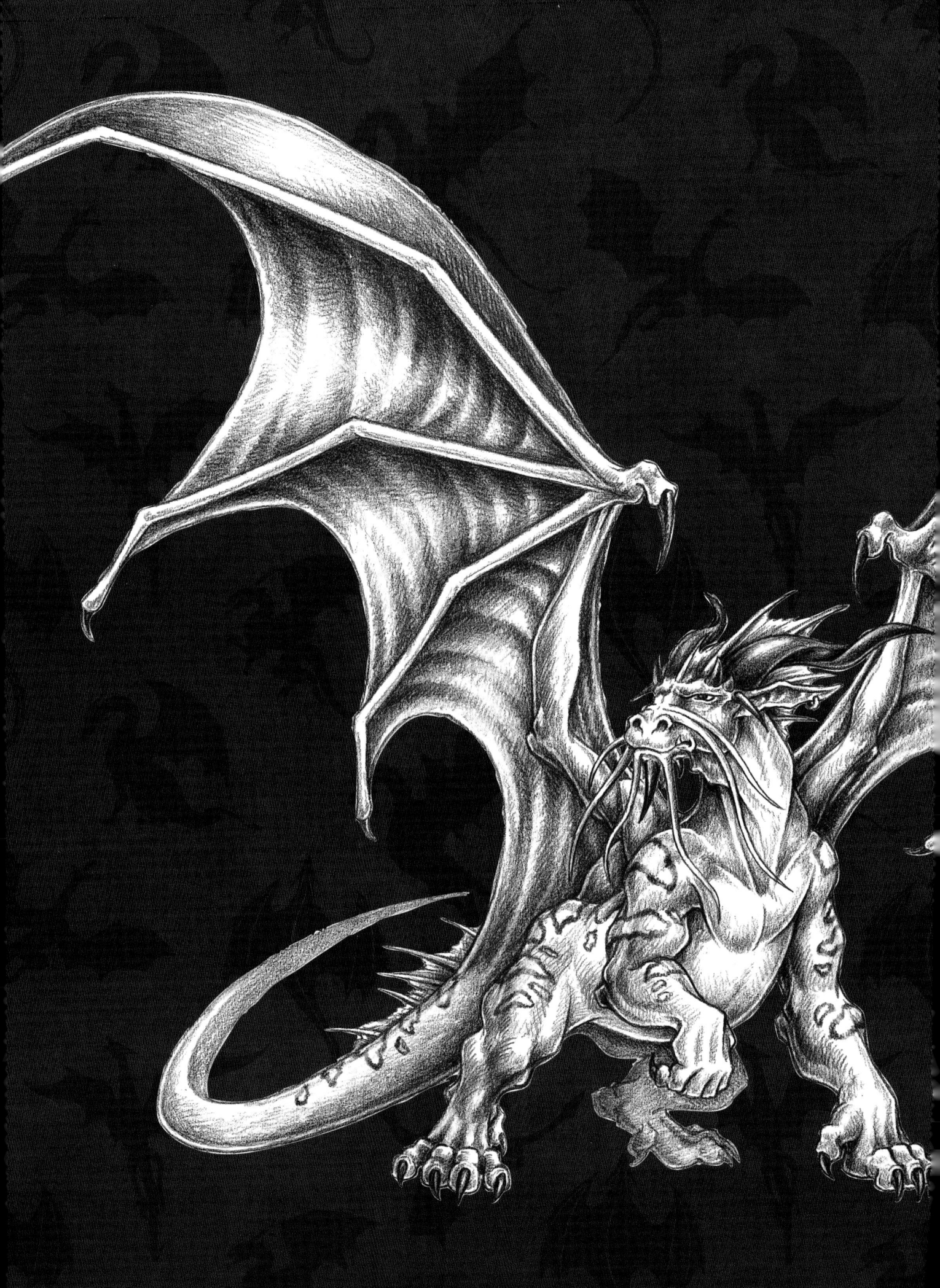

Dragons:
A Visual
Compendium

Types of Dragons

Ultimately, there are as many different types of dragons as there are people who want to draw them. Size, shape, texture, details—all of these things are up to the artist, and there's no limit to what you can come up with. However, in terms of the dragons that are described in classic myths and stories, there are several specific types of dragons that show up quite often. Here are four of these types, presented as a place for you to start cultivating ideas.

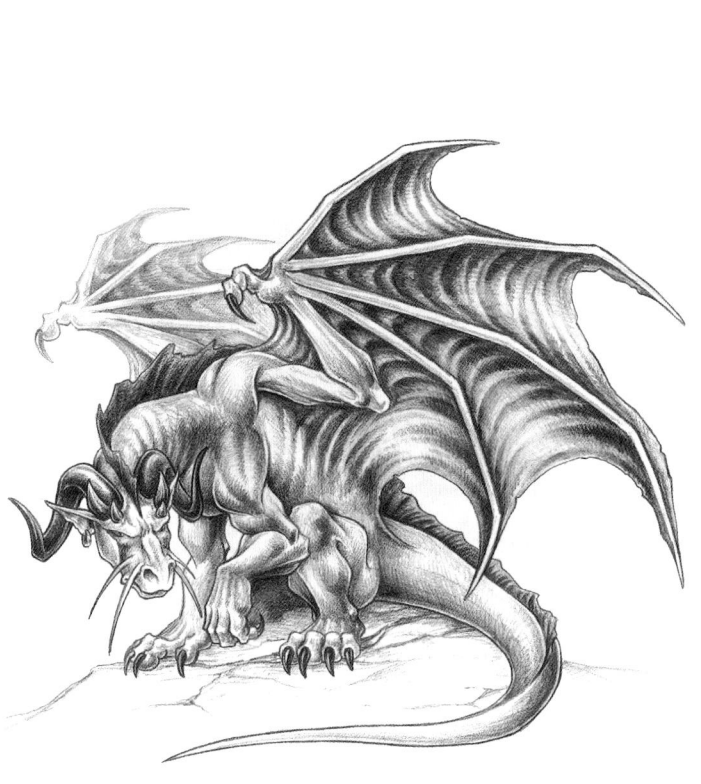

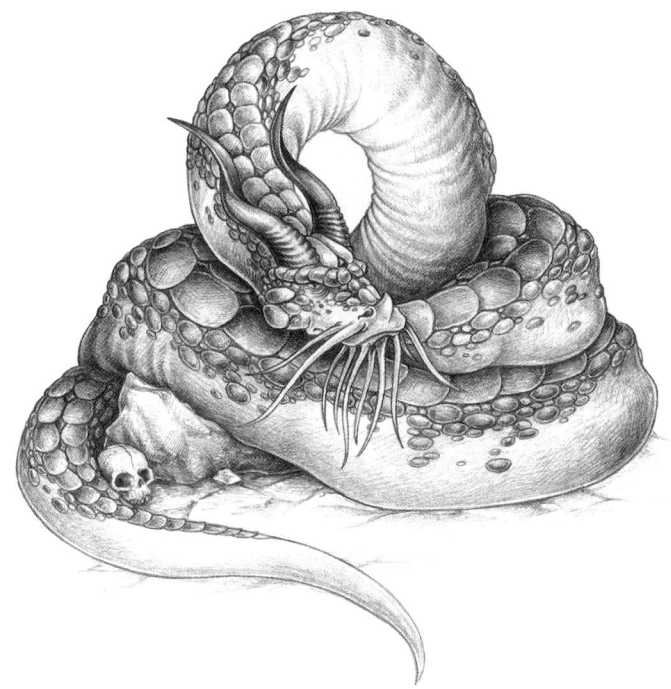

WESTERN DRAGON: LORE & LEGENDS

† In Western culture, this type of dragon is the most familiar: terrorizing kingdoms, dueling with knights, and kidnapping young princesses.

† Occasionally they appear as good guys, providing strength or wisdom, or as the patron who serves the hero with their quest. Their reputation is mixed at best, but they remain a beloved archetype.

† Western dragons usually have four limbs; the forelimbs may or may not end in hand-like paws. Most have two wings, horns, a long tail, and spiky ridges or fins running along the spine.

† See page 34 for a step-by-step tutorial of a Western dragon.

WYRM: LORE & LEGENDS

† The wyrm (pronounced "worm") is a type of dragon with no legs or wings. The word can also refer to dragons in general, or specify that a dragon is very old. But for our purposes, the term refers to limbless dragons.

† There are many examples of wyrms in mythology, such as Jörmungandr, the World Serpent from Norse mythology who grew so long that he could wrap himself around the Earth and grasp the end of his tail in his mouth (see page 46).

† Because wyrms lack wings and limbs, other means must be used to make them look like dragons: Try using thick scales or ridges along the length of its body. The best place to focus on, of course, is the creature's head: Add horns, whiskers, bumps, brow ridges, fins, or perhaps even long ears.

† See page 38 for a step-by-step tutorial of a wyrm.

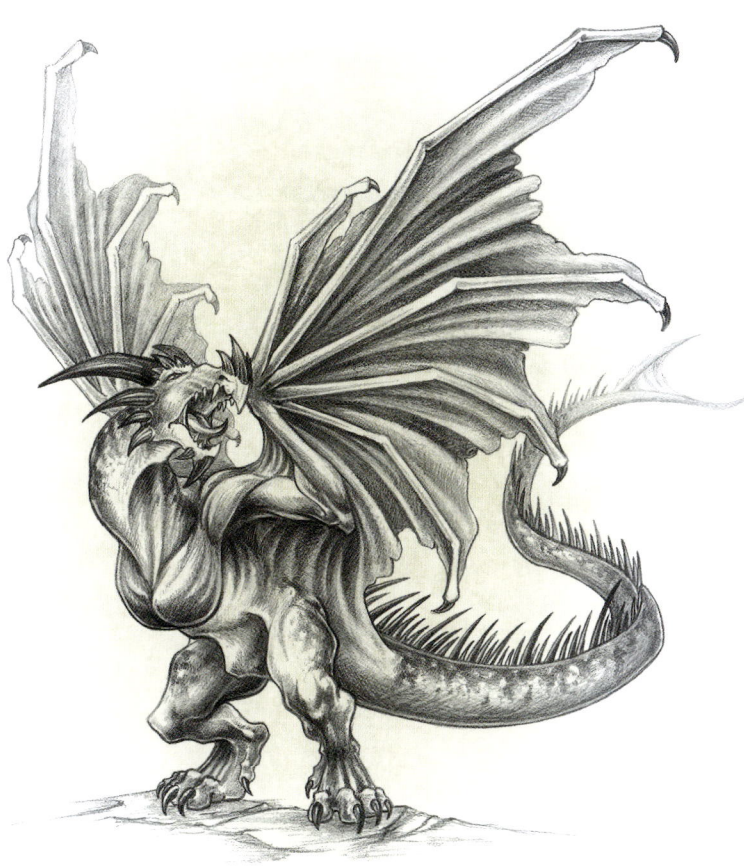

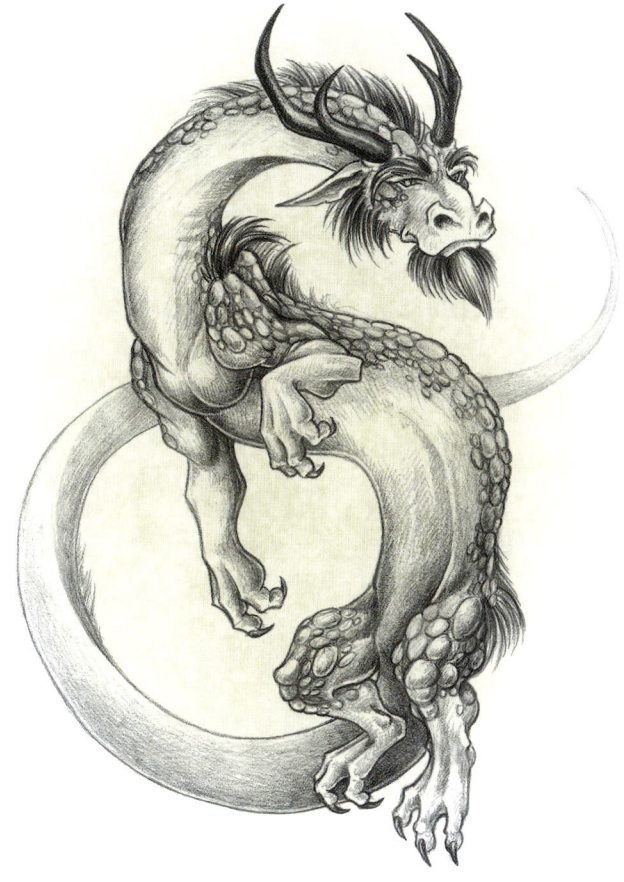

WYVERN: LORE & LEGENDS

† The wyvern is another type of dragon, often regarded as vicious and foul-tempered, and sometimes less intelligent than the Western dragon.

† The exact appearance of wyverns varies slightly from story to story. Most commonly, they have two wings and two hind legs. Like bats, their forelimbs function as their wings.

† Sometimes their tail ends in a spade, other times in a sharp barb, which is usually poisonous. This creature has lots of wicked-looking horns and spikes that make it look especially malevolent.

† See page 42 for a step-by-step tutorial of a wyvern.

EASTERN DRAGON: LORE & LEGENDS

† Whereas dragons often play the role of the villain in Western culture, Eastern dragons are usually respected and considered wise and benevolent. They can, of course, be angered, but aren't usually envisioned as being predisposed to unfounded rage or unprovoked antagonism, as are their Western cousins.

† Unlike Western dragons, Eastern dragons usually don't have wings. Rather, their bodies are very long and slender, and their flight is marked by writhing, coiling movements.

† hey usually have four limbs, with the number of claws on each foot varying according to the type of dragon (and sometimes their rank or status). Their horns usually resemble the antlers of a deer.

† See page 50 for a step-by-step tutorial of an Eastern dragon.

Elemental Dragons

Elemental dragons are those that are related to the elemental spheres: fire, earth, air, and water. These dragons tend to personify their respective element.

† **Eastern Roots** In Chinese and other East Asian mythologies, dragons embodied natural forces—governing rain, rivers, wind, and cosmic balance—more as *personifications of nature* than singular elemental beings.

† **Western Influences** European dragons were physical manifestations of primal power—often tied to fire, earth, or air—and symbolized chaos, greed, or destruction to be overcome.

† **Philosophical Meets Physical** The modern concept merges Eastern elemental philosophy with Western creature mythology, transforming dragons into beings that both embody and wield specific forces.

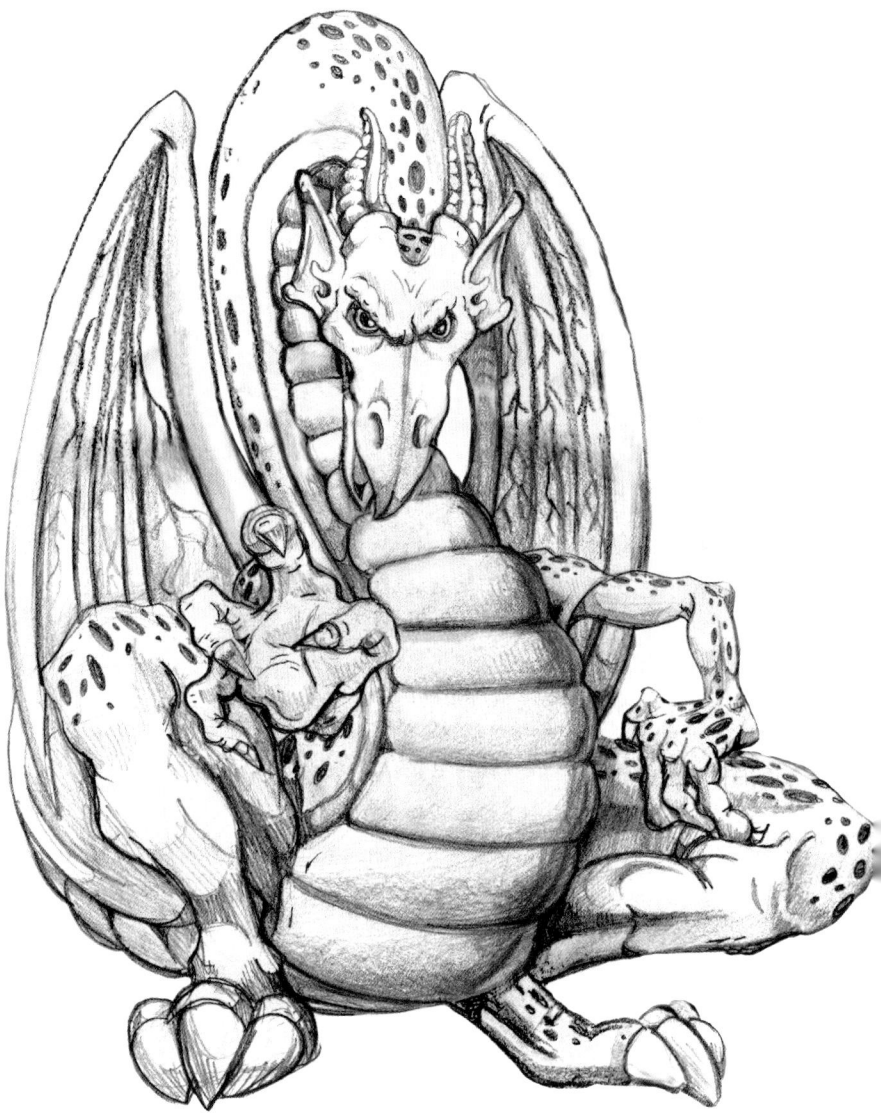

FIRE DRAGON: LORE & LEGENDS

† The most volatile and unpredictable of all elemental dragons, the Fire Dragon embodies raw energy and transformation—feared for its power yet revered for the renewal it brings.

† Often found dwelling deep within dormant volcanoes, this dragon's thick, heavy body and long, sinuous limbs echo the molten rivers it commands, while its scales blaze red, orange, or yellow like living flame.

† Legends link Fire Dragons to the dual nature of fire itself: a force of destruction that clears the way for new life, and a source of warmth, light, and protection for those who wield it wisely.

† In Chinese astrology, those born under the Fire Dragon sign (January 31, 1976–February 17, 1977) are said to be bold, passionate, and destined to ignite change.

WATER DRAGON: LORE & LEGENDS

† Serene yet powerful, the Water Dragon embodies adaptability, intuition, and emotional depth—a creature that shapes its surroundings as effortlessly as water carves stone.

† Unlike its winged kin, the Water Dragon typically lacks legs or wings and does not fly; instead, it glides through seas, rivers, and lakes, its sleek, sinuous form flowing as one with the currents.

† In Chinese astrology, those born under the Water Dragon sign (January 27, 1952–February 13, 1953) are said to be empathetic, intuitive, and deeply adaptable—reflecting the dragon's shifting, transformative nature.

† Real-world Water Dragons—reptiles native to China and Australia—share their mythic namesake's aquatic prowess, remaining submerged for long periods and even possessing a mysterious "third eye" atop their heads.

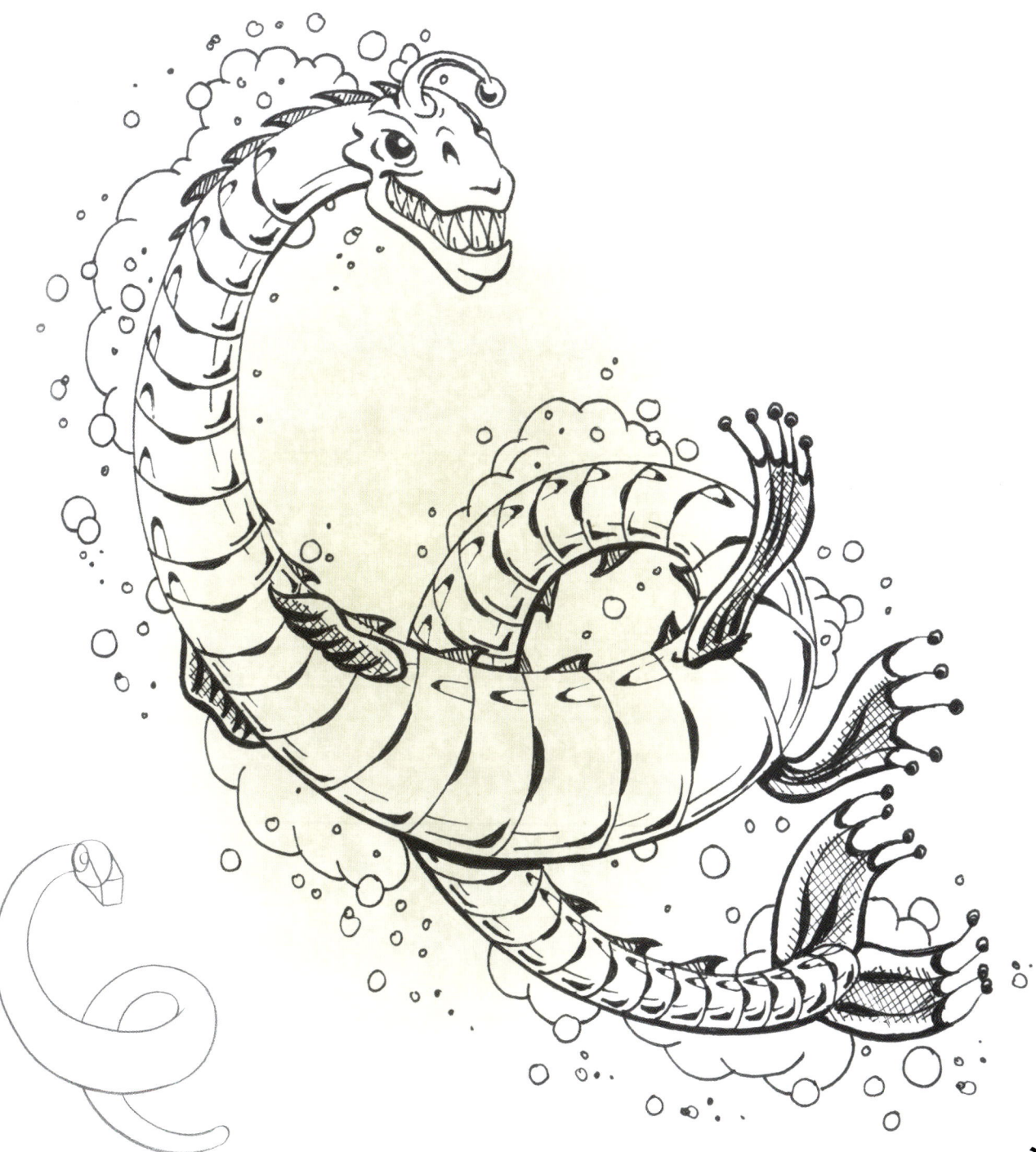

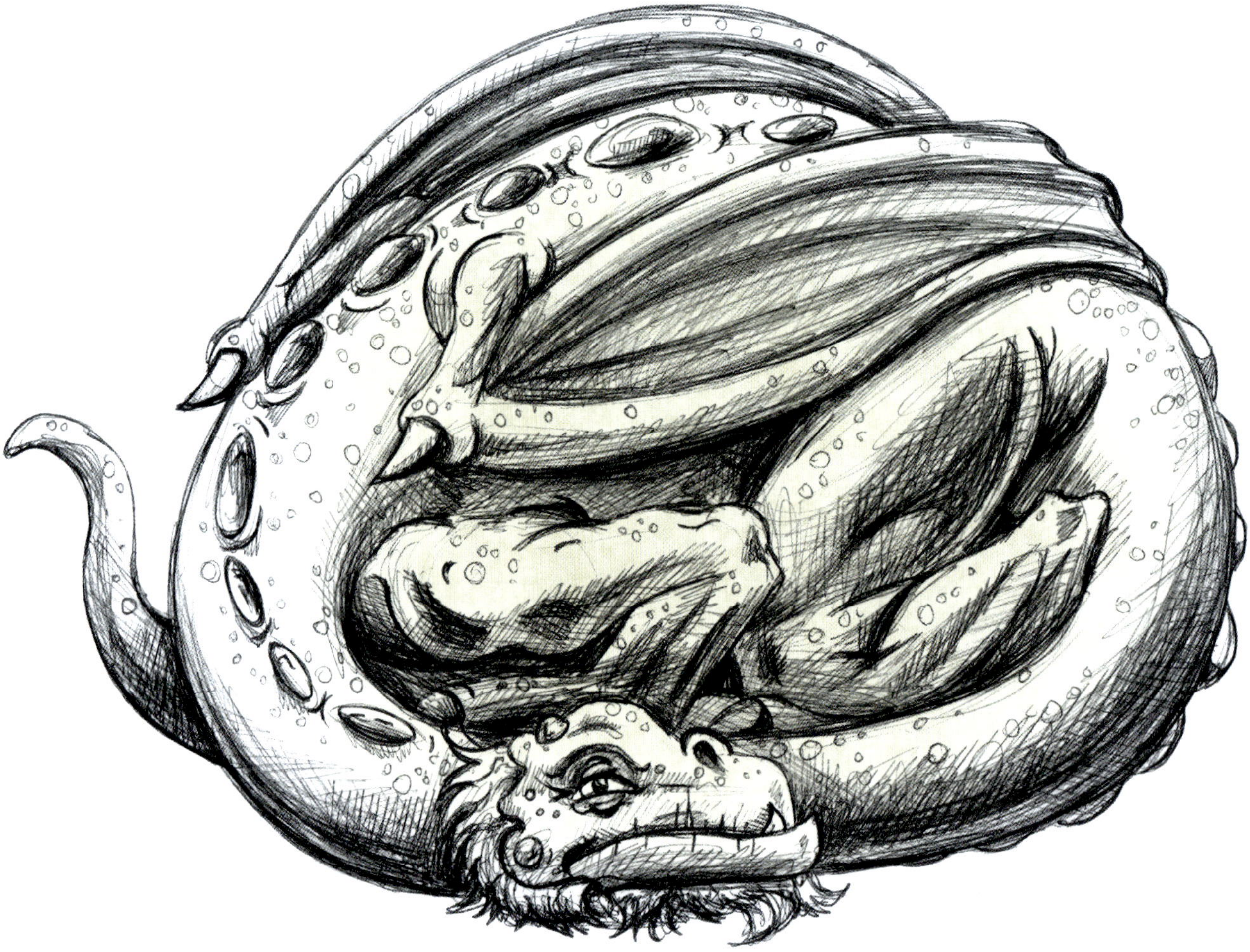

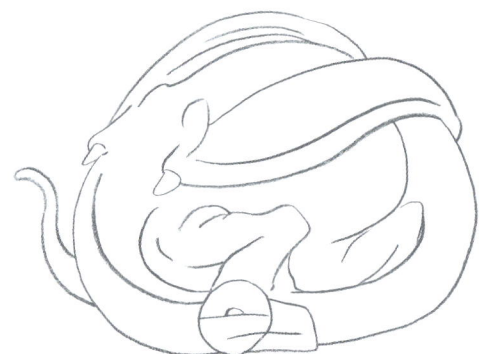

EARTH DRAGON: LORE & LEGENDS

† The most grounded and steadfast of the elemental dragons, the Earth Dragon embodies strength, patience, and stability—a guardian of the natural world and the cycles that sustain it.

† Dwelling among mountains and forests, this dragon is most often seen in green or brown hues that mirror the land it protects. Its heavier body, four sturdy legs, expansive wings, and long neck and tail give it an imposing, majestic presence.

† Known for its practicality and levelheaded nature, the Earth Dragon approaches life—and its relationships—with unwavering responsibility, serving as a stabilizing force amid chaos.

† In Chinese astrology, those born under the Earth Dragon sign (February 6, 1988–February 5, 1989) are said to embody reliability, discipline, and a deep connection to the material world.

STORM DRAGON: LORE & LEGENDS

† Master of winds and weather, the Storm Dragon commands the skies themselves—shaping tempests, summoning lightning, and bending the air to its will.

† Long and sinuous in form, this dragon embodies agility and transformation, often appearing in blue or yellow hues that shift to red, orange, purple, or black when it unleashes its full storm-born power.

† As unpredictable as a thunderhead and as fluid as the wind, the Storm Dragon symbolizes mental flexibility and the courage to embrace change—a force that thrives on motion, evolution, and possibility.

† Legends tell of Storm Dragons soaring through violent skies, their roars mingling with thunder, their breath scattering hurricanes and reshaping the very climate of the world below.

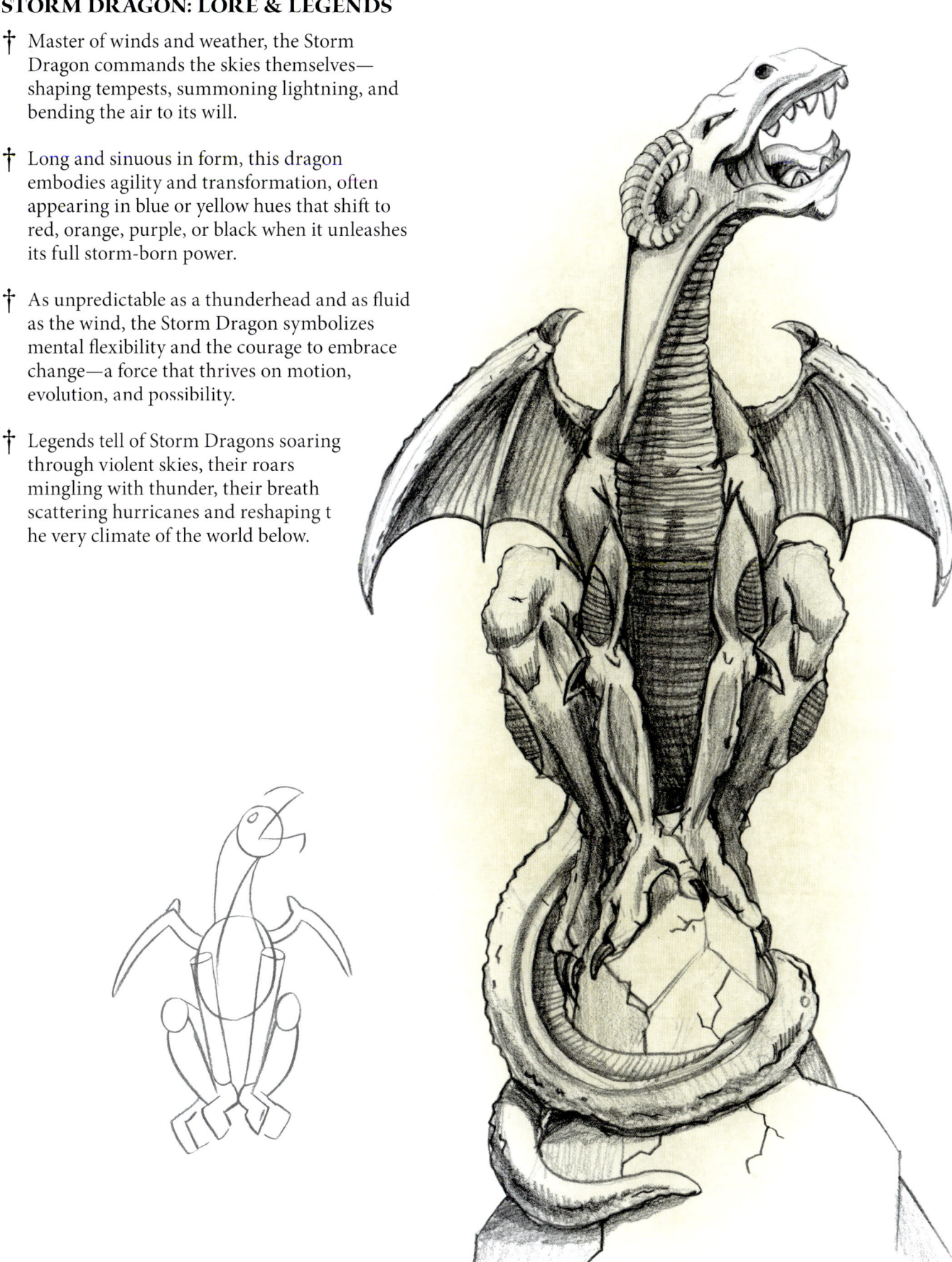

33

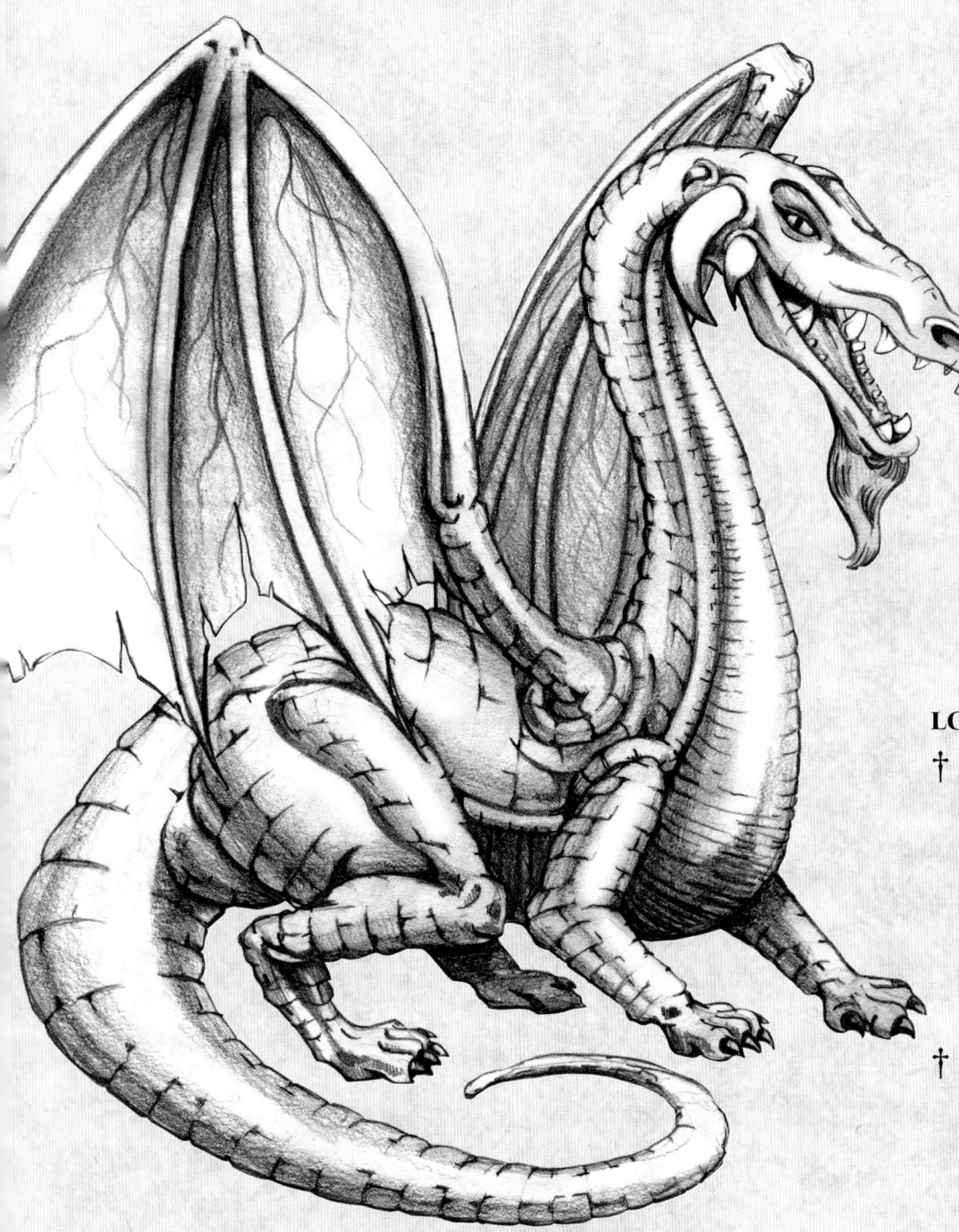

Western Dragon

LORE & LEGENDS

† Most dragons originating in Western mythology have four legs (the forelimbs may or may not end in hand-like paws), a long neck and tail, a thick body with spiky ridges or fins running along the spine, horns, and two batlike wings, which don't grow until adulthood.

† The Western dragon usually is a malevolent, fire-breathing creature that lives underground and hoards treasure, terrorizing kingdoms, dueling with knights, and kidnapping young princesses.

† These dragons also appear as heroes, providing strength or wisdom, or serve as patrons to a protagonist's quest.

† Many contemporary fantasy and romantasy novels feature relationships between humans and dragons, close ties fostered through experiences of military training and conflict as well as romantic connections.

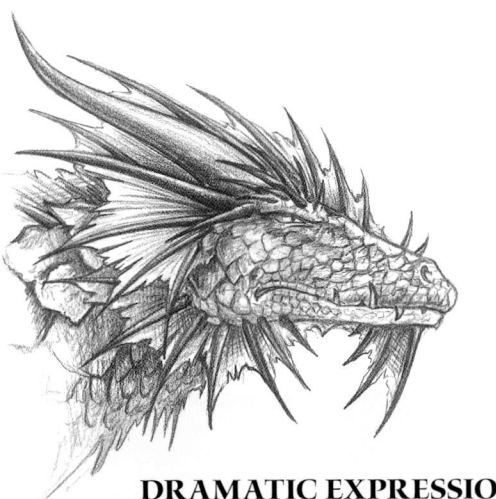

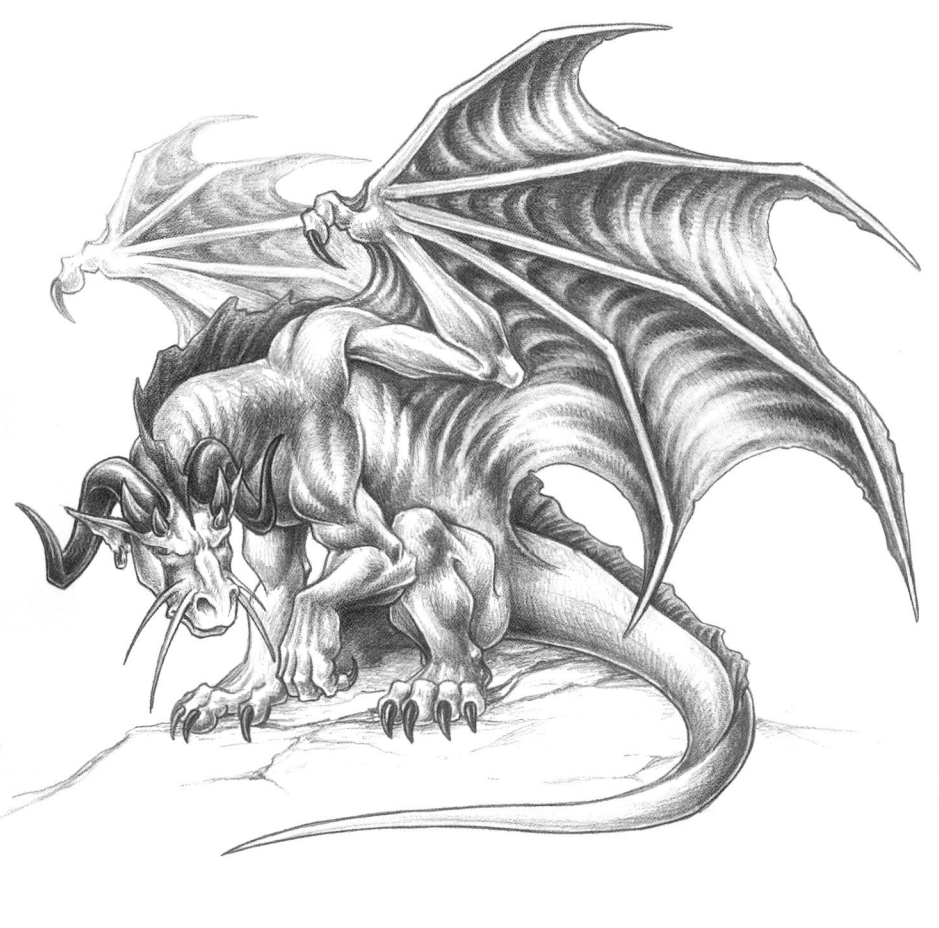

DRAMATIC EXPRESSIONS

Eyes Slanted reptilian eyes suggest a cold, savage personality; large, thoughtful eyes produce an intelligent or kind look.

Horns and Whiskers These features can suggest a dragon's age and personality. An older dragon might have a broken or cracked horn, and one with vast treasures might don an earring or two. Long, drooping whiskers suggest old age.

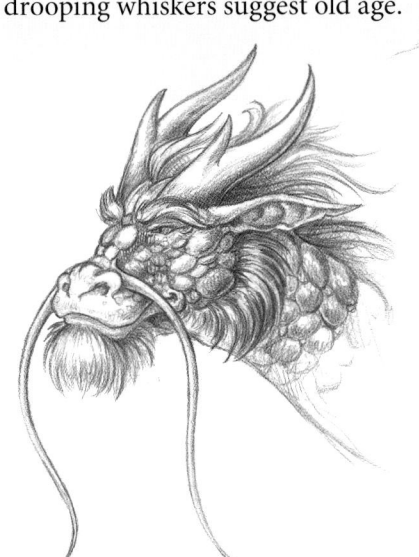

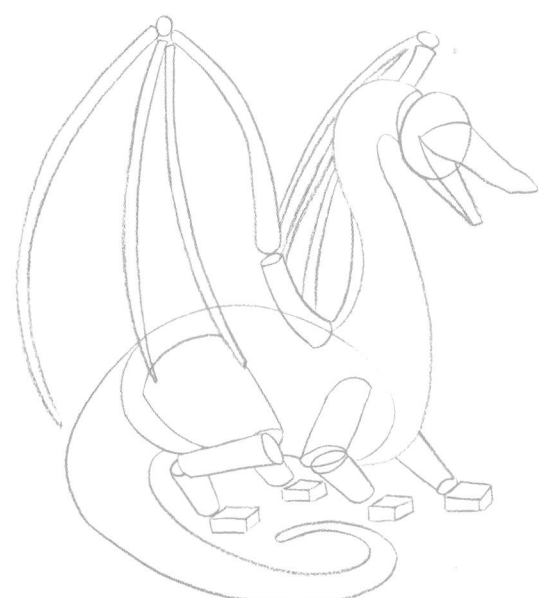

1. Use a 2H pencil to construct the dragon with simple shapes. This will help you understand how individual parts exist in real space and interact with one another.

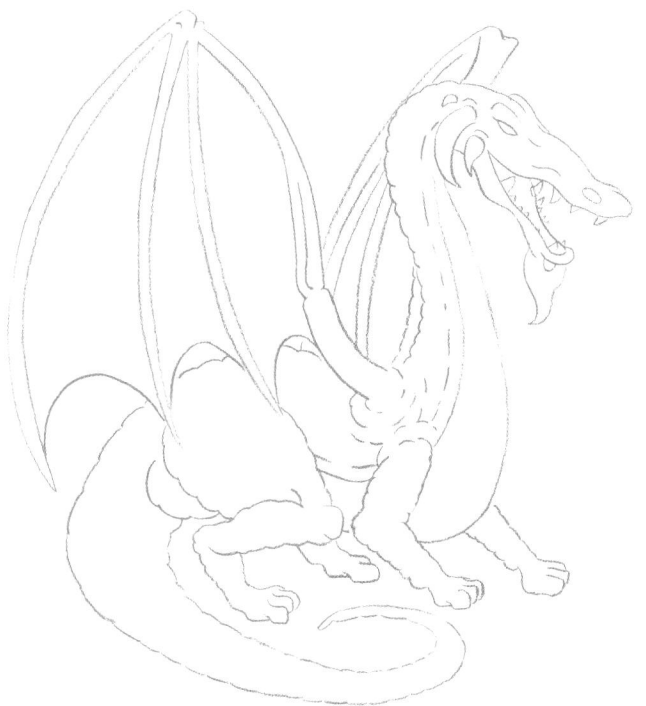

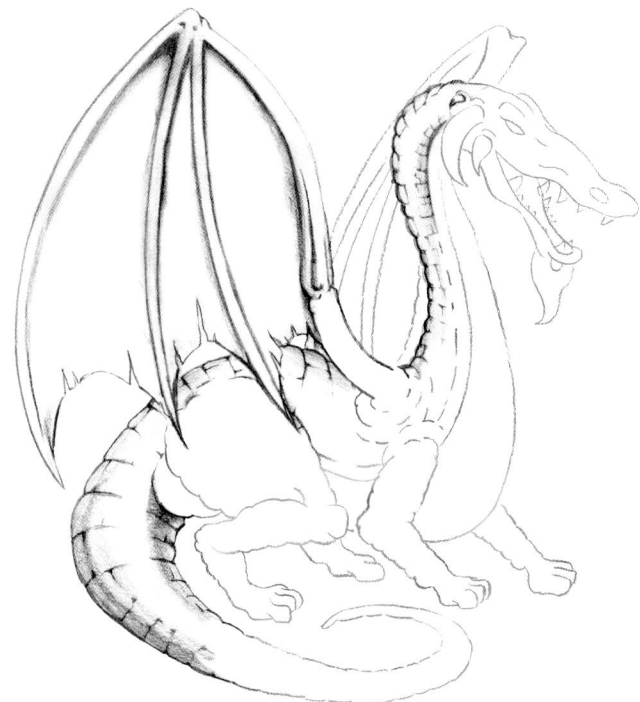

2. Develop the contour lines around the basic shapes with a 2H pencil. Add the eye, teeth, beard, and horns to the head. Erase the lines when you're happy with the drawing.

3. Add tone and texture with a 2B pencil: the hard, rough texture of the skin and the leathery, thin surface of the wings.

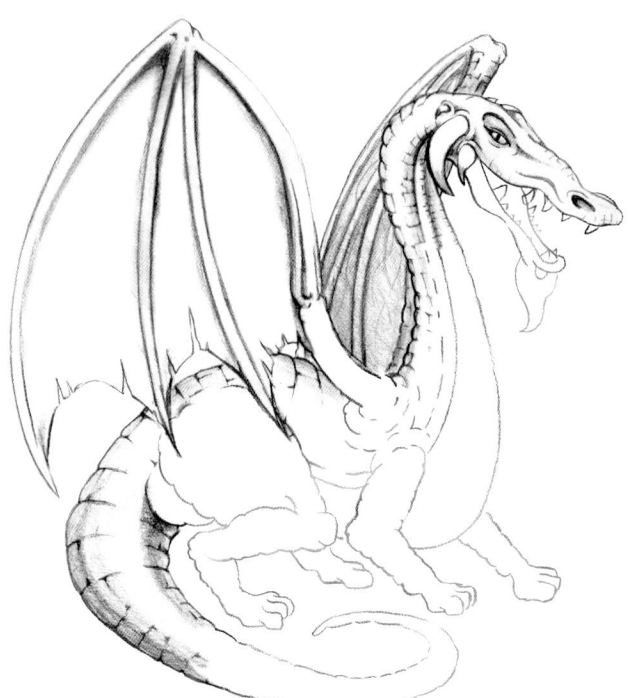

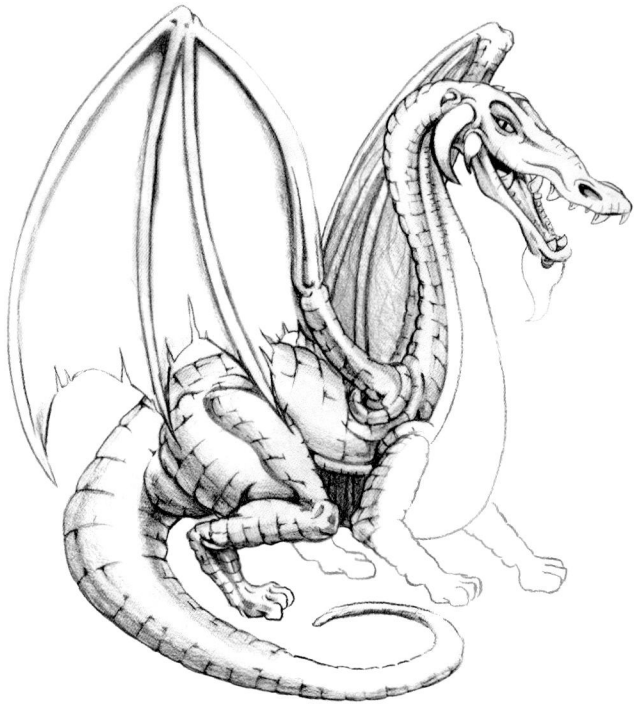

4. Darken the far wing to give it more contrast and provide a sense of depth. Shade the top of the head, detailing the pupil, brow, and nostril, and darken some of the teeth.

5. As you continue to shade the dragon's body, add "cracked" scales that follow its form. (The scales are smaller at the end of the tail than they are at the beginning, which is wider.) Shade inside the mouth, making the back of it the darkest area.

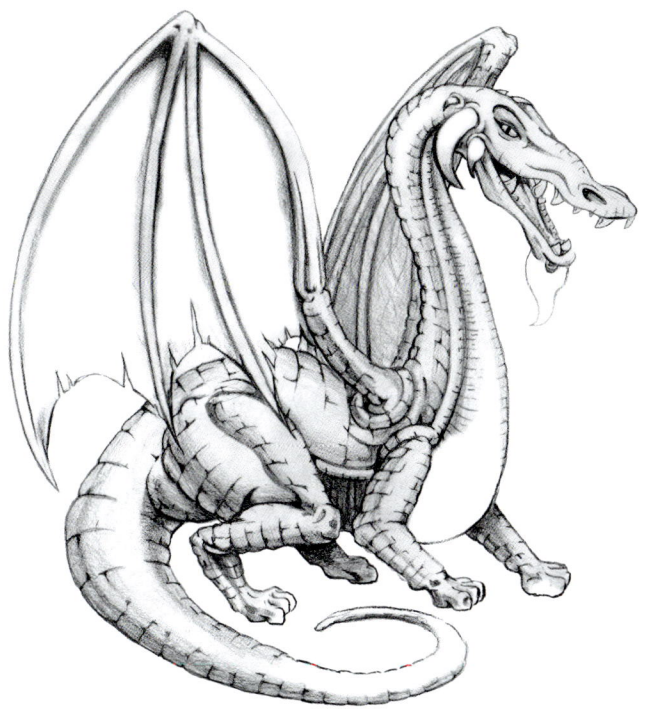

6. Shade the rest of the body except the belly. From the top of the neck down toward the belly, draw short horizontal lines. Add scales to the front legs and refine the paws.

To finish, shade the dragon's front by adding more horizontal ridges to the belly. Shade inside the wings, first creating veins with a blunt 2B pencil, then detailing with a sharp 2B. Draw claws on the paws and shade the beard with curved lines to show its form. Use a vinyl eraser to remove errant marks and lift out highlights on the teeth and horns.

See page 34 for the finished drawing.

DUELING DRAGONS

In this aerial fight, the figures aren't limited by having to maintain their footing, so they're free to twist and turn around each other in space. Start by working out ideas for a composition in your sketchbook. This composition has a circular flow and gives a sense of the motion of the two dragons tumbling through the air, constantly circling each other.

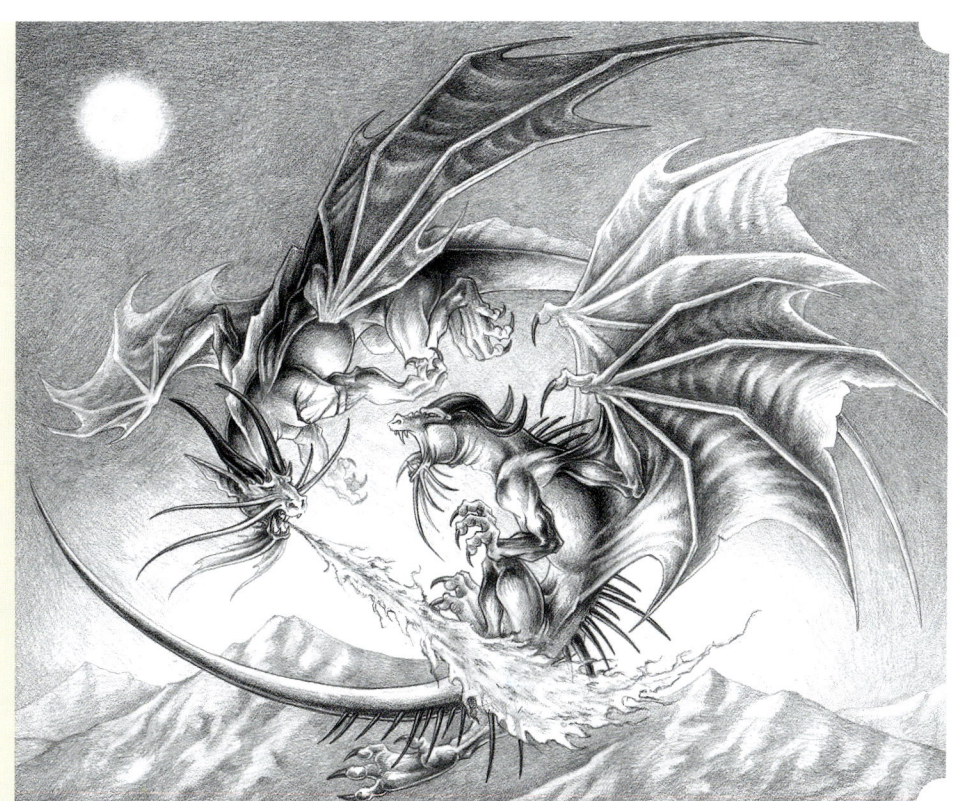

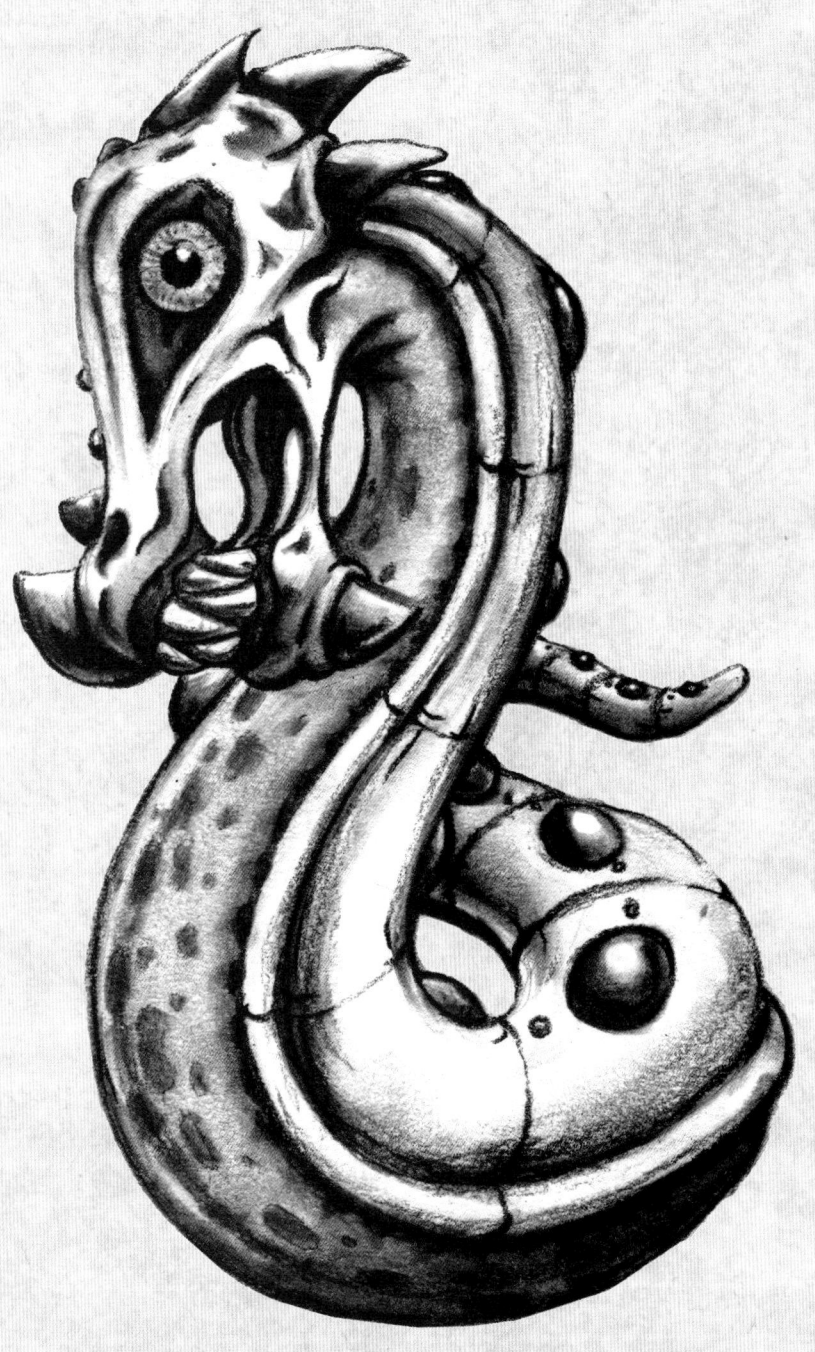

Wyrm

LORE & LEGENDS

† Among the oldest dragon types in European folklore, the wyrm is a serpentlike dragon with a long, slender, wingless body, more reptilian and primal than its later, more elaborate kin.

† Known for its mean-spirited and territorial nature, the wyrm spends much of its existence hoarding and fiercely guarding treasure, often lurking near lakes, rivers, or other bodies of water.

† Legends tell of wyrms with uncanny regenerative powers— even when cleaved in battle, they were said to rejoin their severed parts, making them nearly impossible to kill.

† Ancient depictions often show the wyrm devouring its own tail, forming the ouroboros, a powerful symbol of eternity, cyclical renewal, and the unending nature of life and death.

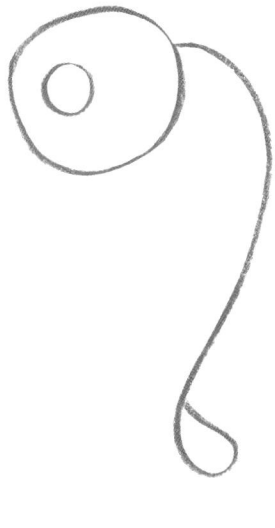

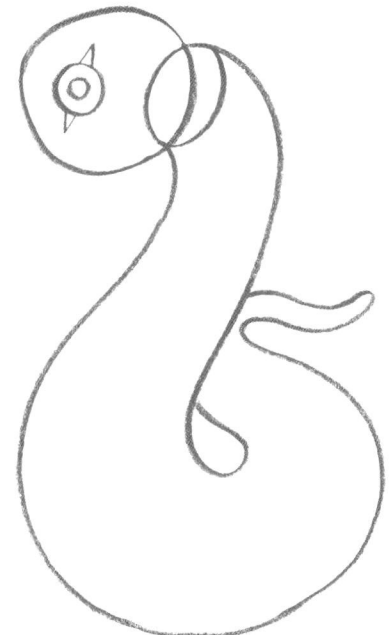

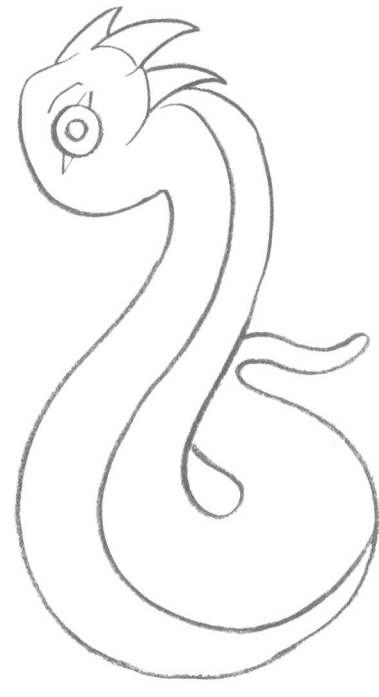

1. With a 3H pencil, draw a large circle for the head, with a smaller circle inside for the eye. Then add a long, curved line that forms a teardrop shape at the end for the foundation of the wyrm's body structure.

2. Building on the original line, draw an S-shaped body that tapers at the end into a rounded tail. Then draw a smaller circle inside the eye for the pupil, using two triangles to define the eye.

3. Draw a curved line down the center of the body to separate the back from the belly. Add three spikes to the back of the head, adjusting and refining as needed. Then add a crease above the eye.

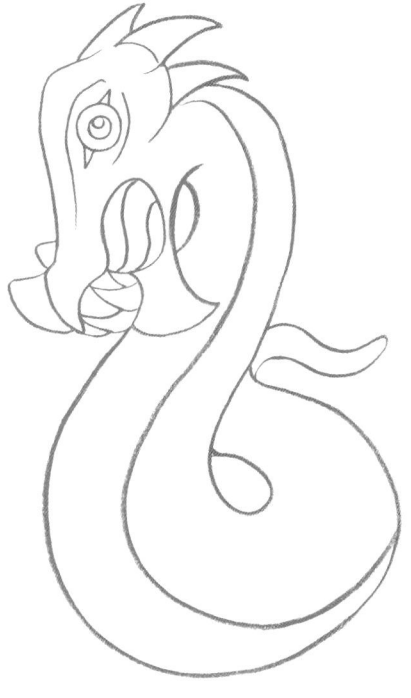 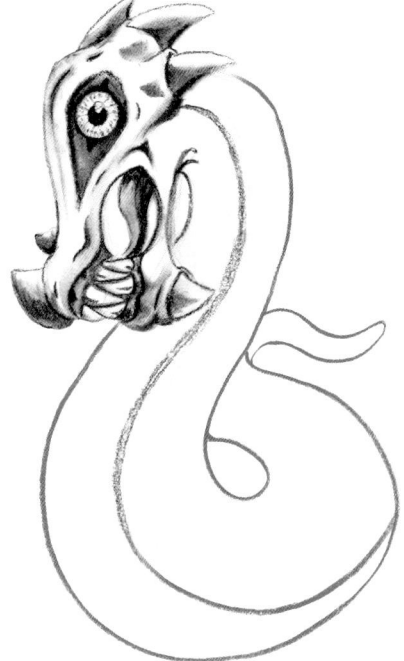 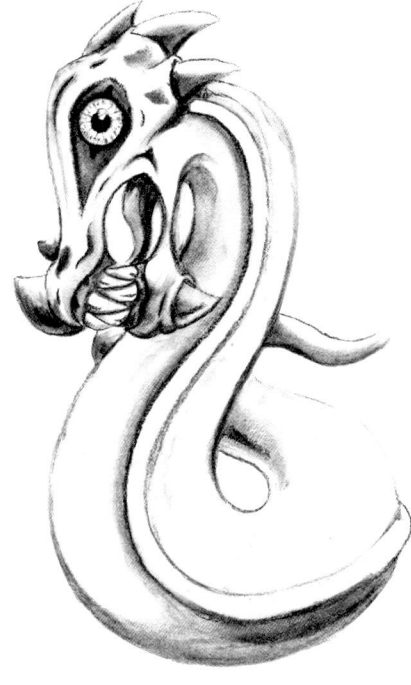

4. After extending the head to accommodate the large, angular jaws—including three horns—add the huge teeth. Draw a pupil in the eye, and extend the line above the eye to reach about halfway down the nose.

5. Because this wyrm has slick skin, use a medium charcoal pencil to add smooth, blended tone. Blend large areas with a stump and tight areas with a color blender (see page 11). Make the teardrop-shaped area around the eye very dark and the iris very light to create contrast. Leave highlights on the tops of the horns on the head, as well as on the tips of the horns on the jaw.

6. Still using the medium charcoal pencil, continue adding tone to the body of the wyrm, blending the charcoal to create the smooth texture.

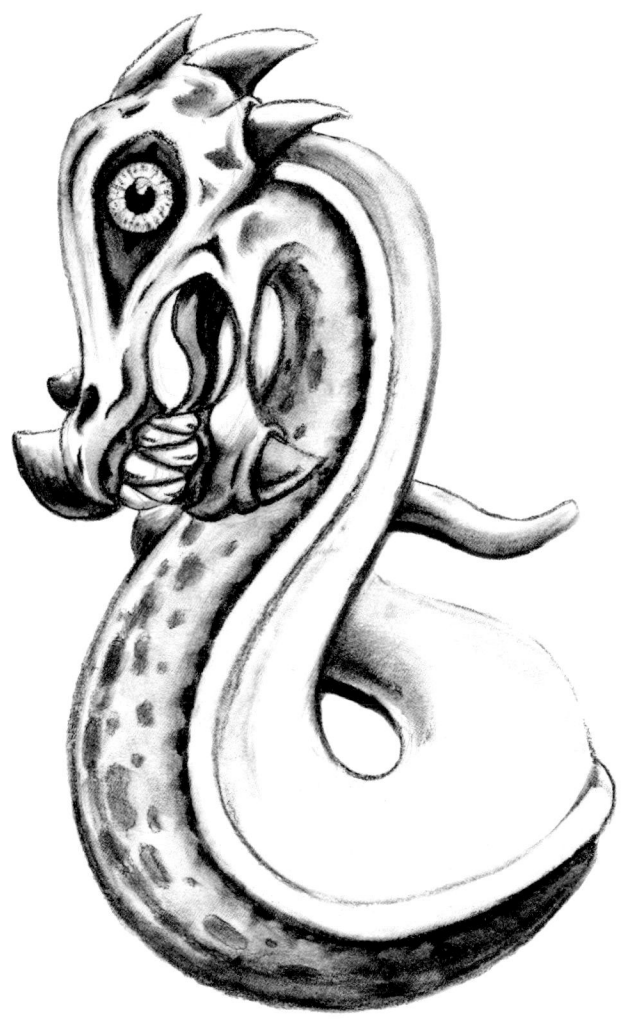 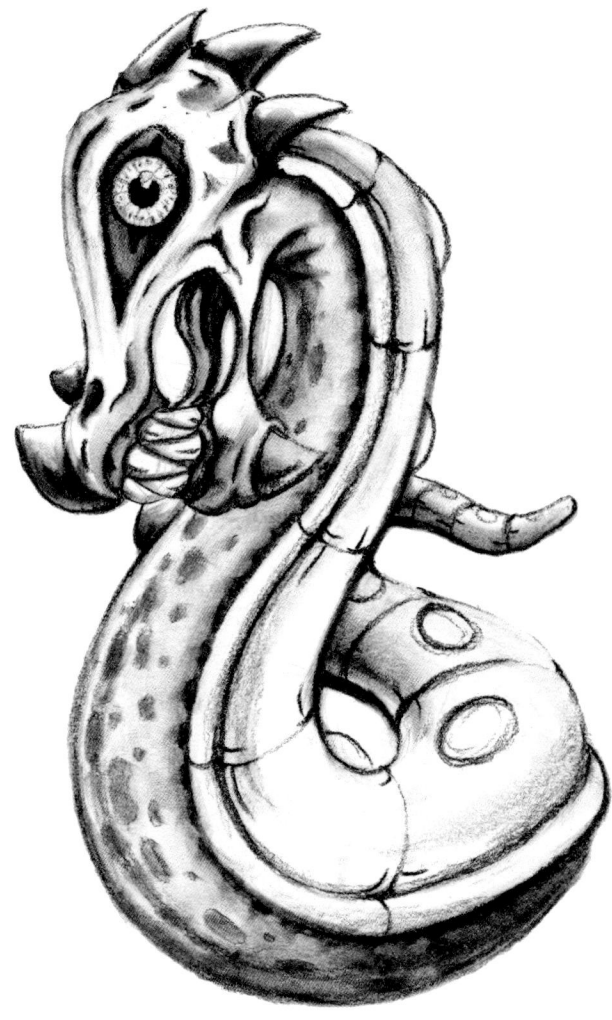

7. Strengthen some of the outlines. Then give the wyrm some belly spots to liven him up. Make the simple shapes with the charcoal pencil, then blend them with a stump.

8. Making some rough segmenting on the wyrm's back gives it an armored appearance. Draw round spikes that extend from the back of the neck to the tip of the tail, and add some cracks on the segments to show texture.

To finish, use the medium charcoal pencil to shade the round spikes, making them lightest at the top. Add some small spots in between the spikes for good measure. Use a charcoal pencil sharpened to a fine point to darken some areas of the face, adding more details.

See page 38 for the finished drawing.

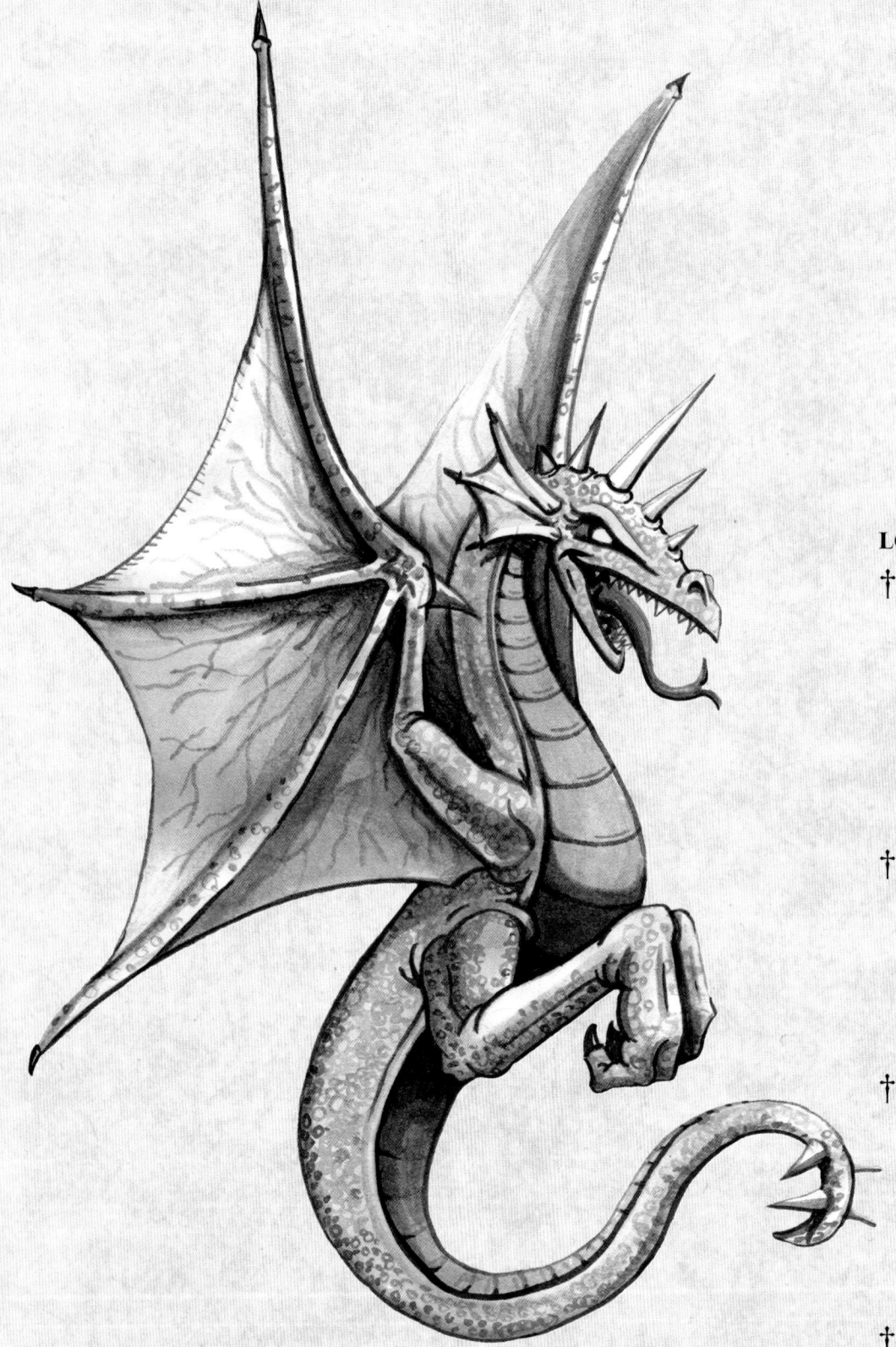

Wyvern

LORE & LEGENDS

† Closely related to the lindworm, the wyvern is a fierce, carnivorous dragon known for its two powerful legs, batlike wings, and long, barbed tail—but notably lacking forearms, which distinguishes it from its four-limbed dragon cousins.

† Agile and energetic in both flight and combat, the wyvern is a relentless predator, swooping down from the skies to seize prey with its talons or strike with its venom-tipped tail.

† During the medieval period, wyverns became powerful symbols in heraldry, representing strength, protection, and martial prowess—often emblazoned on shields, banners, and royal crests.

† Despite their smaller size compared to true dragons, wyverns are no less formidable; their speed and aggression make them feared hunters and cunning defenders of their territory.

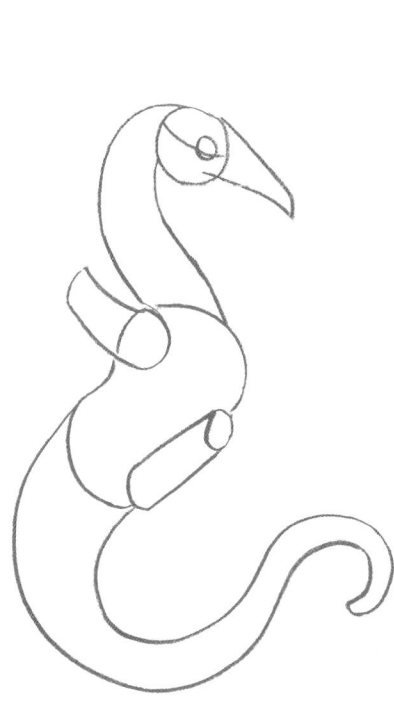

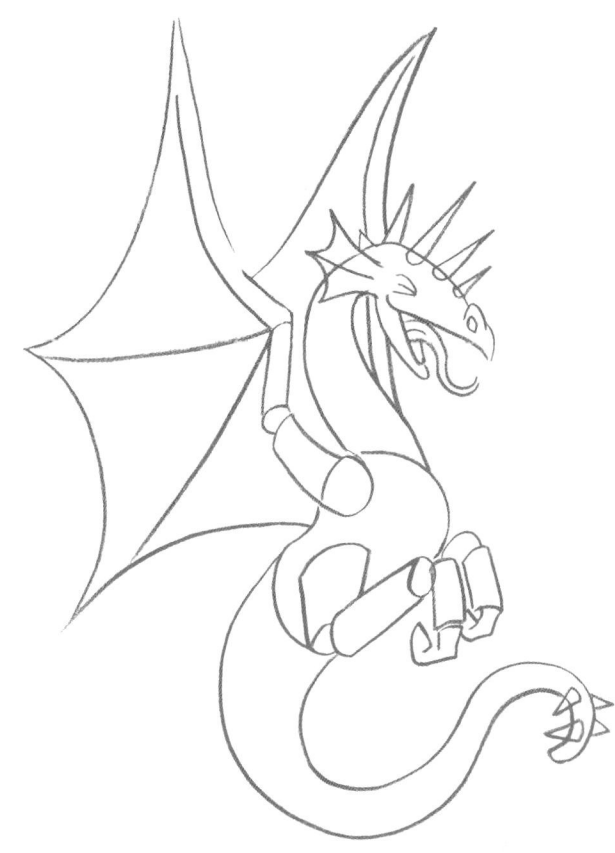

1. With a 3H pencil, sketch the basic shapes that make up the wyvern. Using a horizontal facial guideline, place the eye. Then draw a pointed beak and a whiplike tail.

2. Continuing with the basic shapes, add two large, angular wings, a pair of curled legs, and spikes along the head and at the end of the tail. Add a finlike ear that is reminiscent of the wings. Then draw the lower jaw, adding a long, curled tongue. Refine the eye a bit and add a large nostril.

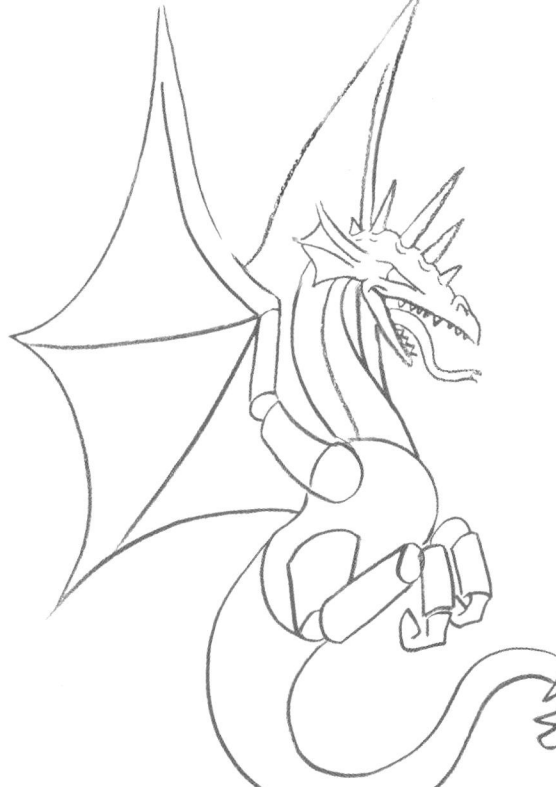

3. Focusing on the head, extend the eye and add small, sharp teeth. Change the shape of the tongue and give it a forked tip. Refine the spikes on top of the head, adding ridges where they protrude from the head. Then refine the ear.

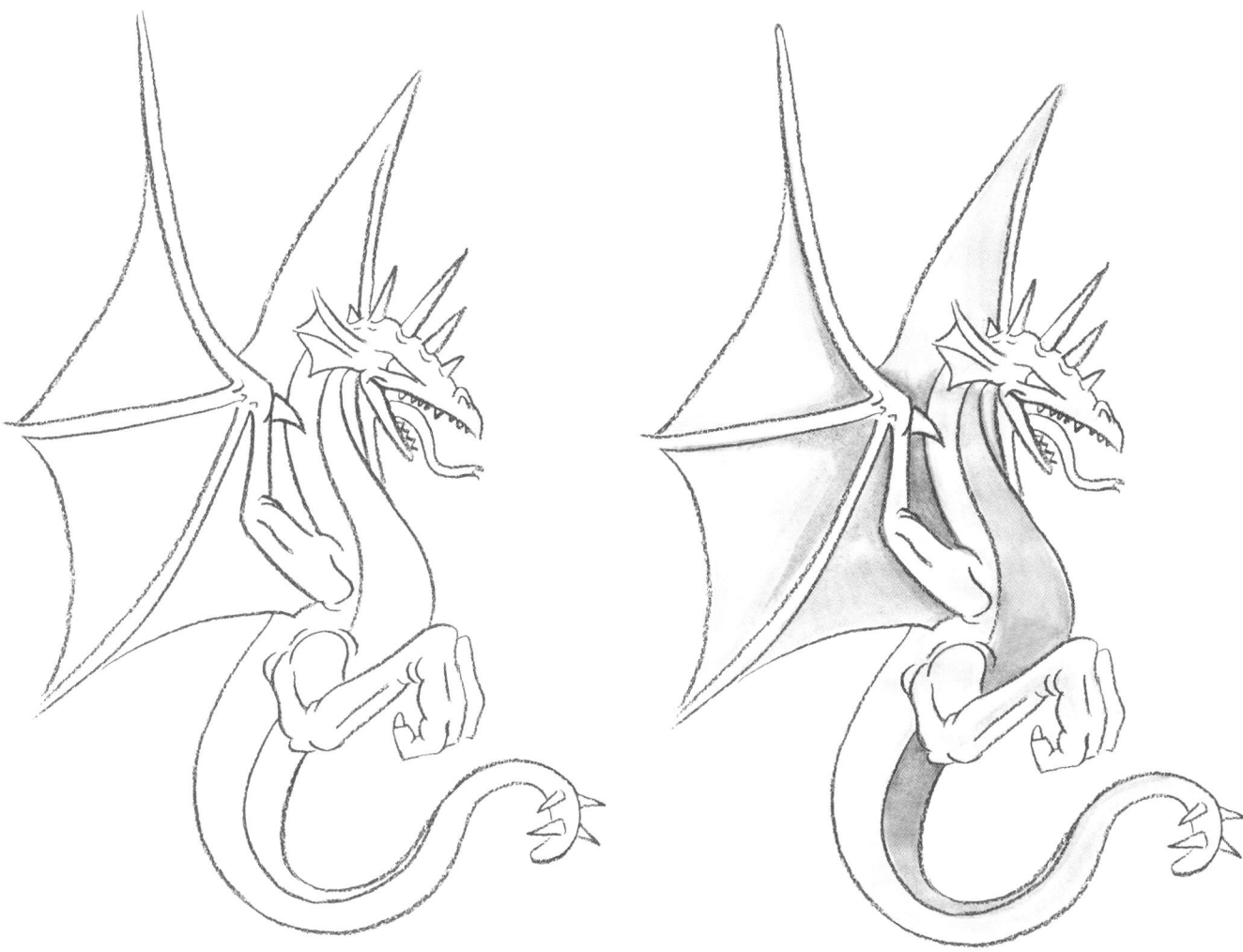

4. Building on the initial wing structures, add definition and connect the base of the wing to the body. Then refine the legs, using the basic shapes to create their forms. Add a claw to the foot, then draw a line to delineate the front of the tail. Erase any unwanted lines.

5. To create a sleek, subtle tone, dilute some India ink to make a wash (see page 11), applying it all over the body with a small flat brush. Let that layer dry, then apply another wash over the belly and the front of the tail, as well as around the wing bones.

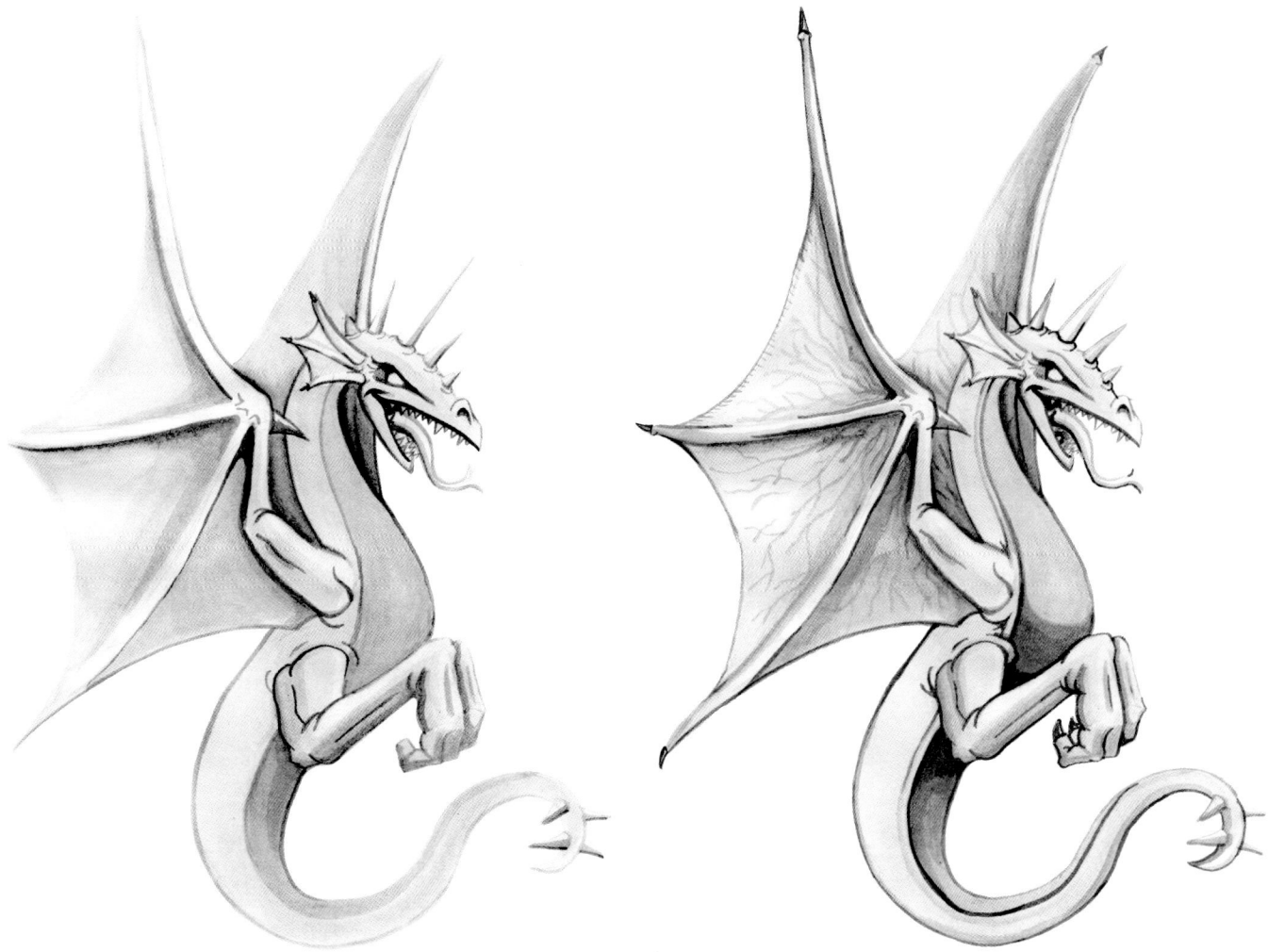

6. After the wash dries, erase any visible pencil lines. With a small, round detail brush, add details with a much darker wash (this time using more ink and less water). Use the dark wash sparingly, because the black is so powerful; it's much safer to start light and build to dark than the other way around.

7. Still using the detail brush, go back to a medium-thin wash to "draw" small veins on the wings. Then add spikes at the tips of the wing bones with less-diluted ink, using this same dark mix to outline the bases of the spikes on the head. Deepen the shading on the underside of the tail and the belly area, and use the same dark ink to outline the ridge of the curved body and tail.

To finish, use a light wash to add small spots all over the dragon's body to indicate its scaly texture. This makes the smoother areas (the wings, horns, and belly) stand out more. Once the ink dries, use a 3B pencil to draw curved lines across the dragon's belly and add some detail shading. Use the same pencil to indicate a soft shadow cast from the wing on the upper thigh, and make crisp cast shadows from the tail spikes.

See page 42 for the finished drawing.

Legendary Western Dragons

JÖRMUNGANDR: LORE & LEGENDS

† Known as the World Serpent or Midgard Serpent, Jörmungandr is an immense sea dragon of Norse mythology, so vast that he encircles the entire world and swallows his own tail, forming a living ouroboros that binds creation together.

† Born of the trickster god Loki and the giantess Angrboda, Jörmungandr is a primordial force of chaos and balance—a reminder that even the gods cannot escape destiny.

† Prophecies foretell that he and his nemesis, Thor, the god of thunder, will face each other in a cataclysmic battle at Ragnarök, the end of the cosmos—a clash that will claim them both and signal the rebirth of the world.

† As a sea serpent, Jörmungandr dwells in the oceans that encircle Midgard (Earth), stirring the tides and causing storms with his movements beneath the waves.

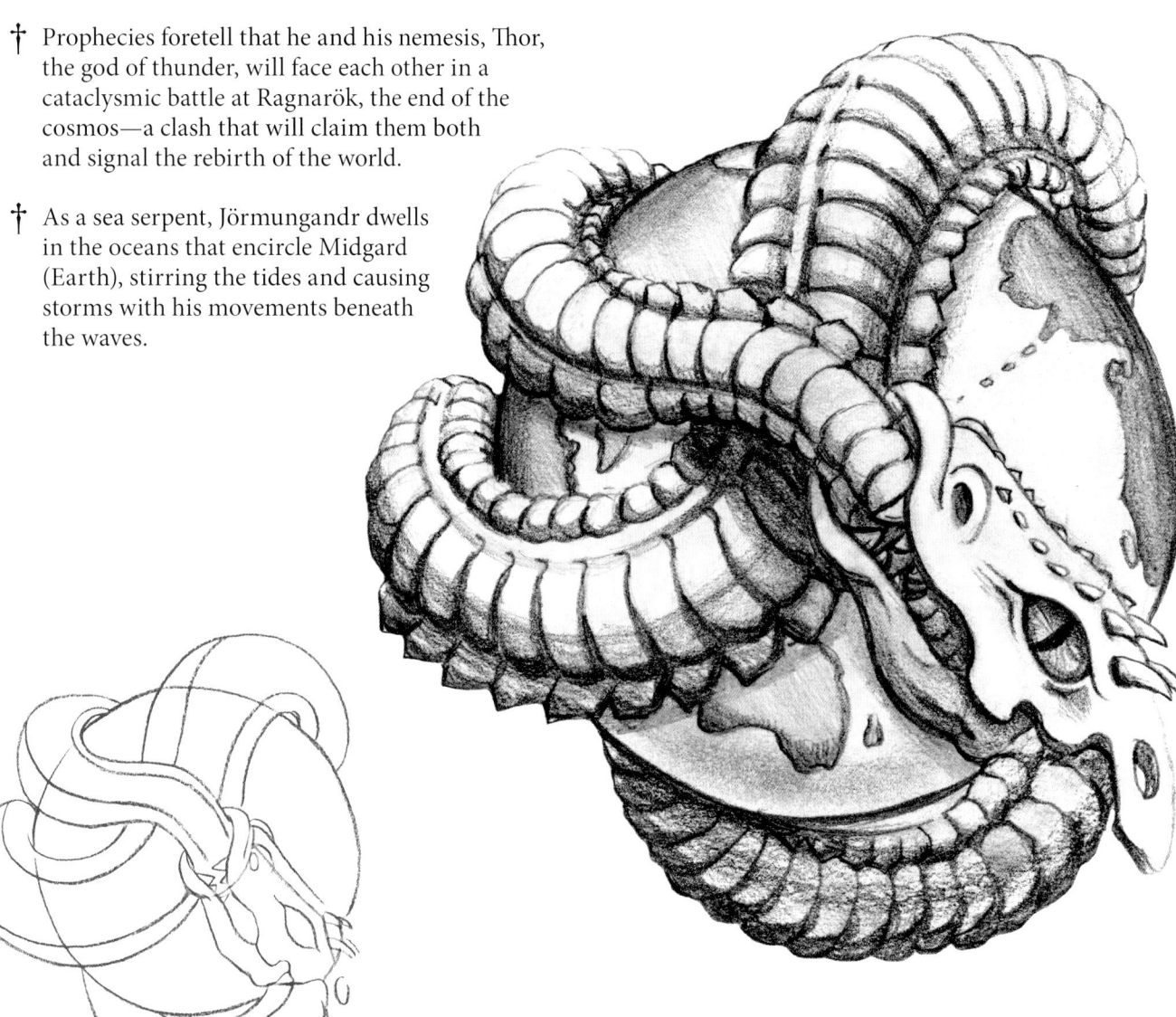

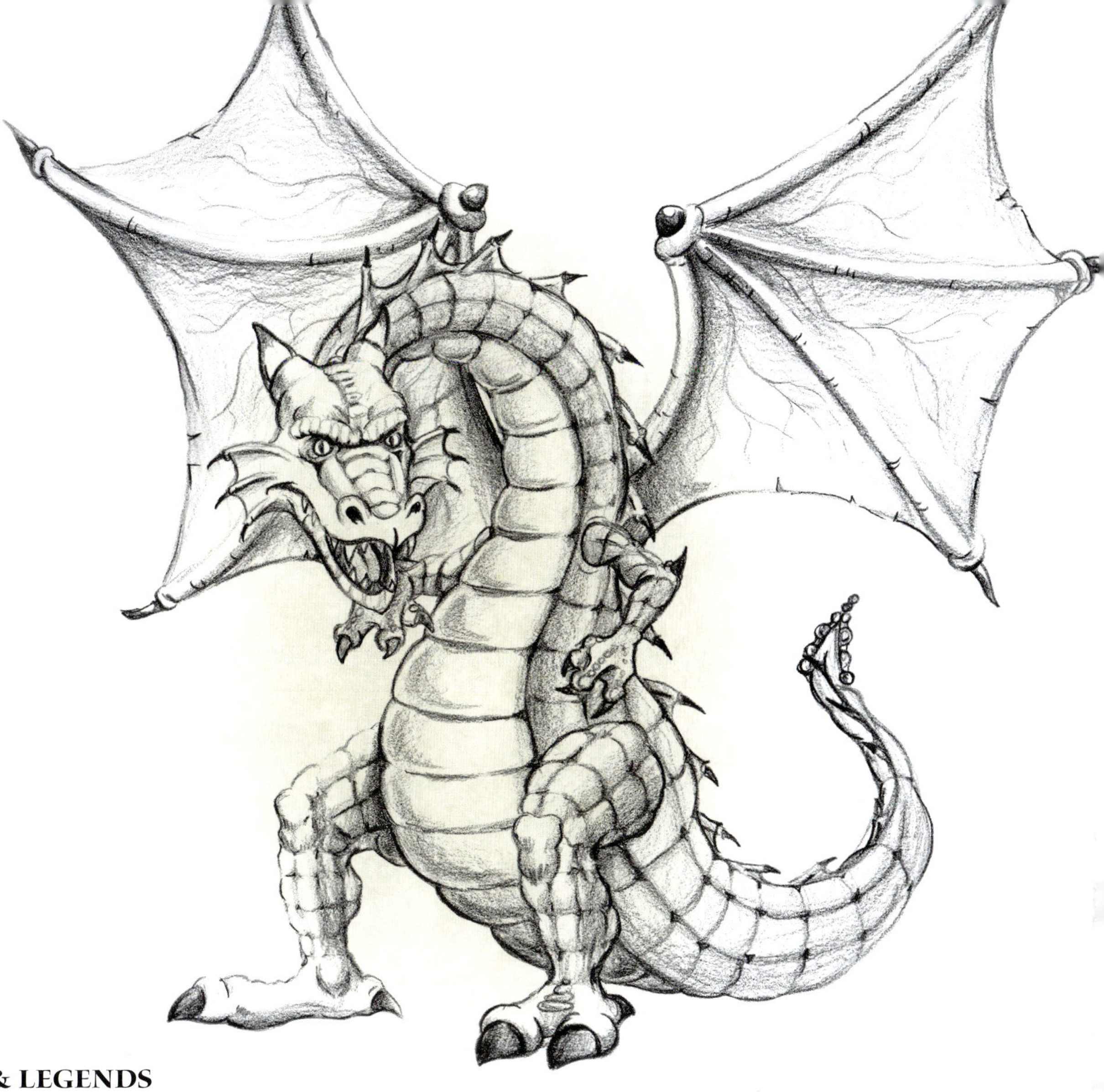

FAFNIR: LORE & LEGENDS

† Once a dwarf and the son of the dwarf-king Hreidmar, Fafnir began his descent into monstrosity after conspiring with his brother Regin to murder their father and seize his immense treasure. But greed soon consumed him—unwilling to share the hoard, Fafnir abandoned his kin and, through his selfishness, was slowly transformed into a dragon.

† As a dragon, he withdrew into the wilderness to guard the cursed treasure, a living embodiment of avarice and corruption.

† Determined to avenge his father's murder and his brother's betrayal, Regin sent his own son, Sigurd, to slay Fafnir. Sigurd hid in a covered pit and drove his sword upward as the dragon passed over him.

† After the battle, Sigurd cooked and tasted Fafnir's heart, gaining the mystical ability to understand the language of birds. Only then did he learn that the treasure Fafnir guarded so jealously was cursed, dooming all who claimed it.

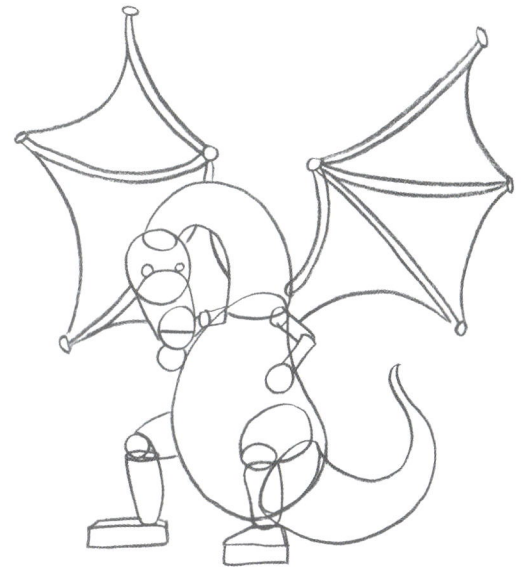

47

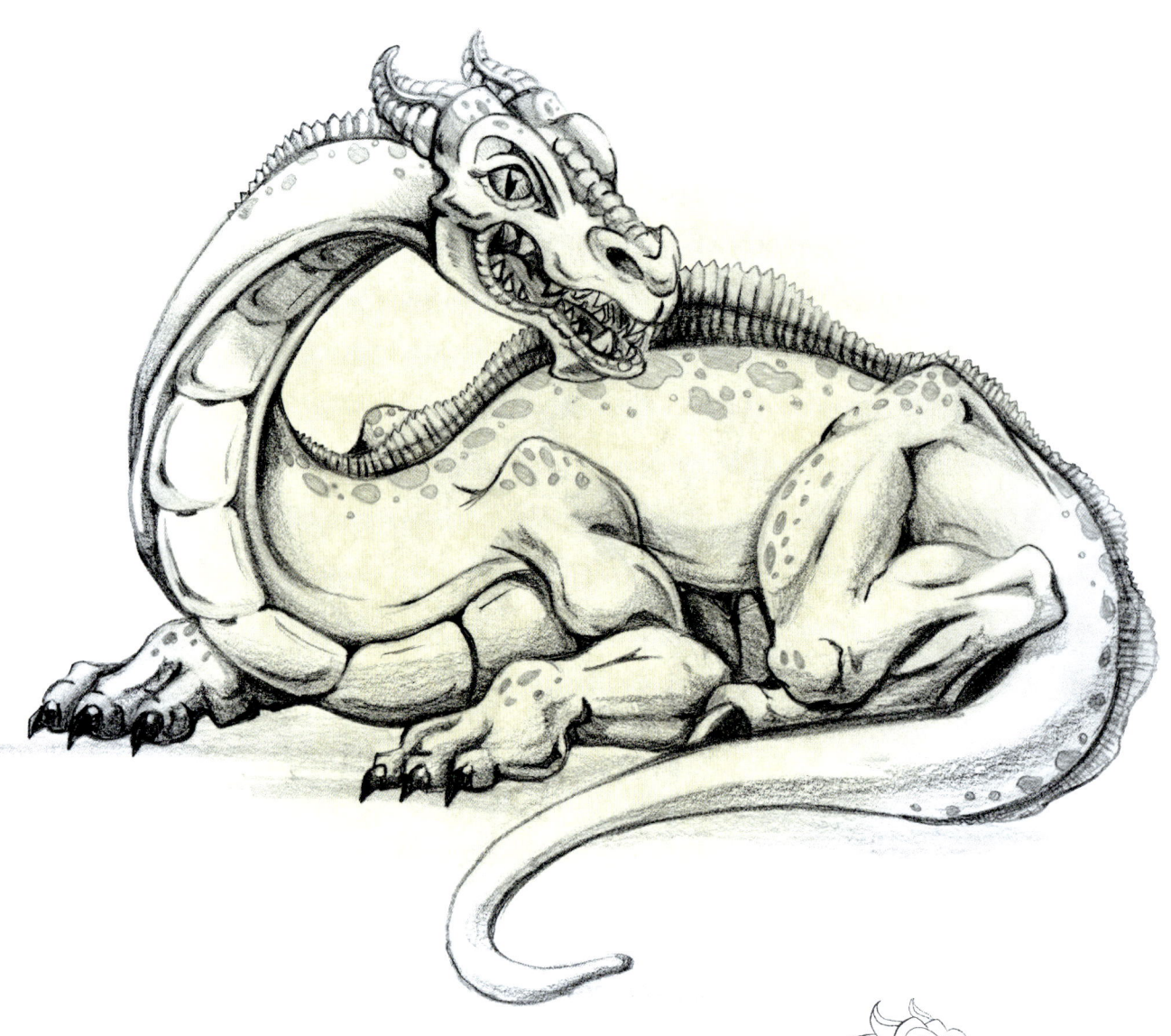

DRACHENSTEIN: LORE & LEGENDS

† This wingless firedrake hails from German mythology. The tale comes from the same origin as Fafnir's story (see page 47)—but in this rendition, Drachenstein was born a dragon. He was slain for hoarding a treasure, but it was his own, not ill-gotten gains.

† Fierce and proud, he dwelled deep within remote caverns, guarding a vast treasure that was rightfully his, amassed not through theft or murder but by the slow accumulation of wealth over ages.

† Despite this, tales tell that Drachenstein was hunted and slain for his hoard, a fate that casts his story in a more tragic light—a reminder that even rightful possession can incite envy and violence.

BEOWULF: LORE & LEGENDS

† One of the most iconic dragons in Western mythic literature, the Beowulf Dragon is famed as the creature that brought about the death of Beowulf, the legendary warrior-king of the Geats.

† According to the epic poem—the oldest known work of English literature—the dragon attacked Beowulf's kingdom in a rage after a thief stole from its treasure hoard, laying waste to the land in fiery vengeance.

† Determined to defend his people, Beowulf sought out the beast in its lair and engaged it in a final, climactic battle. Though he ultimately slew the dragon, the victory came at a terrible cost: the creature's venomous bite sealed the hero's fate.

† Accounts of the monster describe a formidable foe capable of breathing fire, spitting acid, and delivering lethal poison, making it one of the deadliest dragons in the Western mythic tradition.

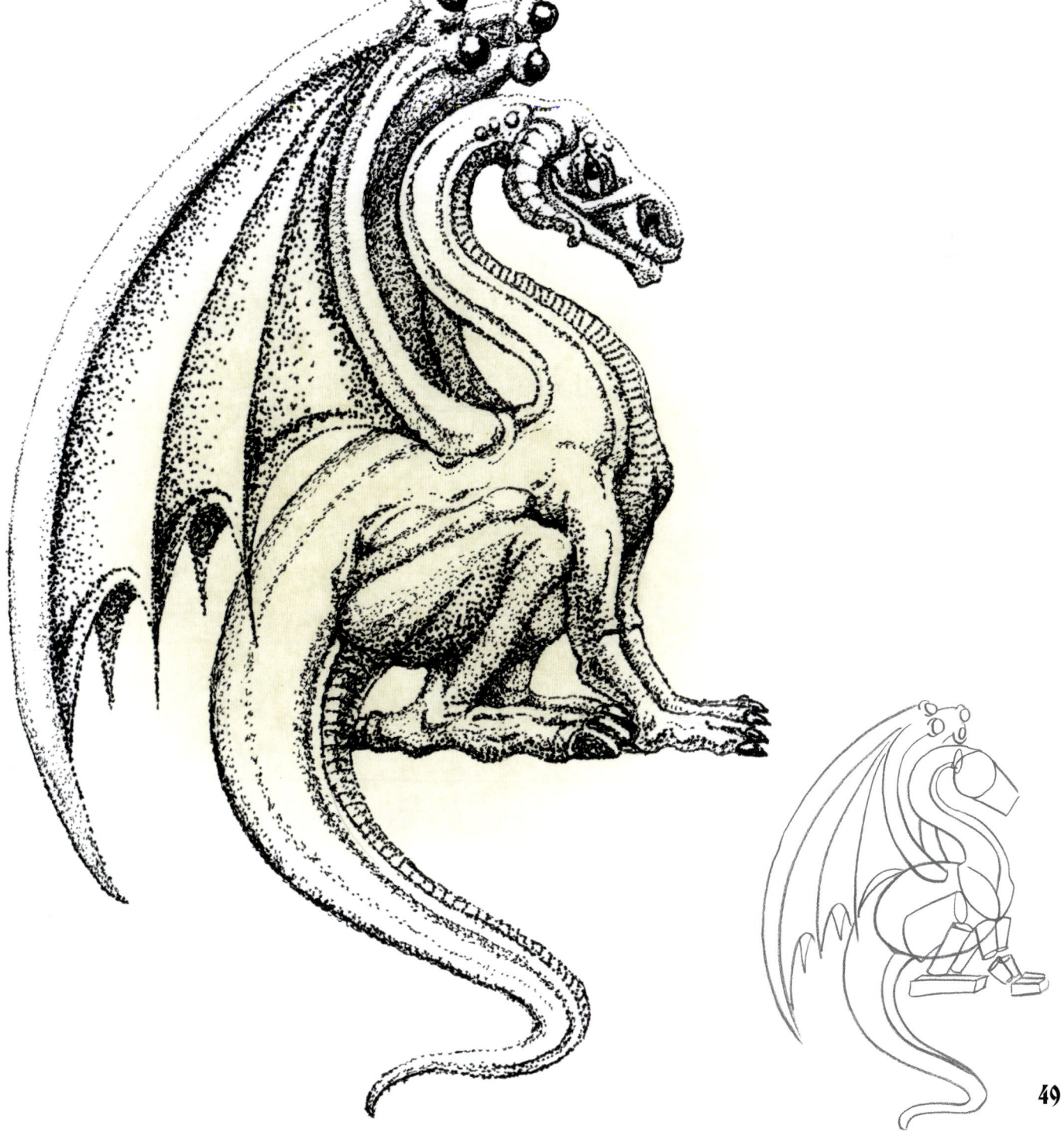

49

Eastern Dragon

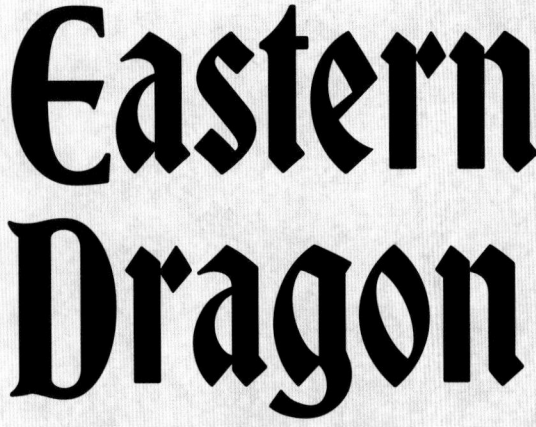

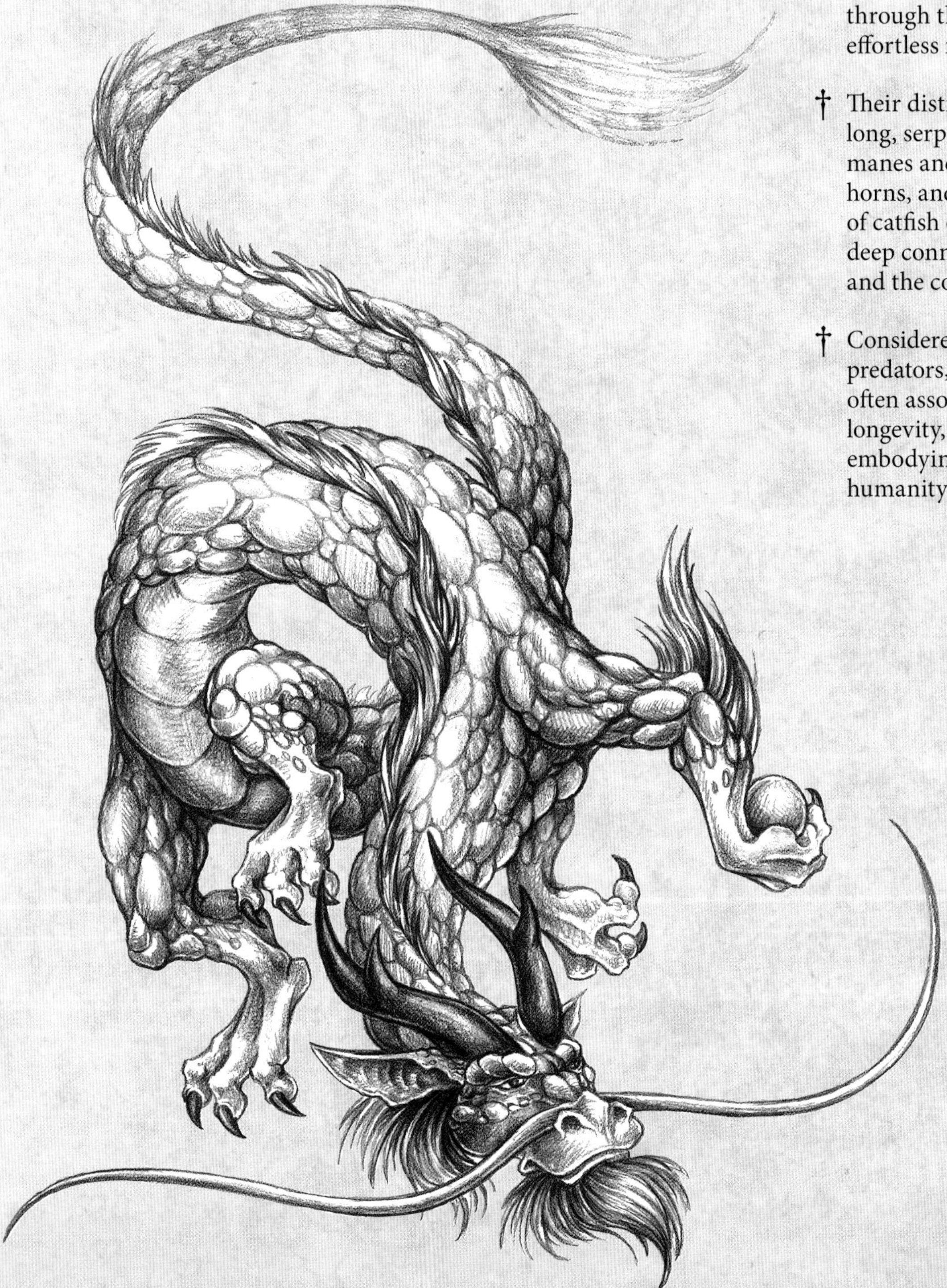

LORE & LEGENDS

† Across China, Japan, and East Asia, dragons are revered as benevolent, wise, and powerful beings—guardians of rivers, rain, and prosperity, and symbols of strength, good fortune, and spiritual balance.

† Unlike their Western counterparts, Eastern dragons are not winged beasts of fire and destruction but graceful, celestial creatures that float and undulate through the air, moving with effortless majesty.

† Their distinctive appearance— long, serpentine bodies, flowing manes and beards, deerlike horns, and whiskers reminiscent of catfish or carp—reflects their deep connection to natural forces and the cosmic order.

† Considered protectors rather than predators, Eastern dragons are often associated with wisdom, longevity, and leadership, embodying the harmony between humanity and the natural world.

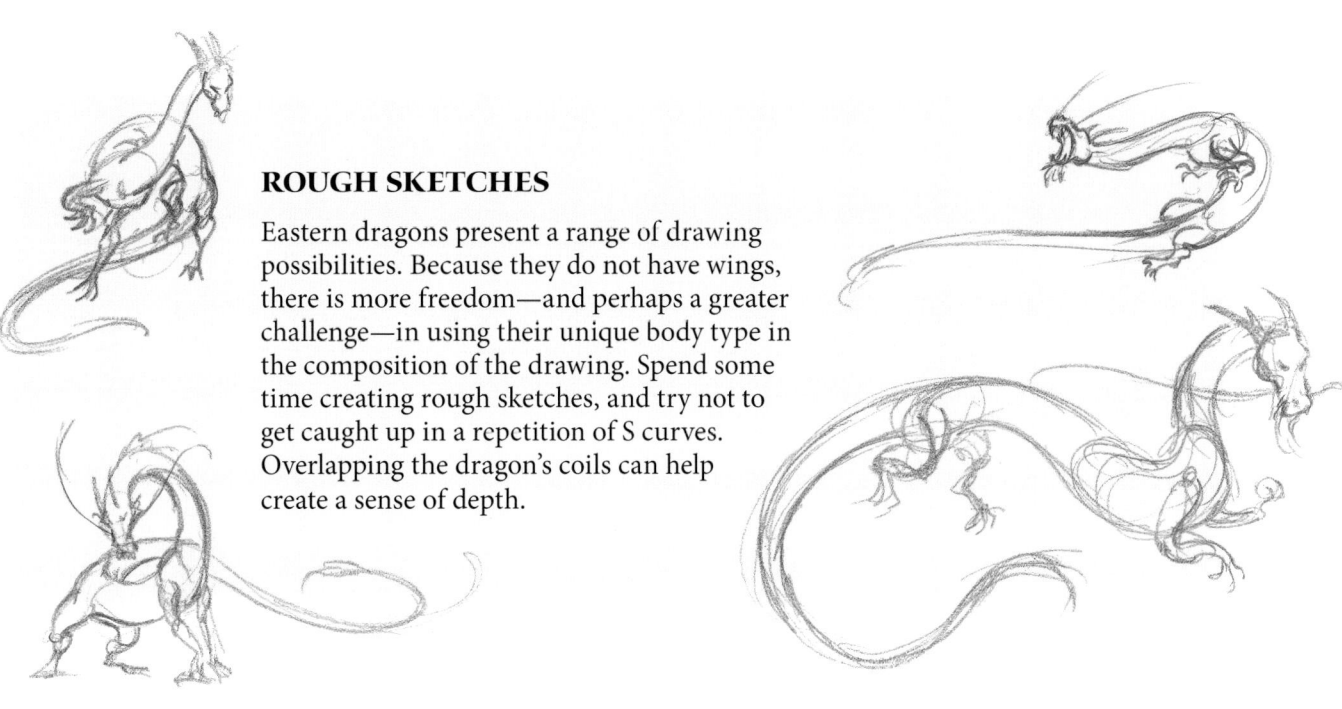

ROUGH SKETCHES

Eastern dragons present a range of drawing possibilities. Because they do not have wings, there is more freedom—and perhaps a greater challenge—in using their unique body type in the composition of the drawing. Spend some time creating rough sketches, and try not to get caught up in a repetition of S curves. Overlapping the dragon's coils can help create a sense of depth.

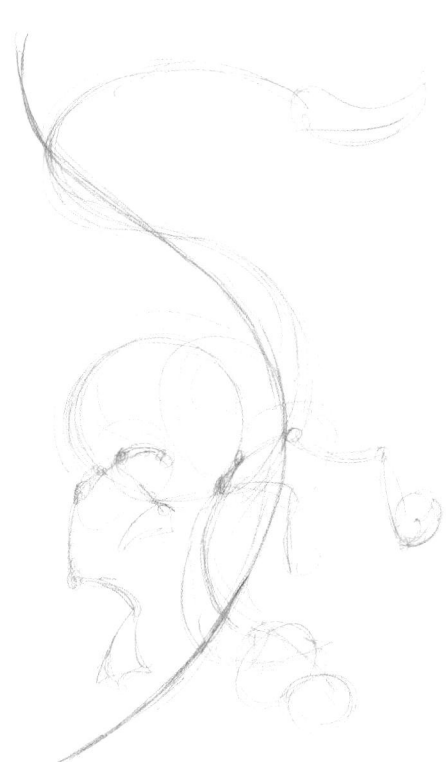

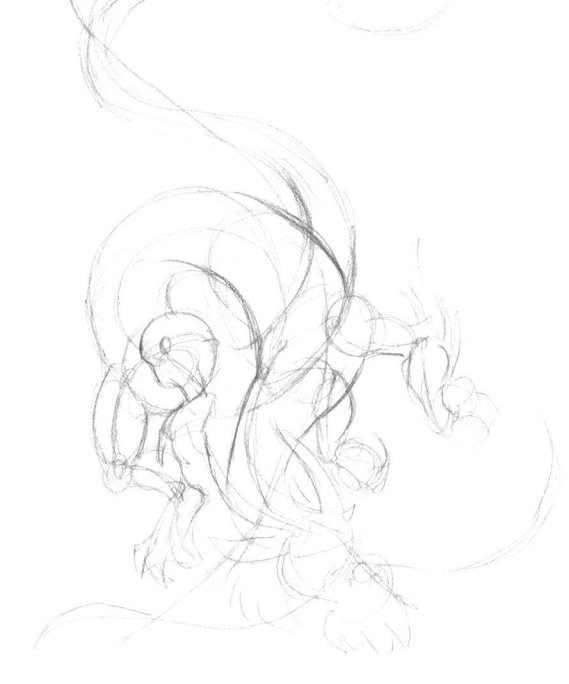

1. Begin by drawing the line of action with an HB pencil. Sketch separate lines to indicate the coil shape of the dragon's body, then rough in lines for the legs. Sketch some rough forms to develop more areas of the body to help you find a pleasing composition. Without wings to fill up the frame, there is more freedom to play around with the coil-shaped body, neck, and tail.

2. Develop the dragon's overall form and sketch the whiskers, toes, horns, and fur. To help position the limbs (and to continue to draw them correctly), lightly sketch the limbs and the rear body through the front body. To emphasize the twisting motion, indicate the backbone and the belly with separate lines so you can see how the body is turning. If you get overwhelmed by this pose, practice drawing simpler poses until you feel more comfortable with this type of dragon, and then work your way up to more challenging poses.

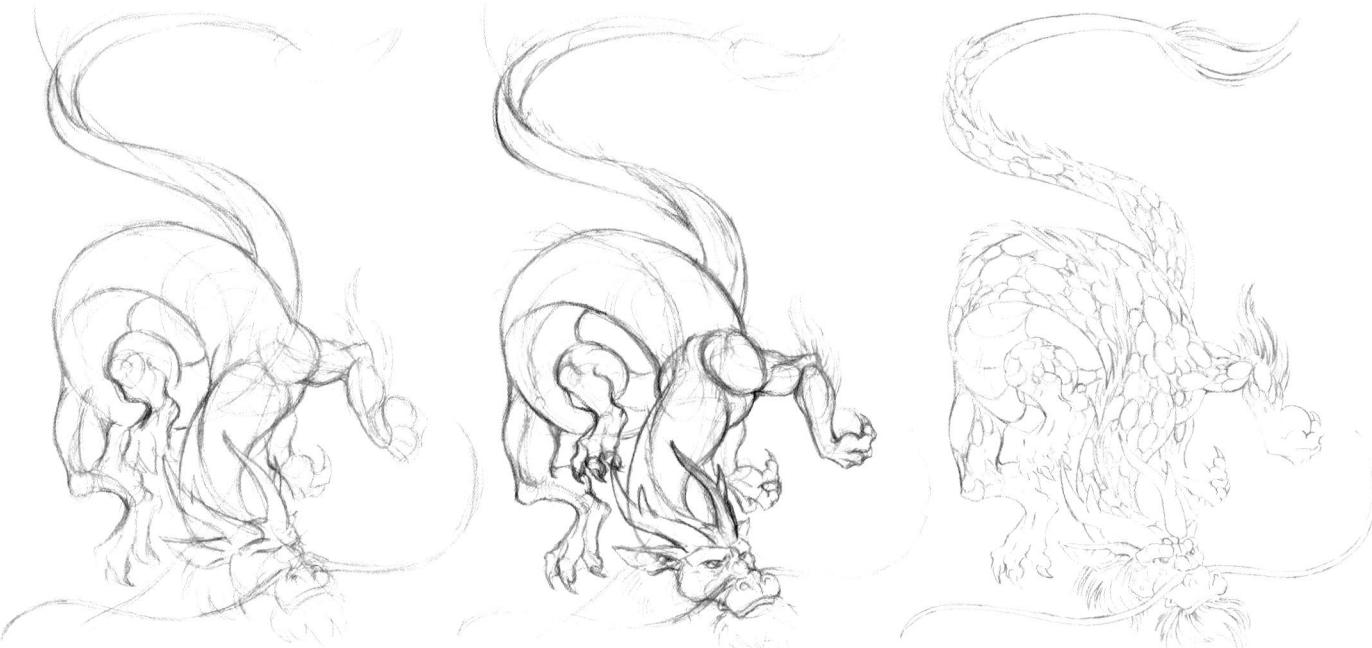

3. Once you're happy with the composition, continue using the HB pencil to develop the form by outlining specific muscle masses. Add more detail to the toes and fur, as well as a few facial features, such as brow ridges and nostrils. More clearly define the shape of the visible ear.

4. Using the HB pencil, clean up extra sketch lines you don't need and darken the lines you want to keep. Further outline the muscle masses and start defining more specific details, including the claws, eyes, horns, and other facial features. Notice the faint outline of the sphere this dragon is holding. Some legends mention Eastern dragons possessing a giant "pearl of wisdom." Details like this are up to you.

5. Transfer the sketch to a sheet of heavier drawing paper so your lines are as clean as possible. Completely erase the remaining sketch lines you don't want. Further define details, such as the claws, horns, and hair, including the mane that travels down the ridge of the spine. By far the most dramatic jump between this step and the previous step is the addition of scales. Sketch them lightly with an HB pencil. Since you're working on a fresh sheet of paper, don't add the scales until the lines are as clean as possible.

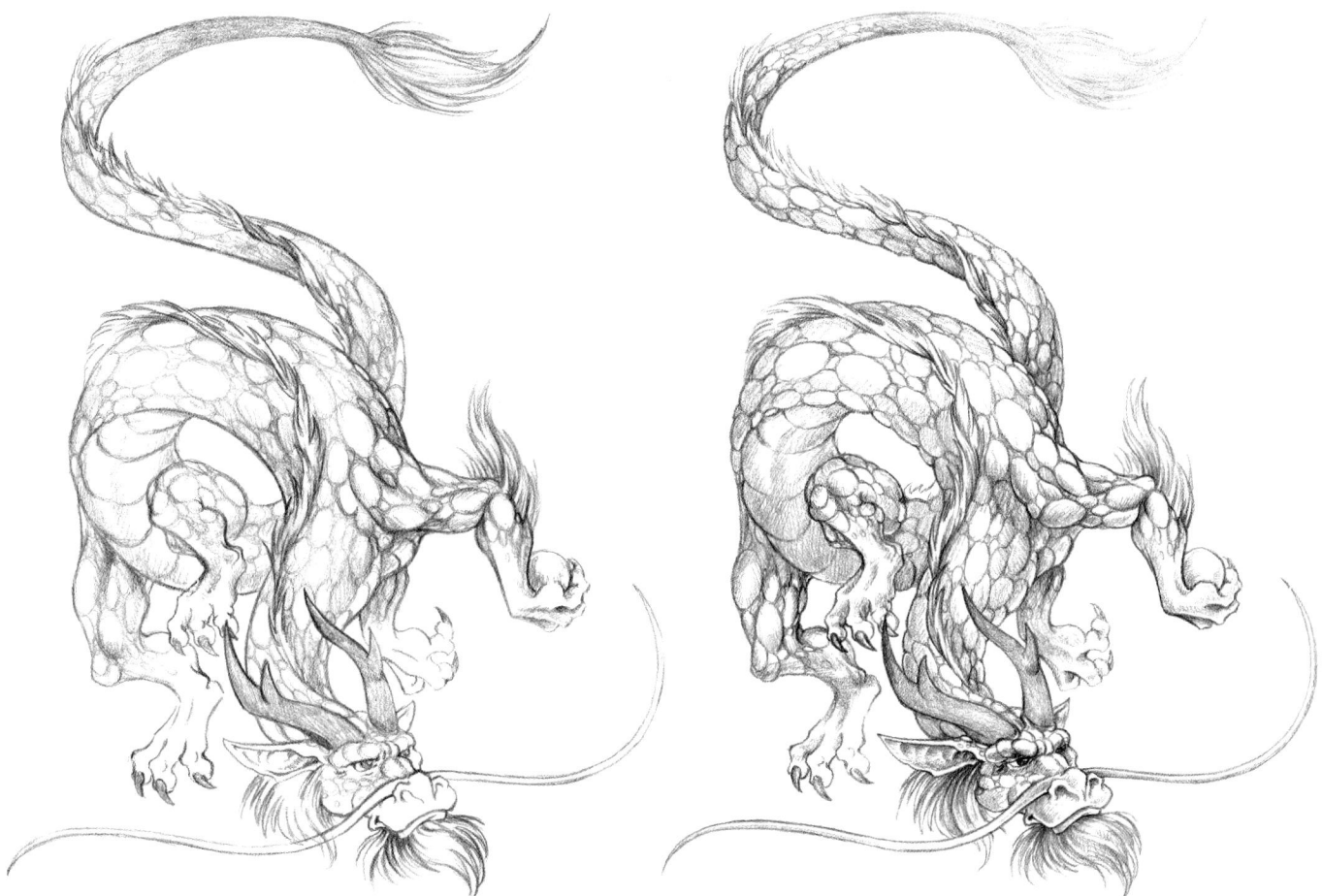

6. Once you've added the scales, start laying down some basic shading using short strokes and hatching with the lighter H pencil; this helps add volume to the dragon's limbs and muscle masses. Work the whole image before developing the shading any further so you'll have a better idea of how the shading will work throughout the image, and you can see which areas need deeper shadows or additional highlights.

7. To develop more shading throughout the drawing, lay down midtones and establish where some of the darker shadows will be by layering shorter, soft strokes using B and 2B pencils. Gradually reduce the detail along the dragon's tail, using atmospheric perspective to make it seem farther away.

To finish, build up the deep shadows using a combination of long and short strokes and some hatching with softer 3B and 4B pencils. Then, using soft strokes with the HB pencil, blend the shadows into the midtones. Lift out highlights with a kneaded eraser. Shade the edges of the scales with a soft pencil and lighten the opposite edges with a kneaded eraser to add volume to the scales and help shape the muscles underneath them. Use the kneaded eraser to lift out highlights on the dragon's horns, as well as in the beard and mane.

See page 50 for the finished drawing.

Eastern Dragons: Myth in Motion

SUI-RIU: LORE & LEGENDS

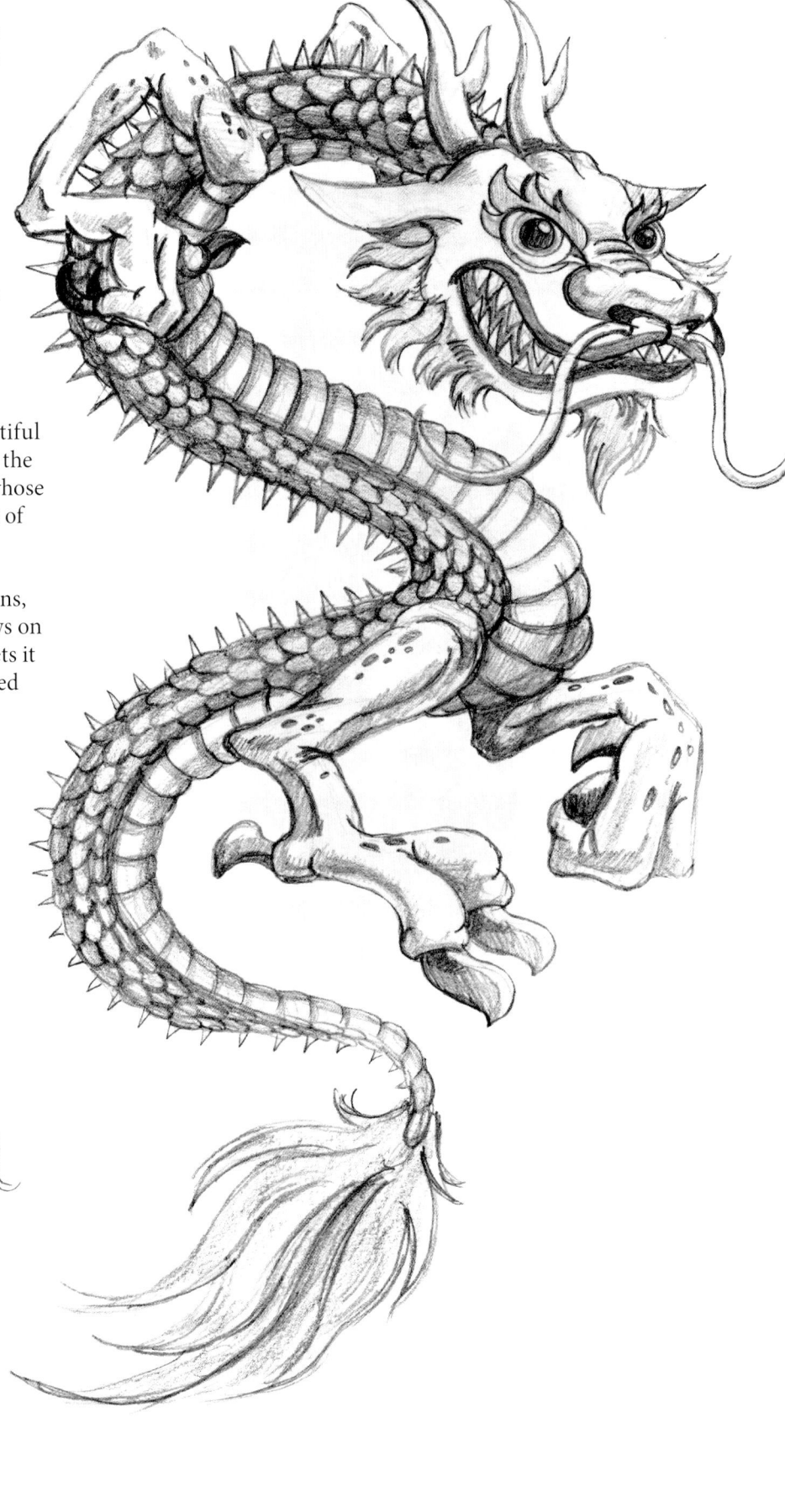

† In Japanese mythology, dragons are rare and deeply revered. Among them, Sui-Riu, the Dragon King of Rain, holds a place of special honor.

† Sui-Riu governs the rainfall that nourishes the land, ensuring bountiful harvests and sustaining life across the islands—a vital force in a nation whose prosperity depends on the balance of nature.

† Like all traditional Japanese dragons, Sui-Riu is depicted with three claws on each foot, a distinctive trait that sets it apart from the four- and five-clawed dragons of Chinese legend.

† Tales describe Sui-Riu as a wise and compassionate guardian, one who responds to prayers for rain and intervenes to restore harmony when drought threatens the land.

54

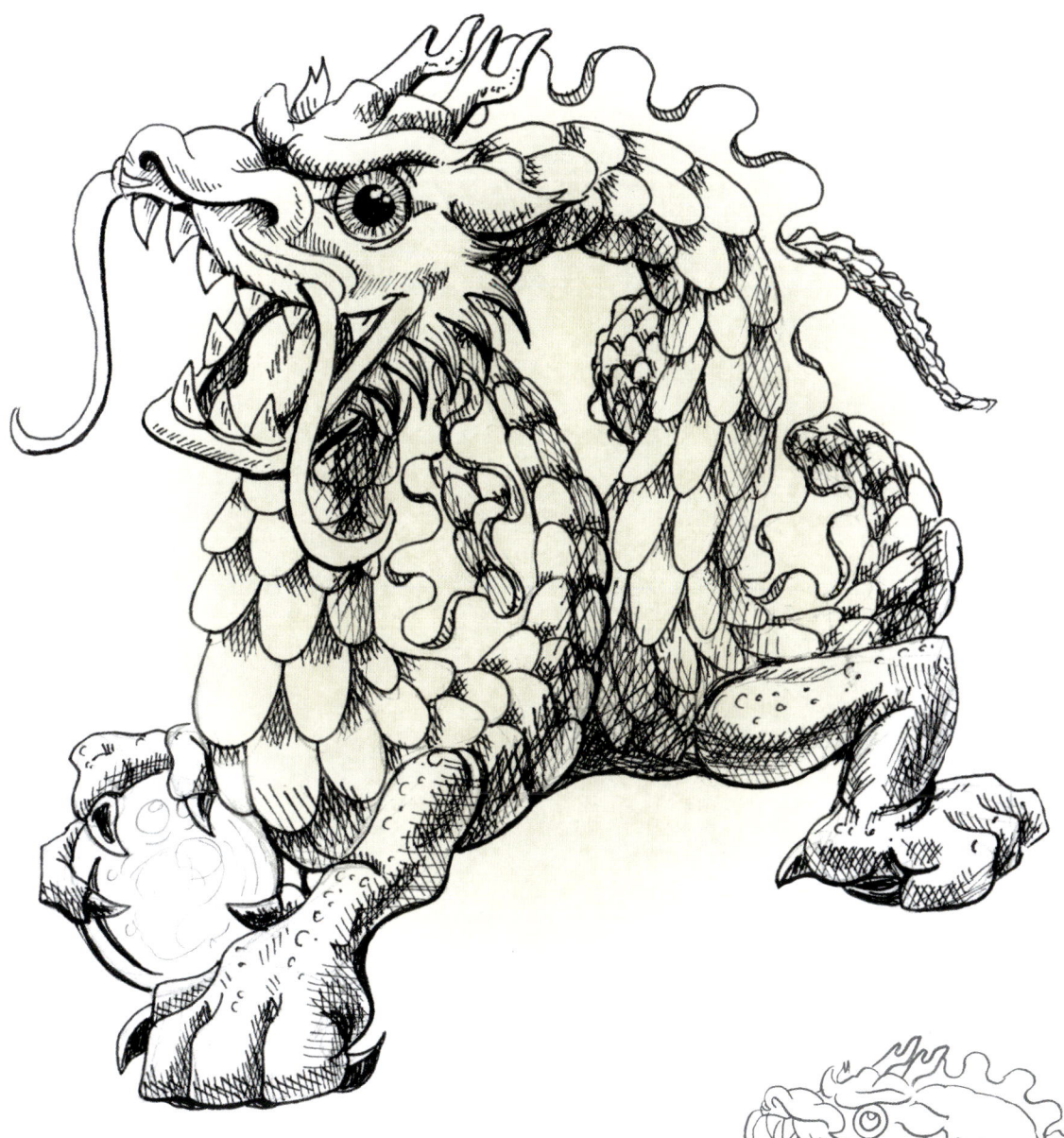

T'IEN LUNG: LORE & LEGENDS

† Known as the Celestial Dragon in Chinese mythology, T'ien Lung is one of the most powerful and revered dragons, tasked with guarding the heavens and the palace of the gods.

† Though totally deaf, this mighty Water Dragon wields immense power, commanding lightning and thunder across the skies—forces that signal his presence and strength.

† T'ien Lung's incredible energy is said to reside within his dragon pearl, a sacred object that symbolizes wisdom, power, and divine authority.

† As a protector of the celestial realm, T'ien Lung represents cosmic order and balance, ensuring that the forces of nature remain in harmony with the will of the heavens.

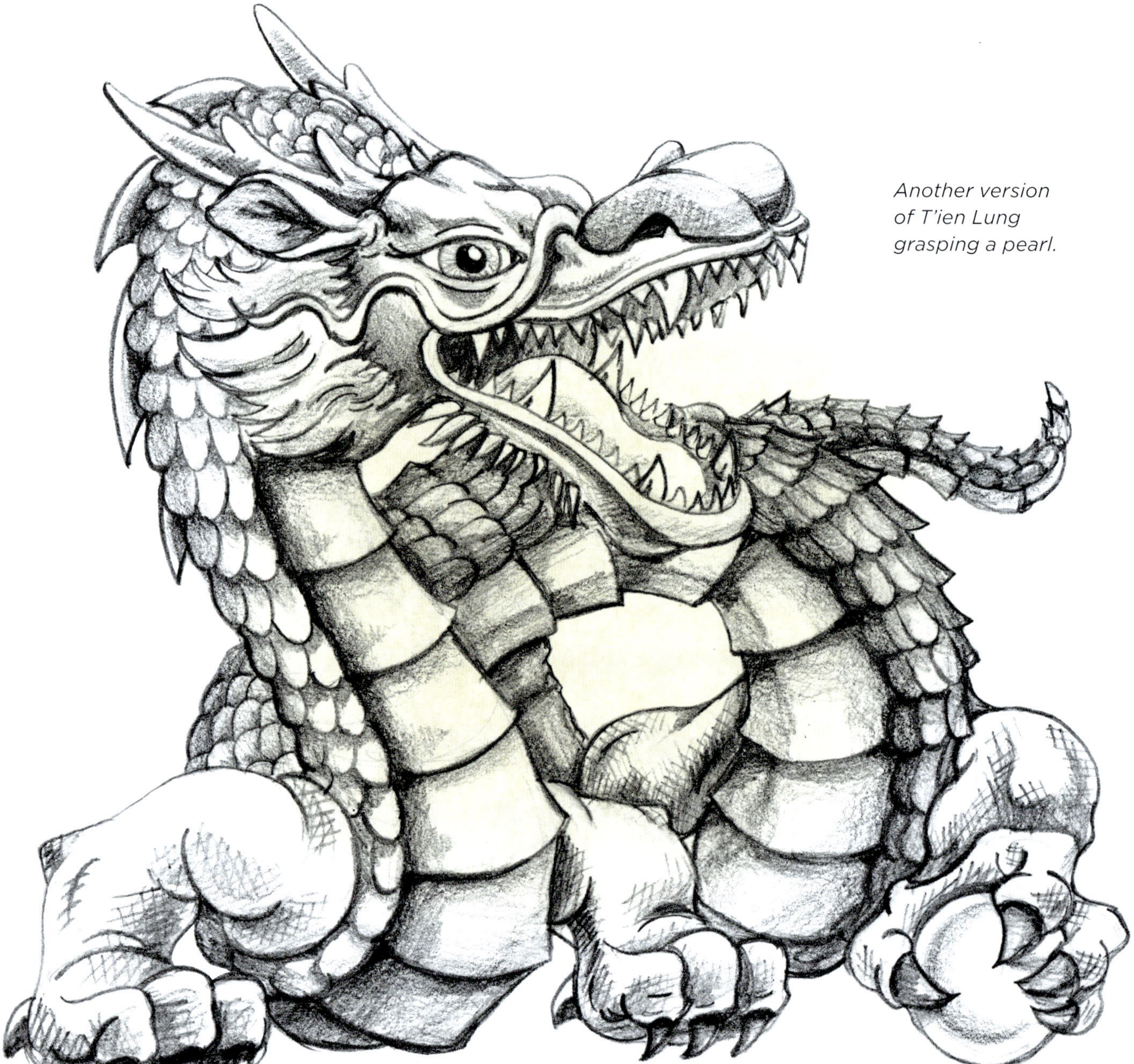

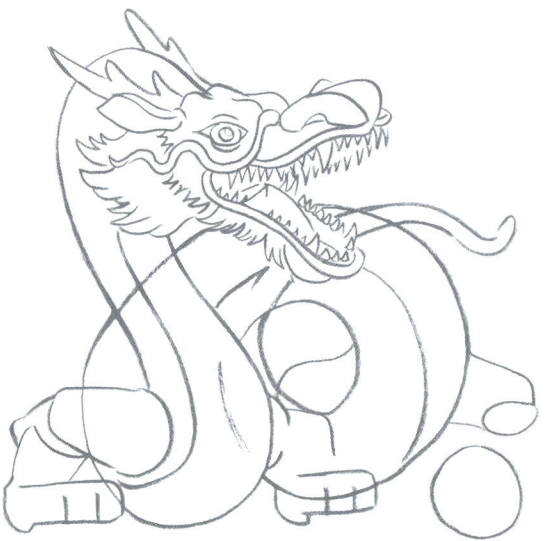

Another version of T'ien Lung grasping a pearl.

Eastern Dragon: Variations

Here are two other variations on the Eastern dragon, showing different features and poses.

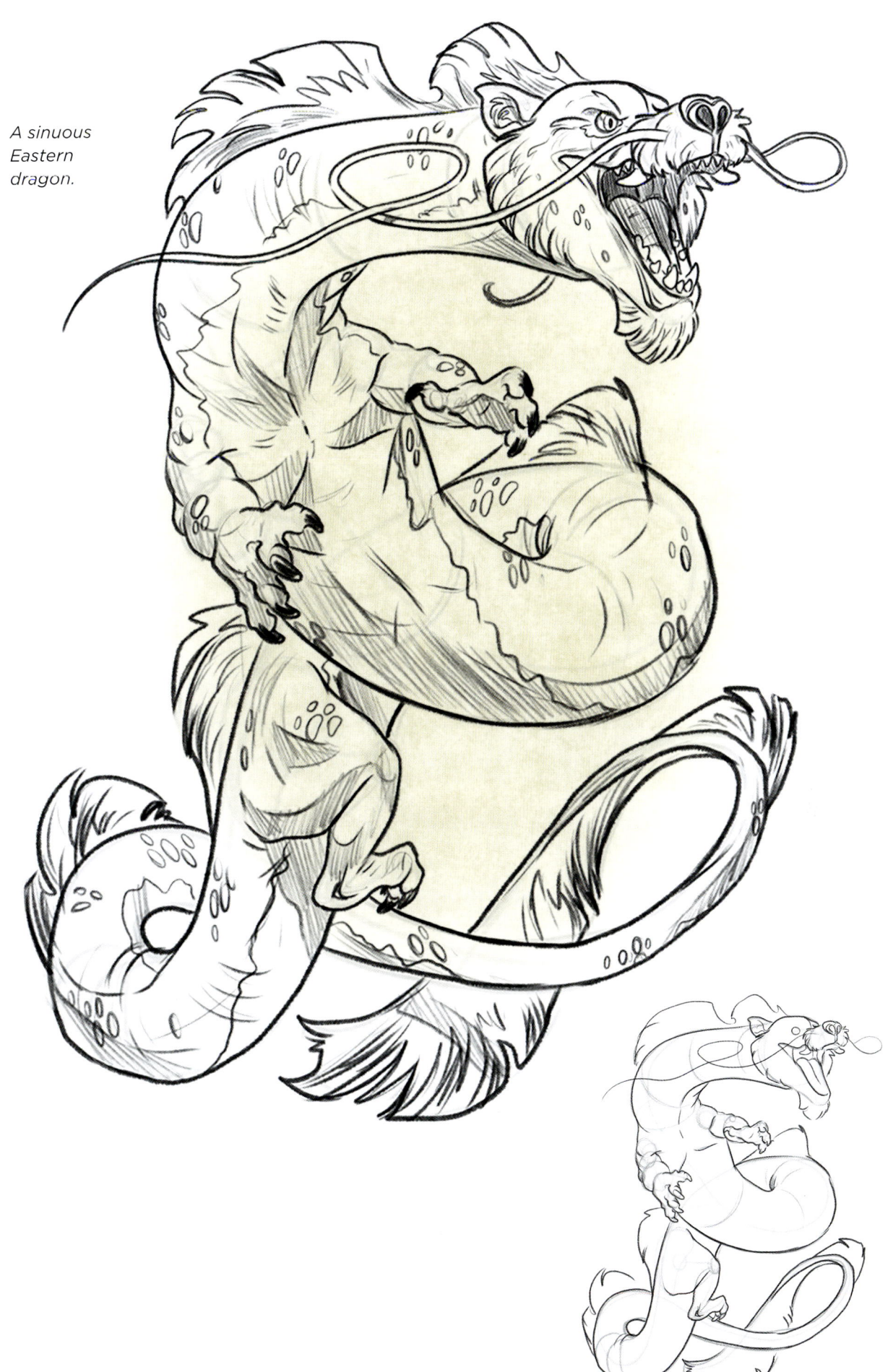

A sinuous Eastern dragon.

Legendary Dragons: Other Traditions

While Chinese and European dragons often dominate myth and legend, cultures around the world have their own powerful interpretations of these extraordinary beings. These legendary creatures reveal the astonishing diversity of dragon lore—and humanity's enduring fascination with their strength, magic, and mystery.

QUETZALCOATL: LORE & LEGENDS

† Known as the "feathered serpent," Quetzalcoatl is one of the most powerful and revered deities of Aztec mythology, classified as an amphitere—a winged dragon with no arms or legs. Majestic and serpentine, he embodies wisdom, creation, and the divine union of earth and sky.

† Quetzalcoatl is credited with teaching the Aztec people agriculture and other essential arts of civilization, guiding humanity toward prosperity and balance. He also possesses the power to assume human form, moving freely between the realms of gods and mortals.

† When Spanish conquistador Hernán Cortés arrived in 1519, Emperor Moctezuma II famously mistook him for the returning Quetzalcoatl—a tragic misunderstanding that altered the course of history.

† The god's name also honors the resplendent quetzal, a bird whose brilliant feathers were treasured as sacred offerings and symbols of divine power in Aztec culture.

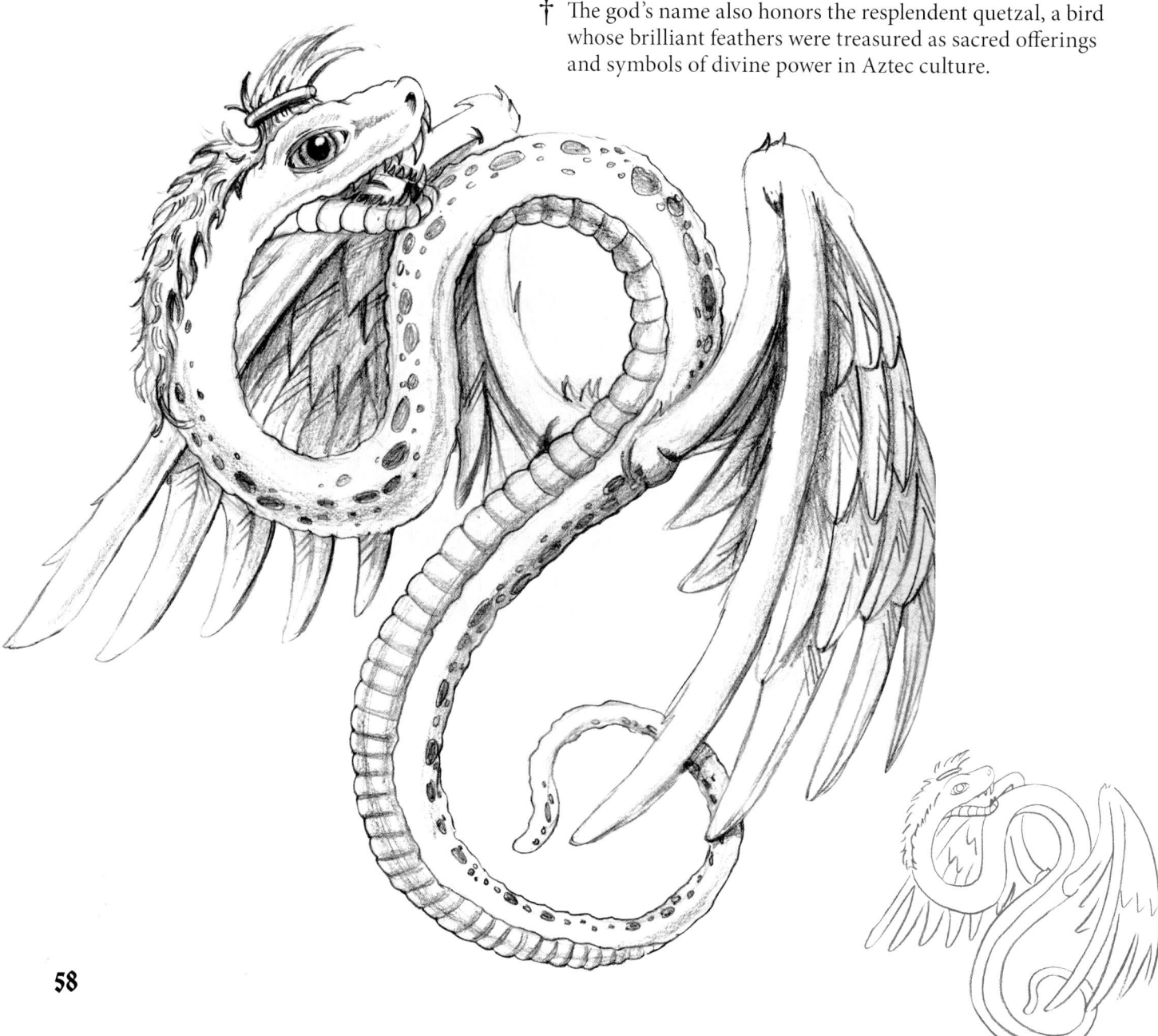

CHELAN LAKE DRAGON: LORE & LEGENDS

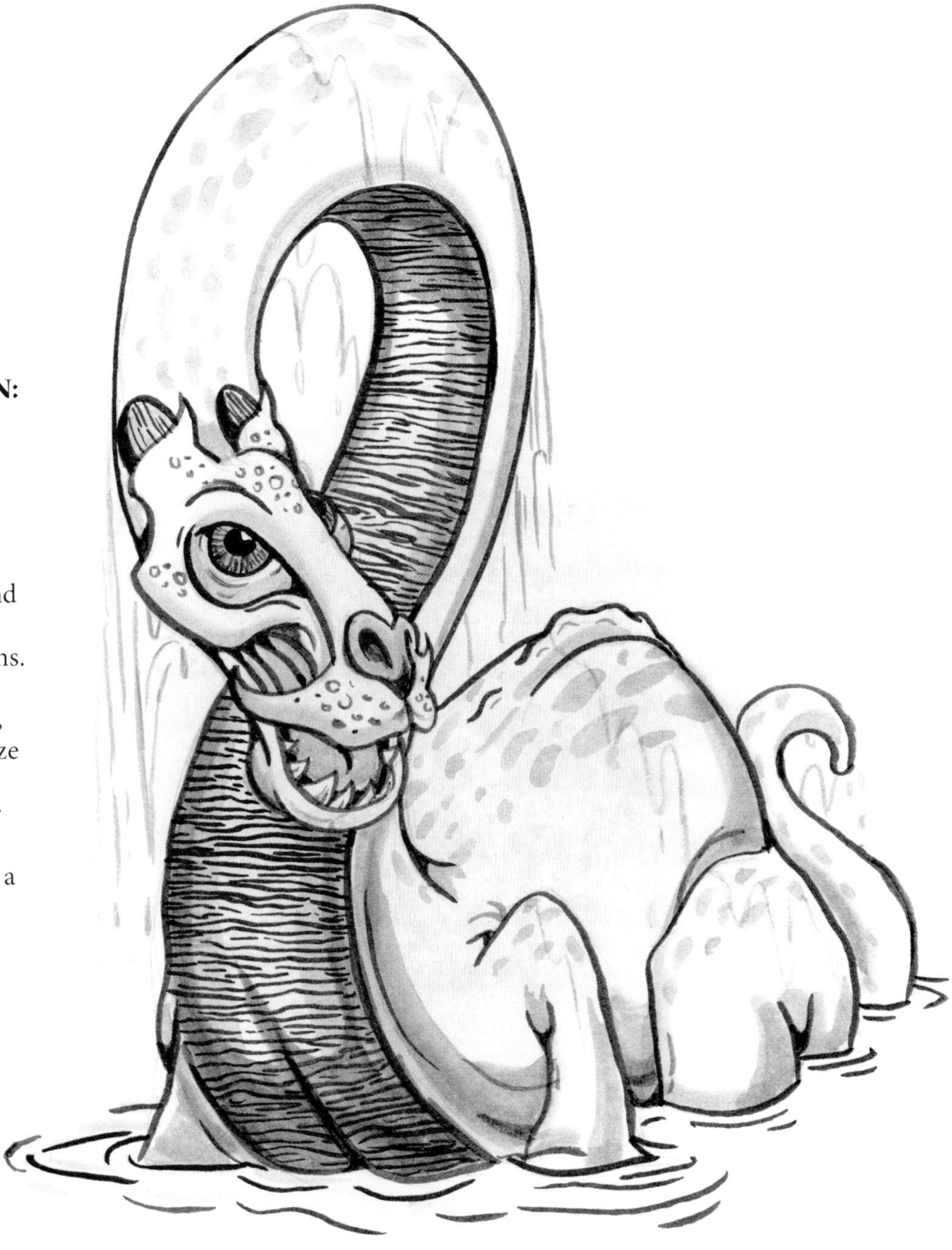

† Hidden beneath the cold, deep waters of Chelan Lake in Washington state lurks a mysterious Water Dragon, a creature of Indigenous legend feared and respected by the Chelan people for generations.

† Said to be fiercely territorial, the dragon is believed to seize fishermen and anyone else who dares to venture too far into its domain, dragging them beneath the surface to a watery fate.

† Unlike many dragons of European tradition, the Chelan Lake Dragon is not depicted as a treasure-hoarding beast but as a guardian of its realm, punishing intrusion and defending the sacred waters it calls home.

† Sightings and stories of the creature often describe sudden disturbances in the lake—ripples without wind, waves without boats—signs that the ancient guardian still patrols the depths.

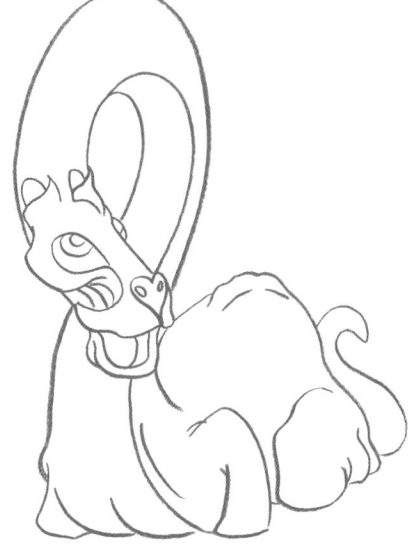

APALALA: LORE & LEGENDS

† In Hindu and Buddhist tradition, Apalala is a revered naga—a divine being with both human and serpentine features—who serves as a powerful river guardian and protector of the natural world.

† Said to dwell within the sacred waters of the Swat River in present-day Pakistan, Apalala uses its strength and wisdom to safeguard the surrounding lands from the depredations of wicked dragons and malevolent forces.

† Because of Apalala's vigilant watch, the countryside it protects is said to flourish, its fields fertile and its people prosperous under the naga's benevolent influence.

† As both a spirit of the water and a defender of order, Apalala embodies the balance between strength and compassion, demonstrating that true power lies not only in destruction but also in preservation and guardianship.

† Worshipped as a symbol of protection, fertility, and renewal, Apalala reminds mortals of the sacred bond between water and life—and the guardians who ensure that bond endures.

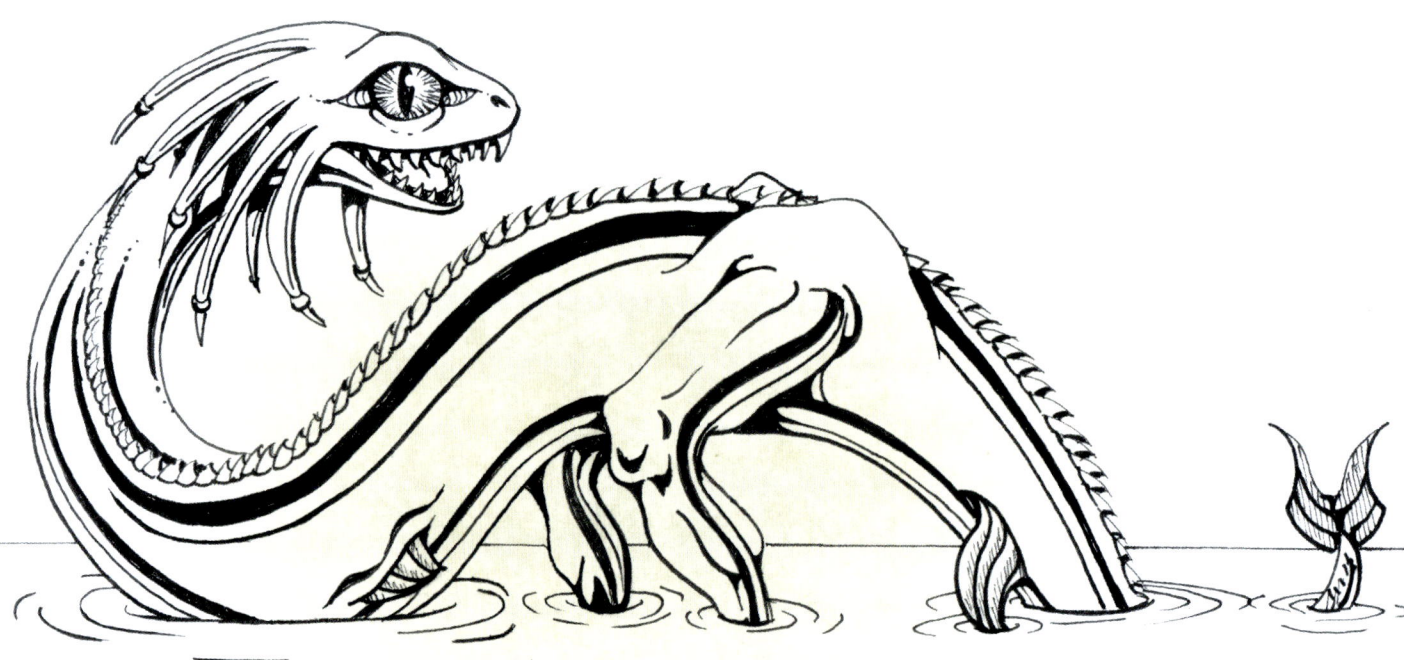

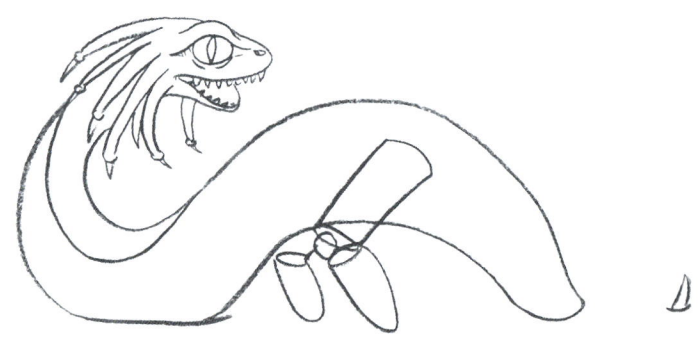

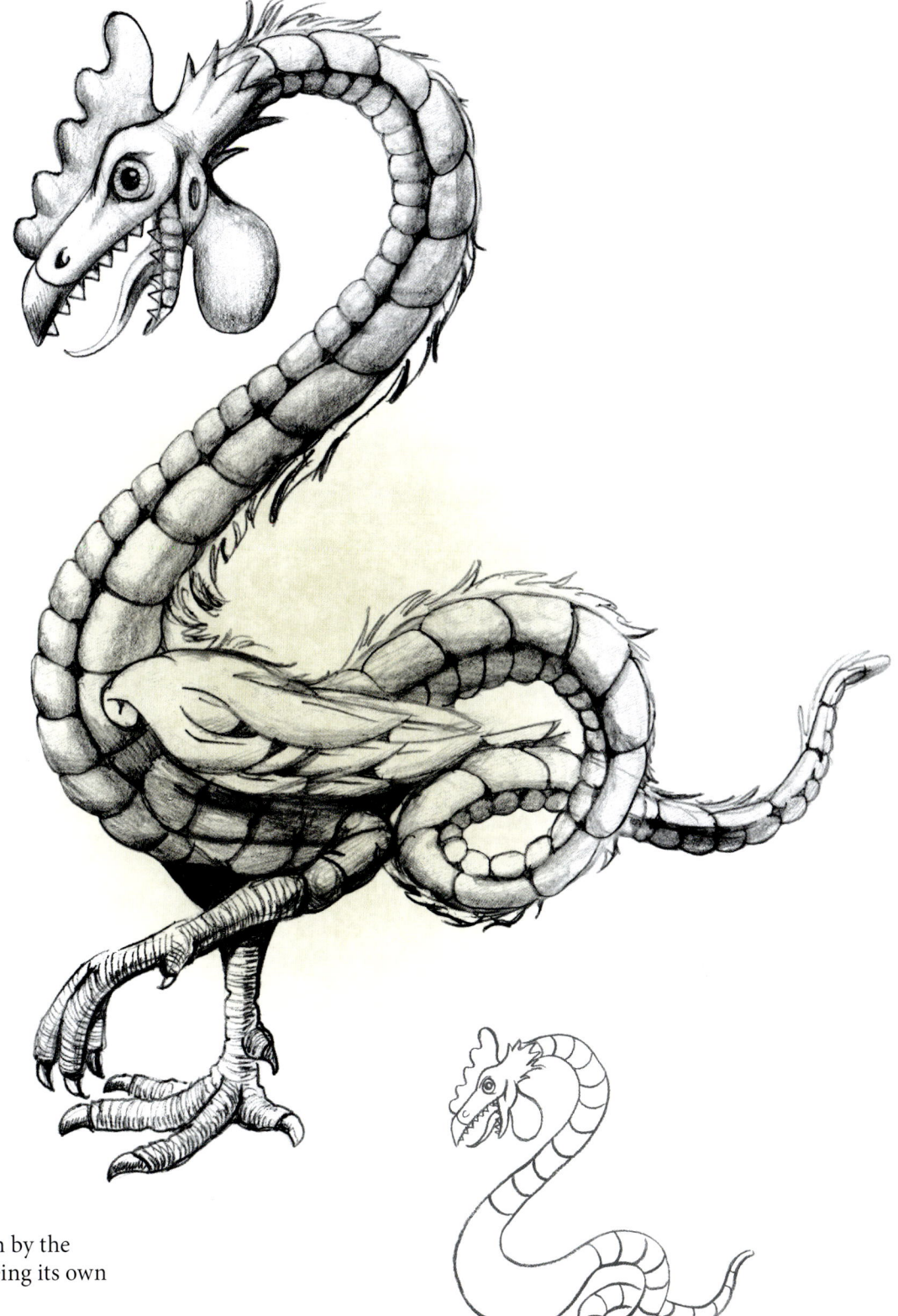

BASILISK: LORE & LEGENDS

† One of the most feared creatures in European legend, the basilisk is said to possess a lethal gaze capable of killing with a single look, while its very presence leaves behind a trail of venom potent enough to poison the land itself.

† Descriptions of the basilisk vary wildly: some depict it as a giant serpent or lizard, while others portray a bizarre, more monstrous form— a three-foot-tall rooster with the fangs and tail of a snake.

† Despite its terrifying powers, the basilisk has weaknesses: It can be slain by the crow of a rooster or by seeing its own reflection in a mirror.

† Folklore holds that hanging a basilisk's corpse within a home will ward off spiders, while mixing its ashes with silver is said to transform the metal into gold—proof that even in death, the creature's presence is bound to potent magic.

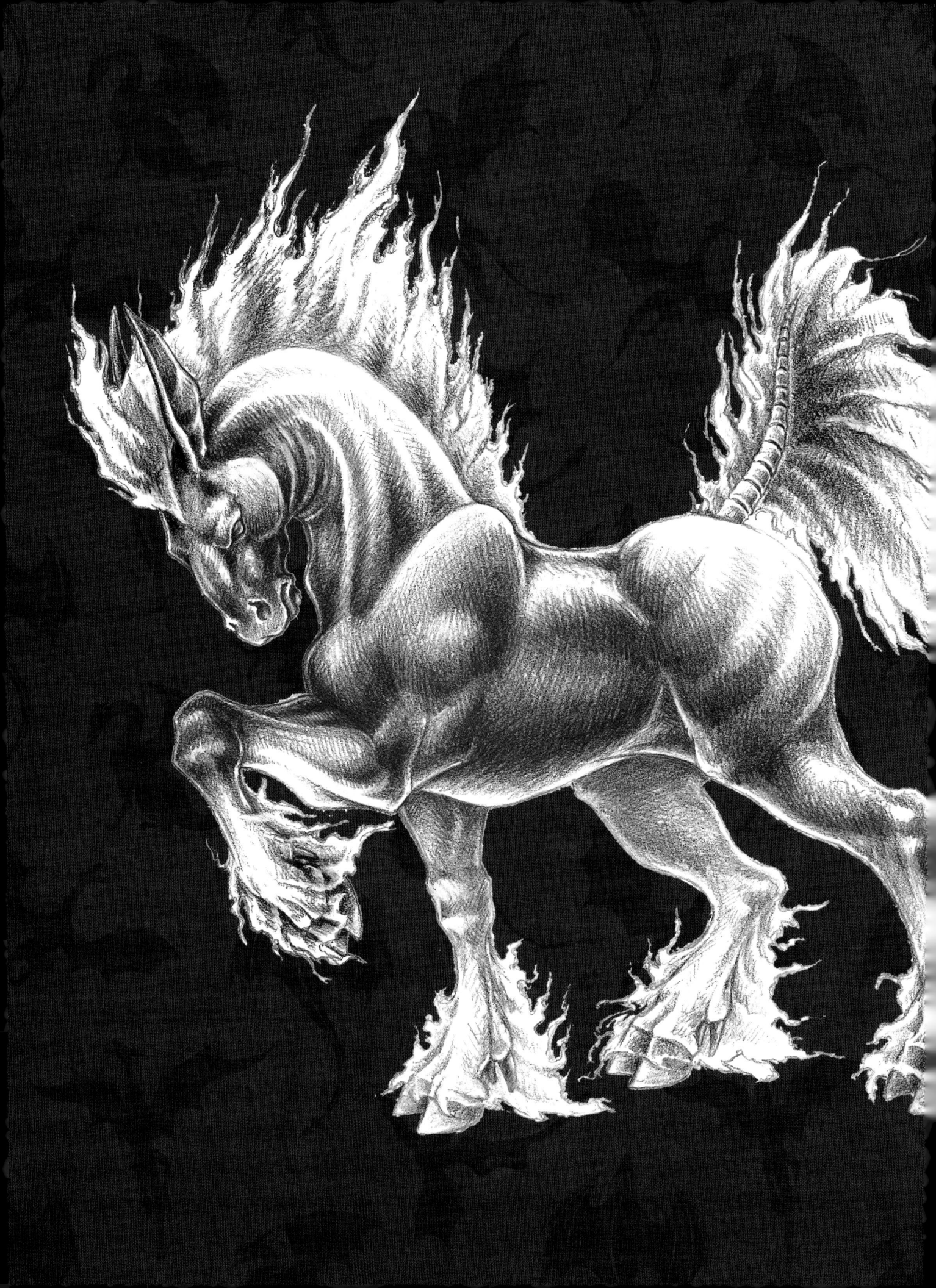

Fantastic Bestiary

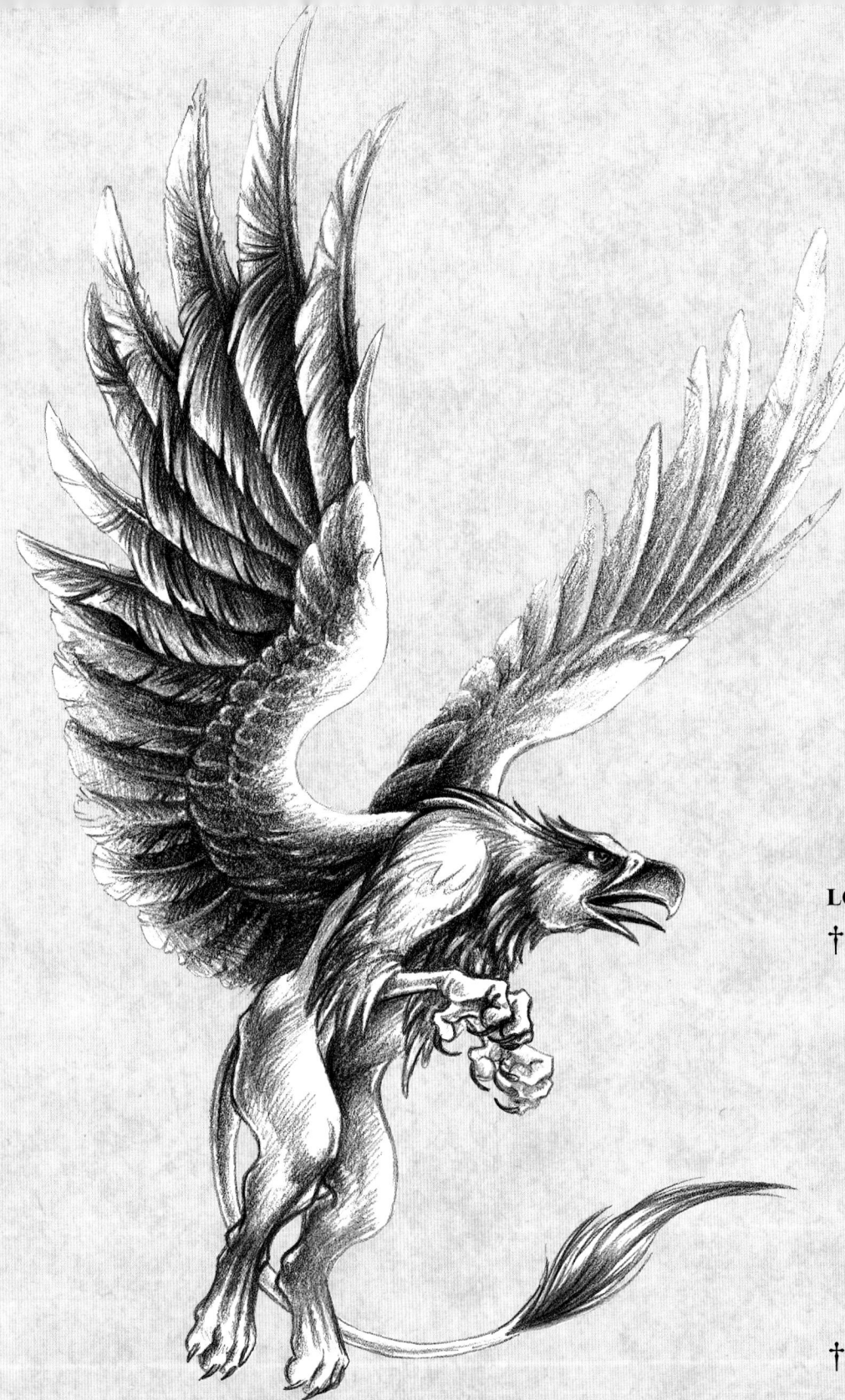

Gryphon

LORE & LEGENDS

† With the body of a lion and the head, talons, and wings of an eagle, the gryphon was said to protect the Scythian steppes (modern Ukraine, Russia, and Kazakhstan) from anyone who attempted to steal the gold and precious stones that were abundant there. As a result, the gryphon (also known as "griffin") was commonly featured on gold coins in Scythia.

† Because a gryphon takes a single mate for life, it has become a symbol of fidelity.

† In Rebecca Yarros's Empyrean series, gryphons are ridden by Fliers, a branch of the military of the kingdom of Poromiel.

COMBINING ANATOMICAL ELEMENTS

Visually, this creature presents a unique challenge in that it combines two very different animals into a unique whole.

The lion's forelegs are effectively replaced with the hind legs of the eagle—as with all birds, an eagle's forelegs are its wings. Keep these parallels in mind when constructing your gryphon:

- The lion's "elbows" become the "heel" of the eagle's leg.
- The eagle's "ankle" becomes the lion's "wrist."

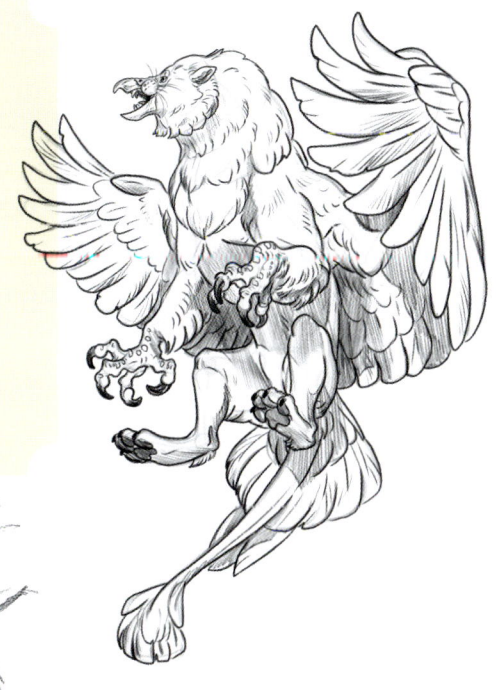

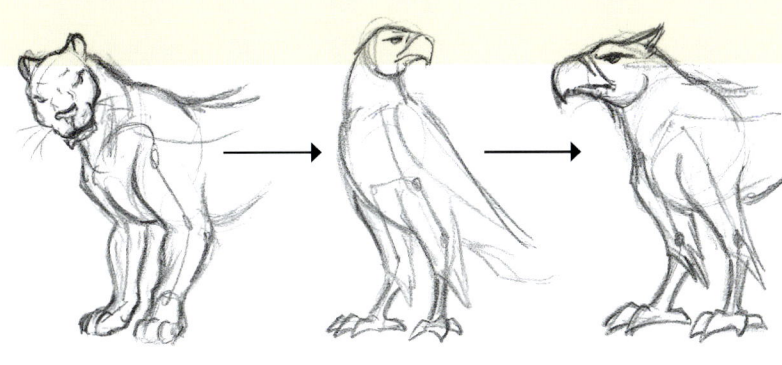

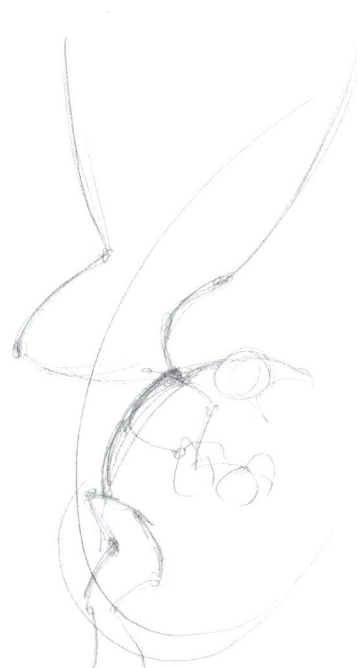

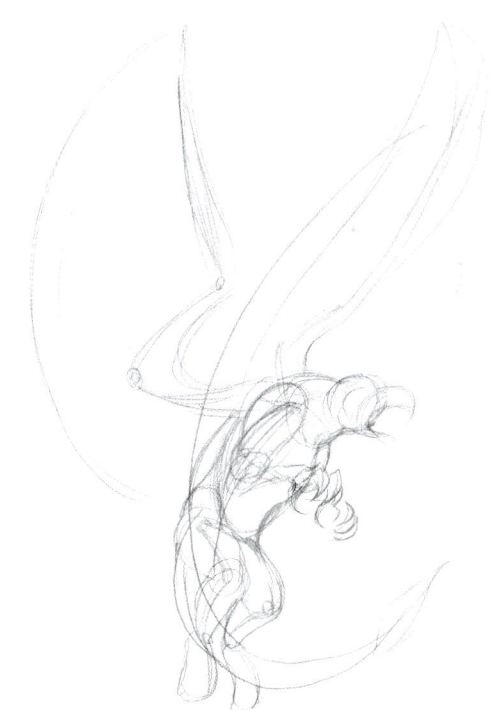

1. Using an HB pencil, indicate the line of action, which denotes the general movement and flow of the figure and thus doesn't need to be in line with the spine. If desired, include the wing bones in your sketch.

2. Build the figure with basic forms and use wide, sweeping arcs to indicate the placement of the wings. This example follows the rule of thumb that a creature's wingspan should be at least two times the length of its body.

65

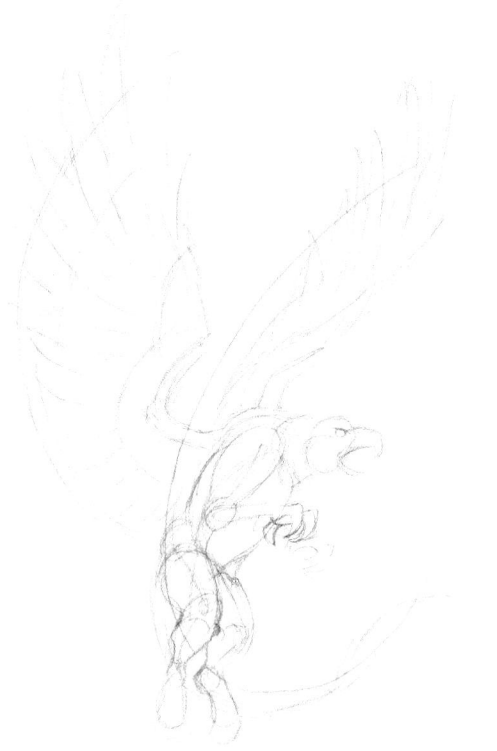

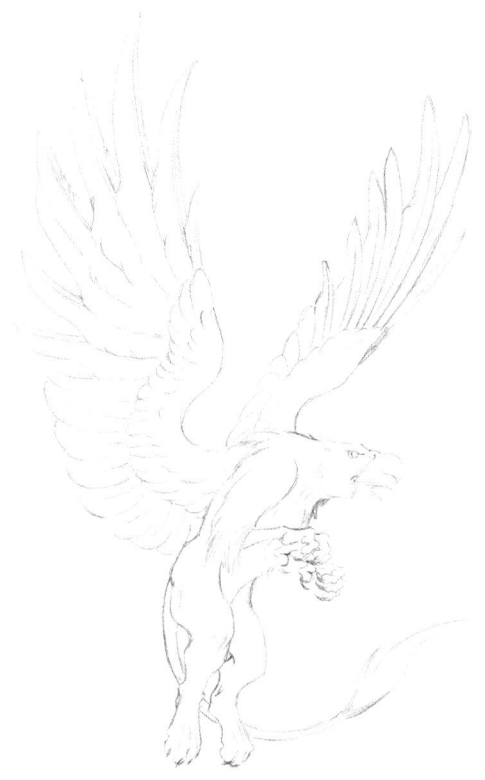

3. Add details to the wings, focusing on the primary feathers, which are the largest. To show that the wing is on the downstroke, curve the lines for the primary feathers back so they look like they're resisting the movement through the air. Show groups of smaller feathers with simple shapes.

4. Add the finer details from head to tail. Tighten up the shapes of the beak and tongue, create brow ridges that end in tufted feathers, define the talons, indicate the lion's paws, and draw the hair at the end of the tail. Also detail the wings, refining smaller feathers with short, curved lines.

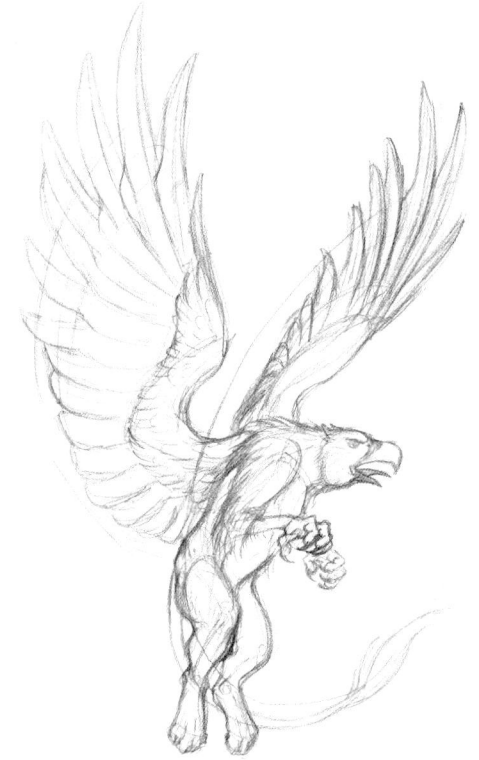

5. Transfer the drawing to a clean sheet of paper, indicating the main shaft on most of the larger feathers. Draw some short lines to show clumps or gaps in the barbs—the parts of the feather that branch off from the main shaft.

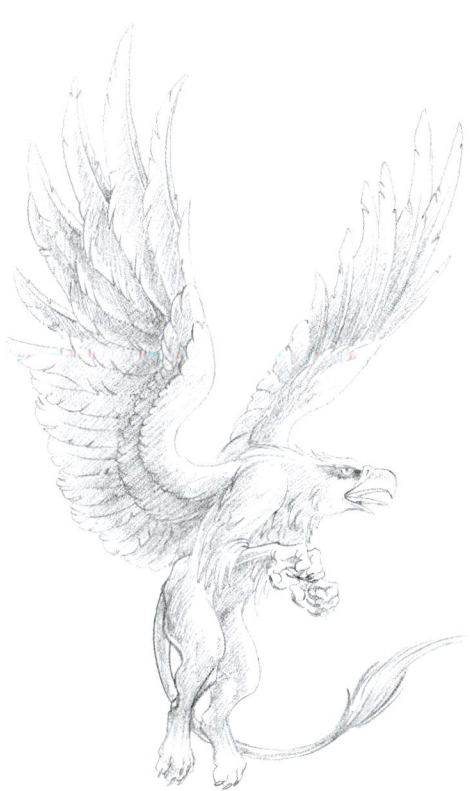

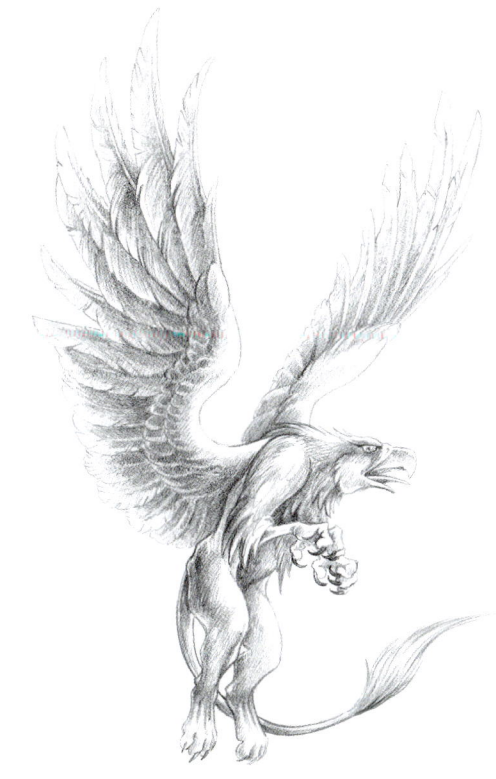

6. Use hatching to establish basic shadow areas. The strokes on the larger feathers should follow the direction of the barbs to help indicate their texture and suggest movement.

7. Use a 2B pencil to darken the deepest shadow areas with hatching, then blend these areas with the lighter ones by adding soft strokes with an HB pencil. Spend time detailing the large feathers; the small feathers are less detailed, but their edges should be kept white so they stand out.

To finish, use the 2B pencil to darken shadows, especially on the wings and face, switching to the HB to blend darker areas into lighter ones. Use a kneaded eraser to lift out highlights and lighten the tips of the right wing to make it seem farther away.

See page 64 for the finished drawing.

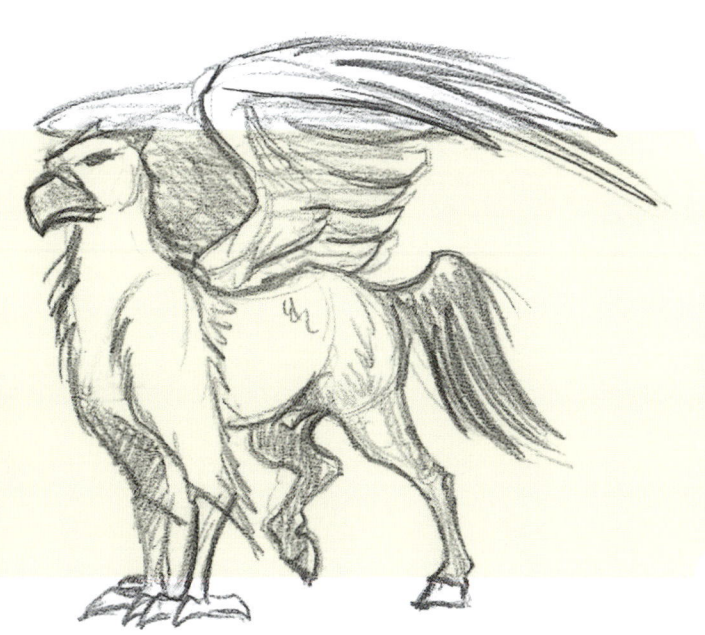

HIPPOGRYPHS

Although the horse is the natural prey of the gryphon, there are rare instances of offspring from the two creatures, called "hippogryphs." Instead of having the rear body of a lion, this creature has the rear body of a horse.

Unicorn

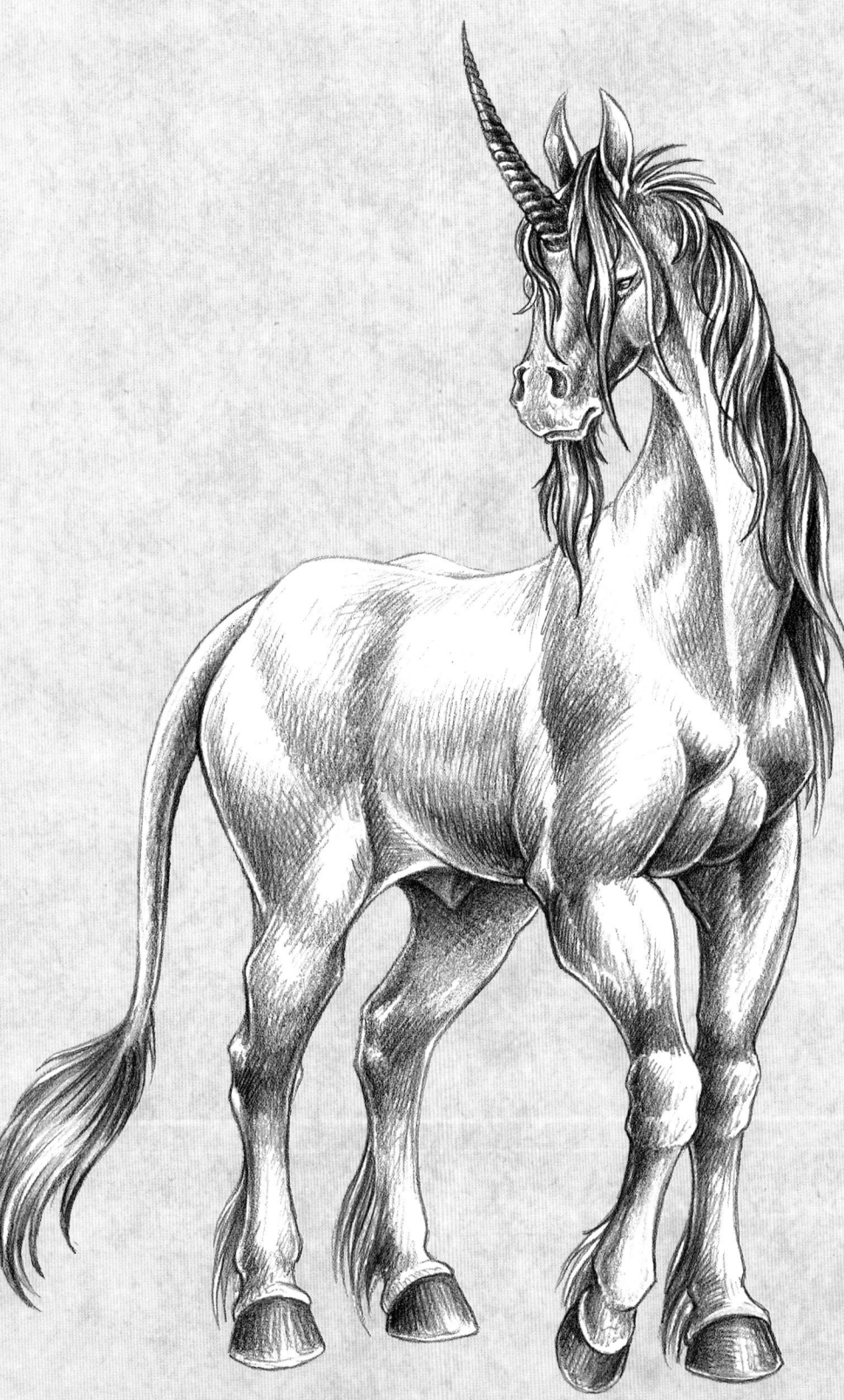

LORE & LEGENDS

† Born of starlight and wild magic, unicorns walk the line between wonder and danger—elusive creatures that reveal themselves only to those whose hearts are true . . . or whose destinies demand it.

† Their spiraled horns are said to purify poison and heal mortal wounds, but in darker tales, they can pierce enchantments—or enemies—with deadly precision.

† Ancient texts describe them as guardians of hidden realms and keepers of forgotten truths, guiding the worthy and banishing the corrupt.

† To capture or harm a unicorn invites ruin; their wrath is rare but unstoppable, and their disappearance from a land is said to herald its decline.

ALICORN: THE UNICORN'S HORN

The primary feature that sets unicorns apart from mundane horses is their single horn, properly called an "alicorn." It is commonly whorled or spiraled, but don't let that hamper your creativity. The world is full of horned creatures of various forms, some with very spectacular (or at least detailed and interesting) horns. Study what exists, and let those images inspire you when it's time to create something fantastic.

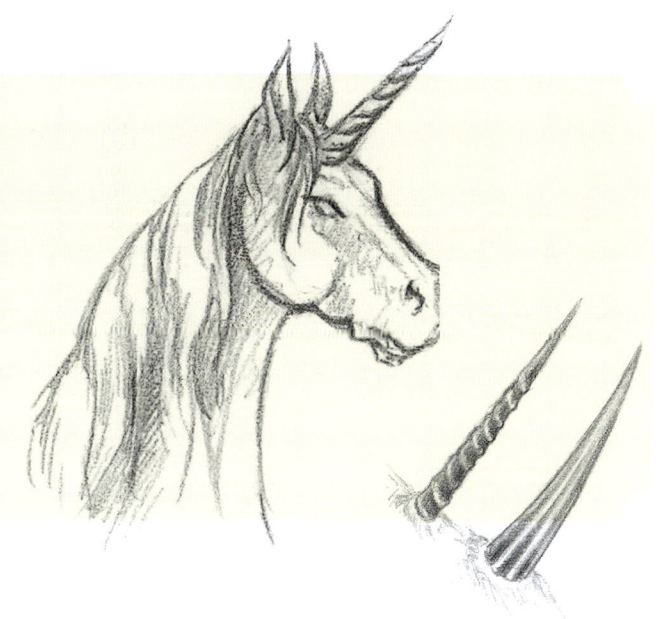

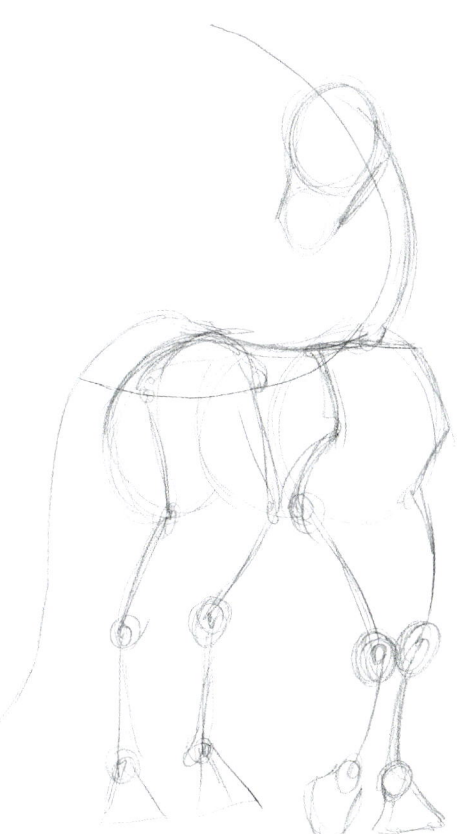

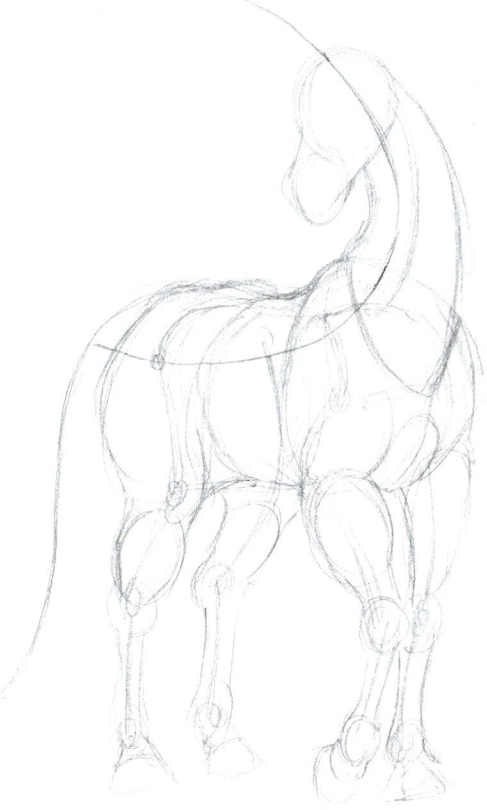

1. Start by drawing the line of action with an HB pencil, then block in the lines of the figure. Although the pose is fairly static and stately, you can add some motion to the composition by drawing the head so the unicorn is looking back over its shoulder.

2. When you're satisfied with the pose, start to round out the figure with basic shapes.

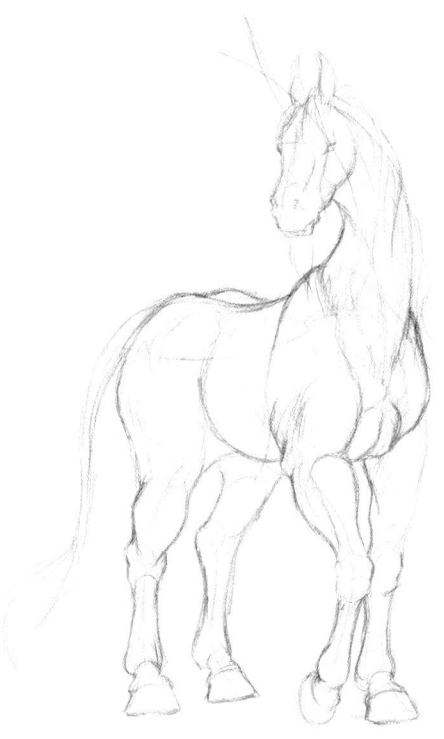

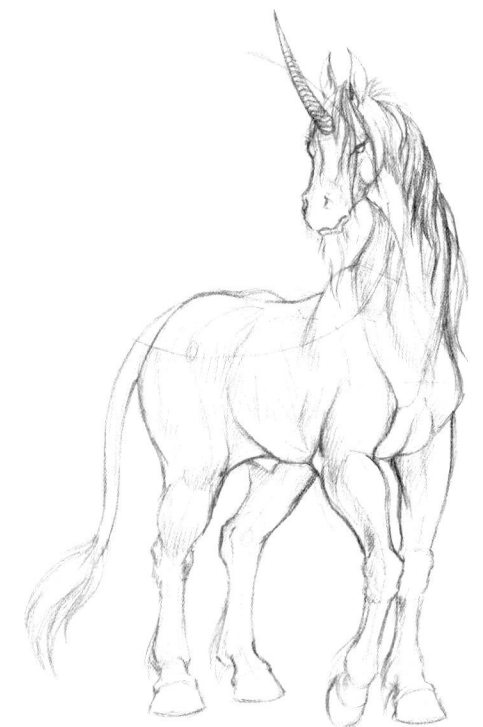

3. Still sketching with the HB pencil, flesh out more of the details: Define the muscles, add the mane and tuft of hair at the end of the tail, and draw the goatlike beard on the chin. Also add the ears, eyes, nose, mouth, and alicorn.

4. Concentrate on the hair: Indicate the way the mane falls in layers, add hair to the fetlocks, and create the long forelock that falls to either side of the alicorn. Also detail the alicorn, making it ridged rather than smooth or spiraled. Lay down hatching that follows the contours of the muscles, especially around the neck.

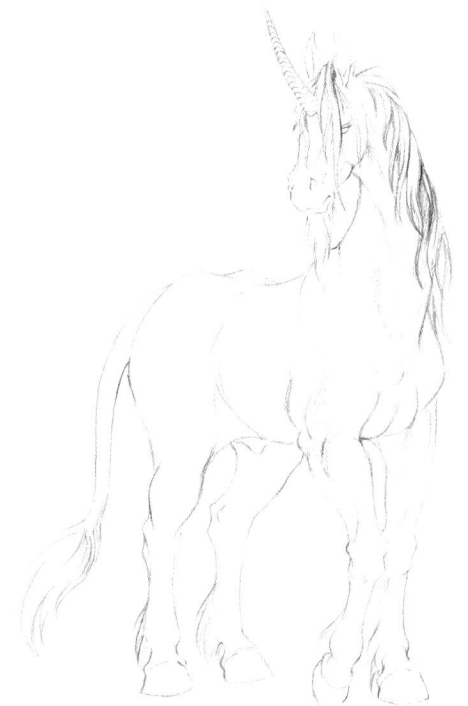

5. Transfer the lines—along with some of the hatching to keep track of the contours of the muscles—to a clean sheet of paper, using a light table if desired.

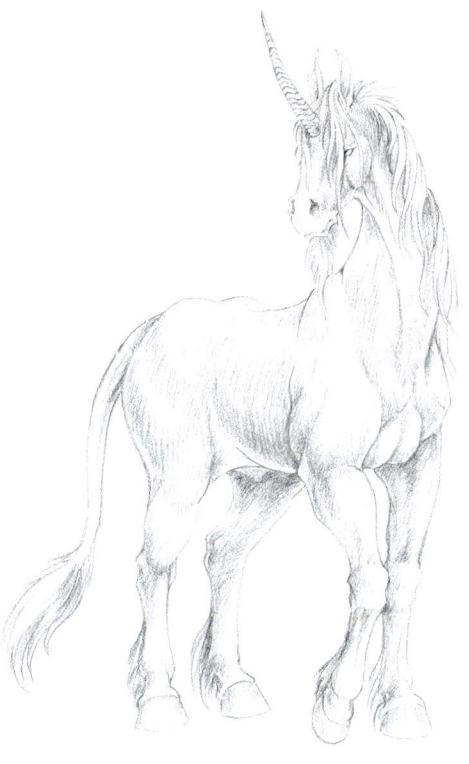

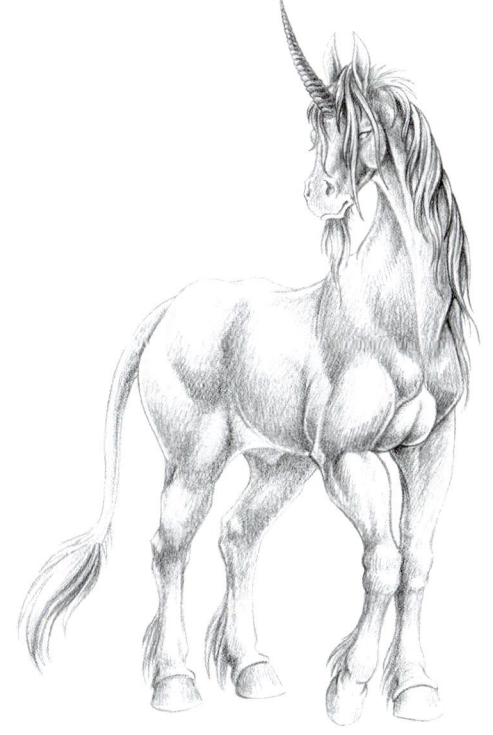

6. Use the HB pencil and hatching to indicate the general shading across the unicorn. For the long hair, use strokes that run parallel to the direction of the hair growth; this makes the hair look smooth and silky.

7. To keep the image fairly light, implying a white or very light coat, use the HB pencil instead of switching to a softer 2B. Slowly build up the shading with layers of hatching, gently blending with short, smooth strokes. Keep the shading on the alicorn and hooves smooth and subtle. To make the hooves look polished, use a combination of vertical strokes and strokes that follow the shape of the hoof.

To finish, use a soft 2B pencil to darken some of the deepest shadows, especially the alicorn, hooves, and darkest strands of hair.

See page 68 for the finished drawing.

OTHER UNICORN FEATURES

Besides the alicorn, another common feature of the unicorn is a lion's tail, rather than a traditional horse's tail. Some unicorns also have split hooves, rather than solid ones.

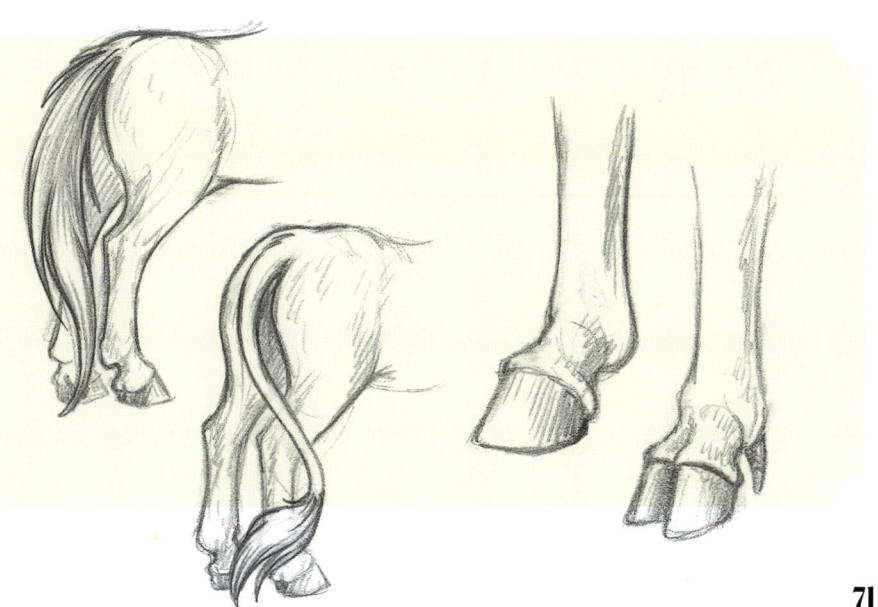

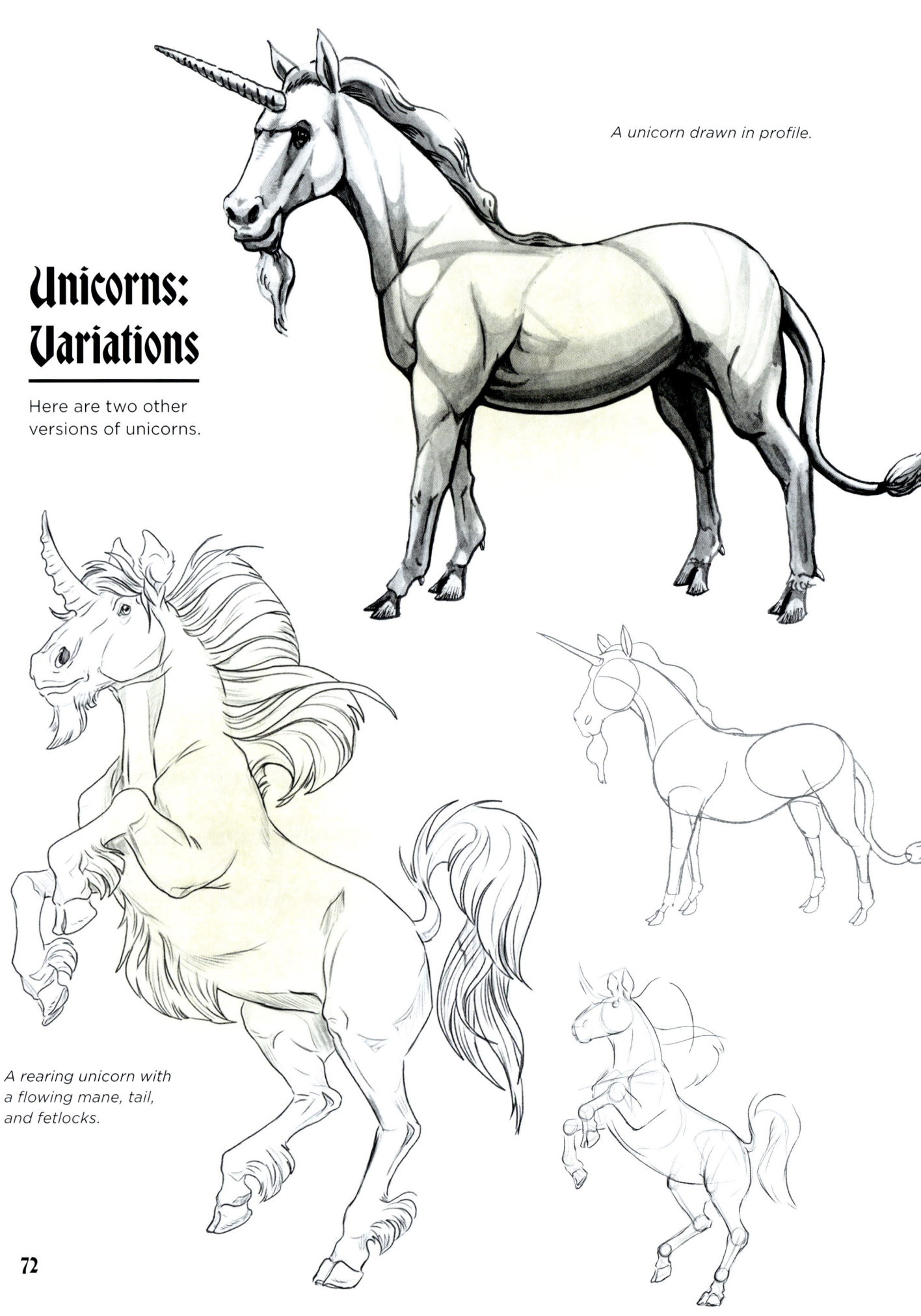

Unicorns: Variations

Here are two other versions of unicorns.

A unicorn drawn in profile.

A rearing unicorn with a flowing mane, tail, and fetlocks.

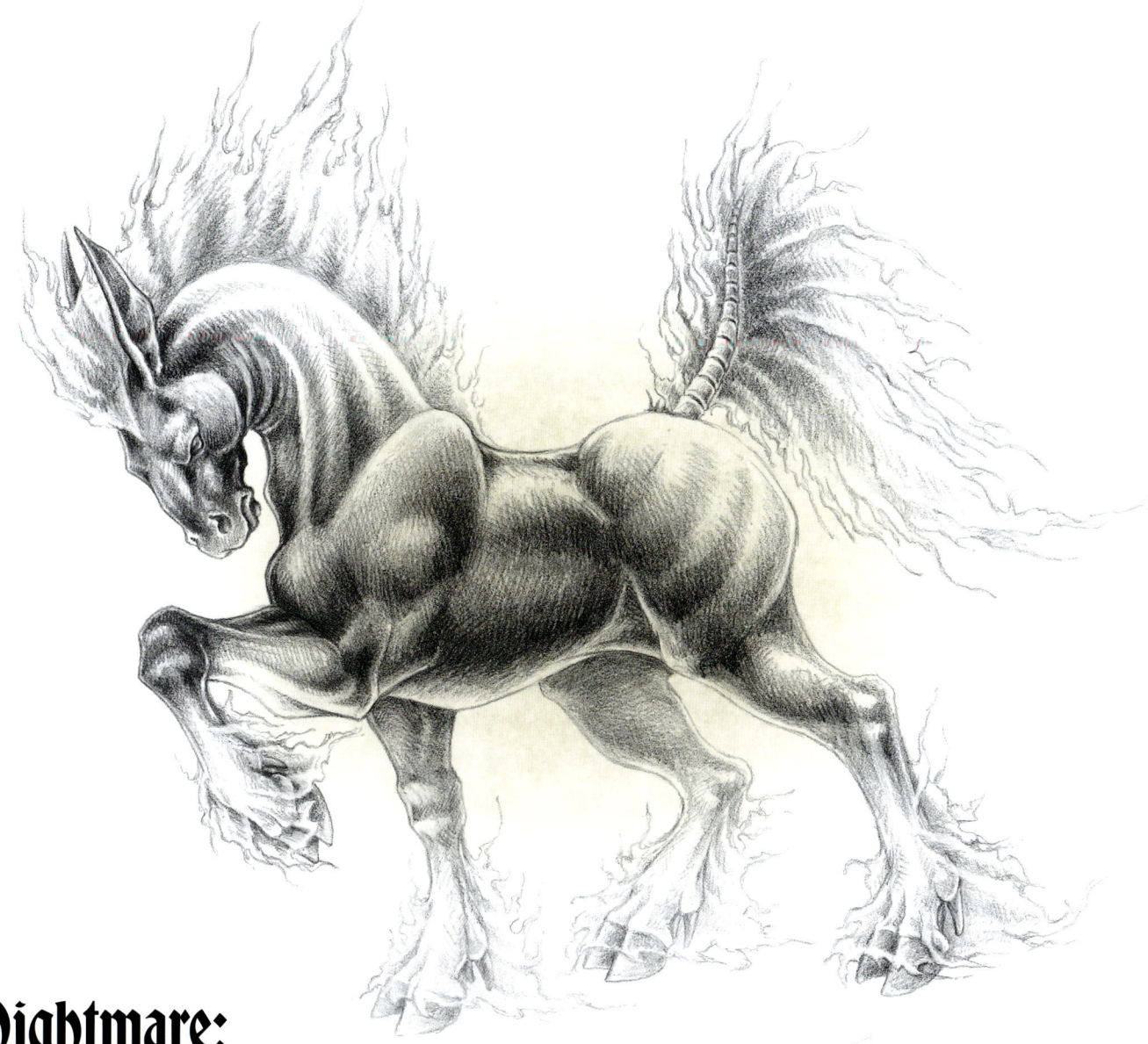

Nightmare: Another Mythical Equine

LORE & LEGENDS

† Though the concept of the Nightmare as a mystical horse is relatively recent, this fiery steed has quickly become a staple of modern fantasy and gaming, often appearing as an antagonist or malevolent spirit true to its ominous name.

† The Nightmare's most striking feature is its blazing appearance: Its mane and tail burn with living fire, casting an otherworldly glow as it gallops through darkness and dream alike.

† Some tales claim that the Nightmare can breathe fire, exhale smoke from its nostrils, or even scorch the ground beneath its flaming hooves, leaving a trail of cinders in its wake.

† Often associated with shadowy realms, cursed riders, or infernal masters, the Nightmare is a creature of both terror and awe—a spectral embodiment of fear itself.

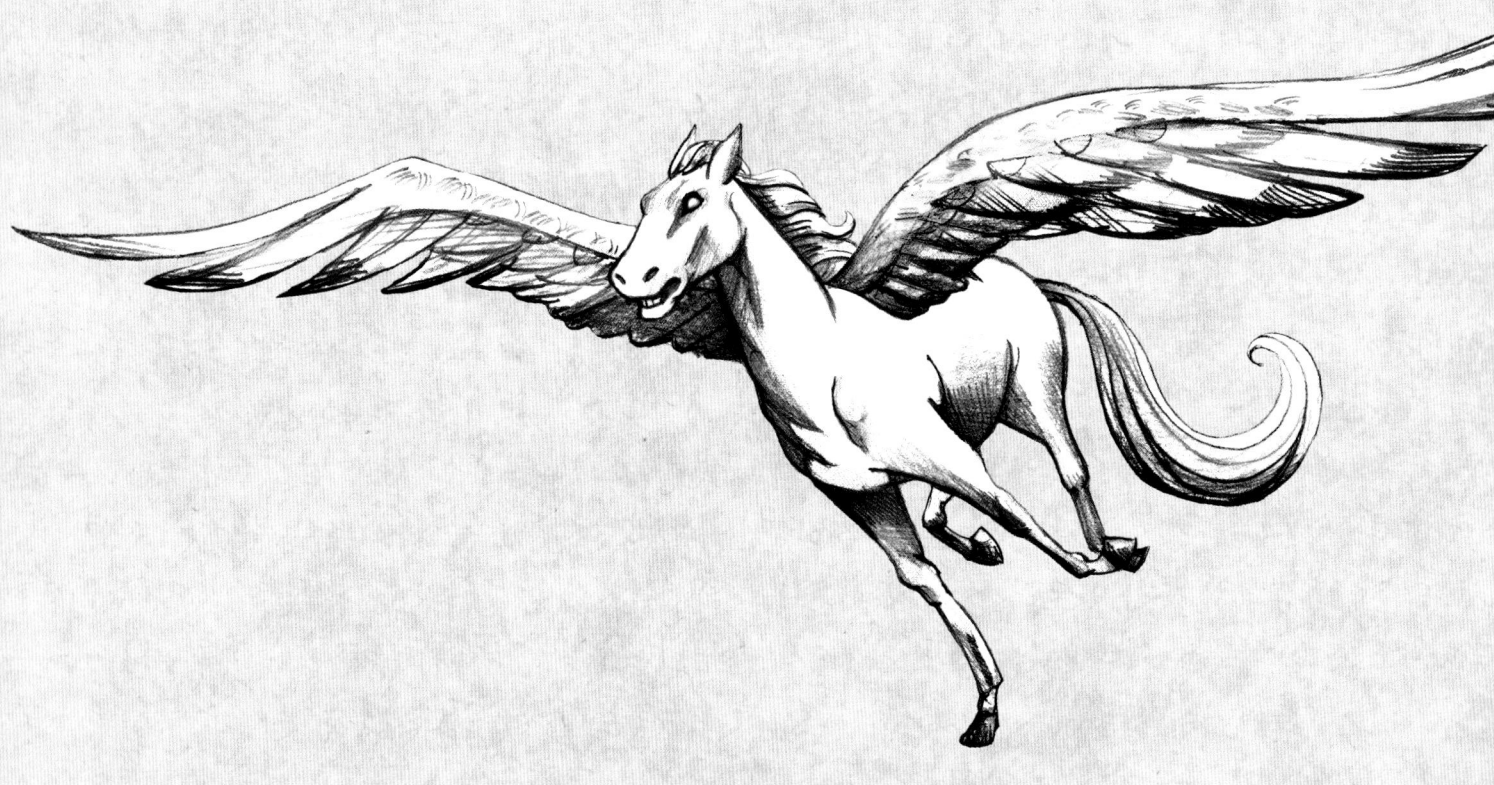

Pegasus

LORE & LEGENDS

† Born of tragedy and divine power, Pegasus sprang from the blood of Medusa when she was slain by Perseus— the immortal offspring of the gorgon and the sea god Poseidon.

† A creature of both earth and sky, Pegasus embodies freedom, transformation, and the enduring link between mortal struggle and celestial destiny.

† Legends claim that each beat of its wings stirs the winds, and where its hooves strike, sacred springs burst forth—gifts from a creature born of both darkness and divinity.

† In the oldest tales, Pegasus's journey ends among the stars—ascending to the heavens and becoming a constellation, an eternal symbol of transcendence and the triumph of destiny over death.

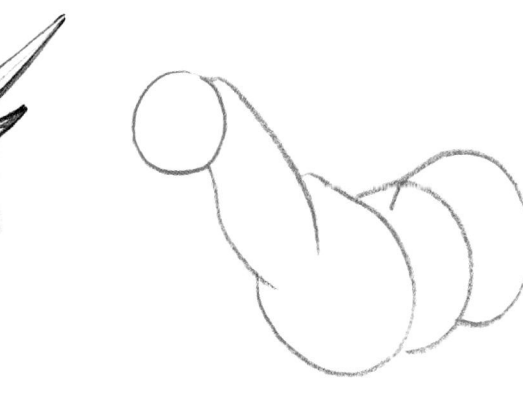

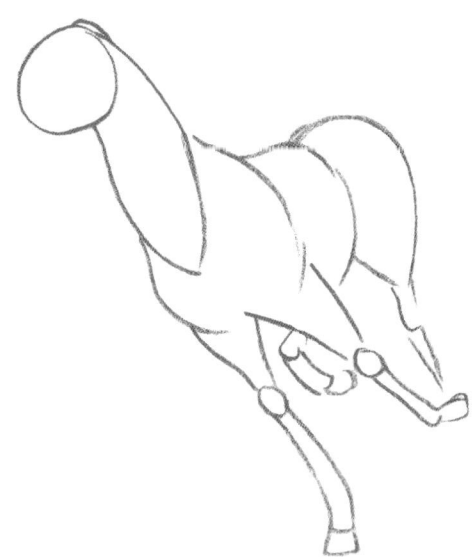

1. Use a 3H pencil to build Pegasus's head and torso with circles. Then connect the head to the torso with two curving lines.

2. Add the four legs, positioning them so it appears as though Pegasus is about to take off in flight. This pose is foreshortened (the front end is closer to the viewer than the back end), so the front legs are larger than the back legs.

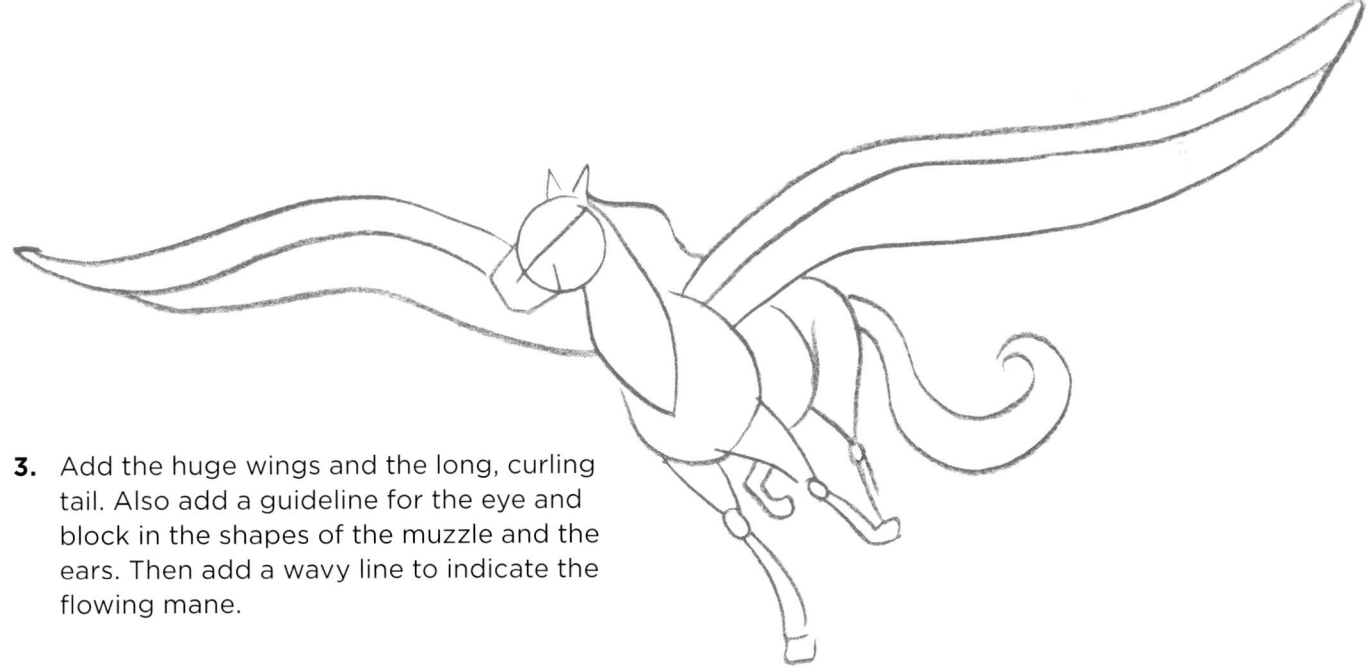

3. Add the huge wings and the long, curling tail. Also add a guideline for the eye and block in the shapes of the muzzle and the ears. Then add a wavy line to indicate the flowing mane.

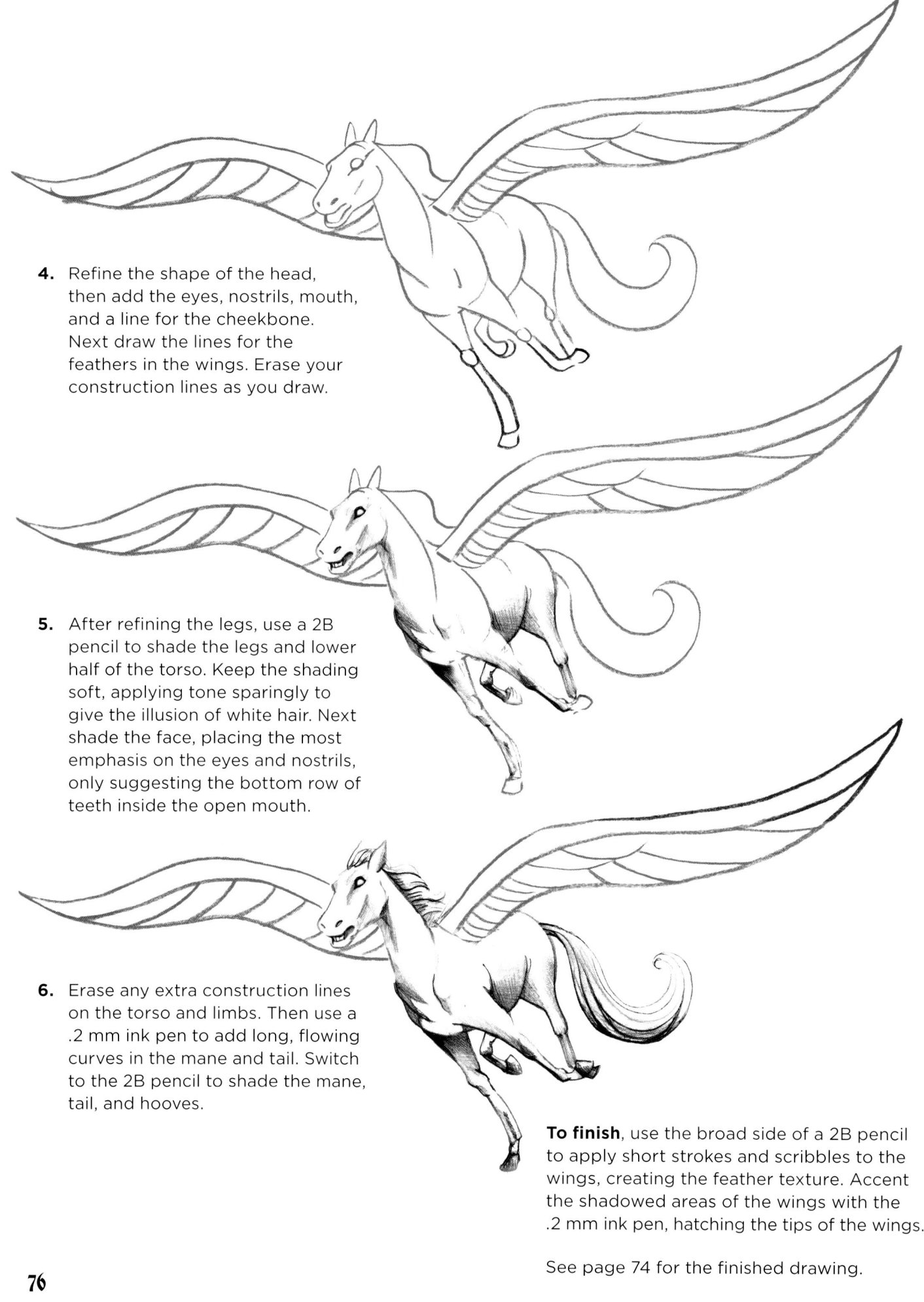

4. Refine the shape of the head, then add the eyes, nostrils, mouth, and a line for the cheekbone. Next draw the lines for the feathers in the wings. Erase your construction lines as you draw.

5. After refining the legs, use a 2B pencil to shade the legs and lower half of the torso. Keep the shading soft, applying tone sparingly to give the illusion of white hair. Next shade the face, placing the most emphasis on the eyes and nostrils, only suggesting the bottom row of teeth inside the open mouth.

6. Erase any extra construction lines on the torso and limbs. Then use a .2 mm ink pen to add long, flowing curves in the mane and tail. Switch to the 2B pencil to shade the mane, tail, and hooves.

To finish, use the broad side of a 2B pencil to apply short strokes and scribbles to the wings, creating the feather texture. Accent the shadowed areas of the wings with the .2 mm ink pen, hatching the tips of the wings.

See page 74 for the finished drawing.

Pegasus: Variation

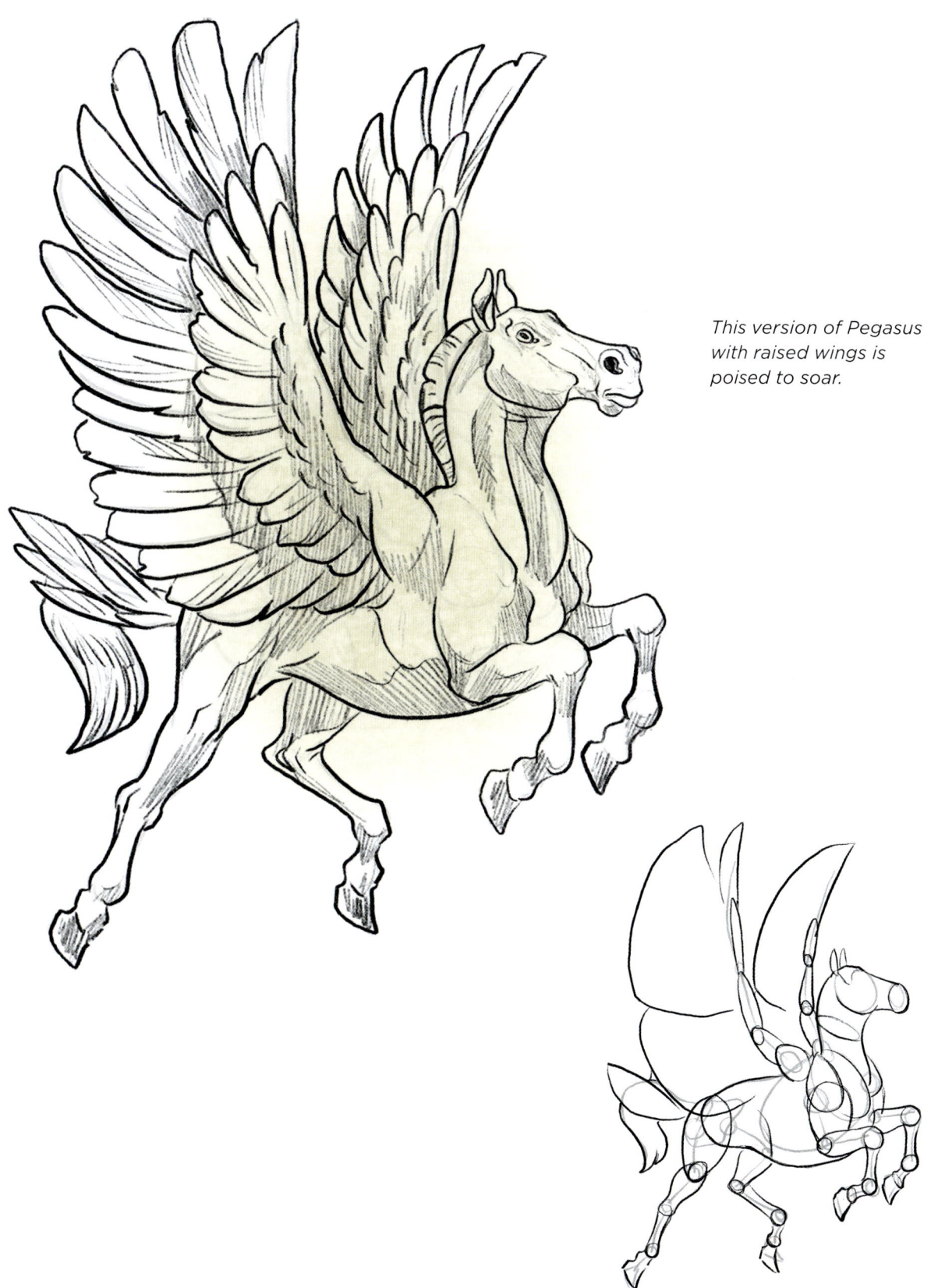

This version of Pegasus with raised wings is poised to soar.

Cerberus

LORE & LEGENDS

† Cerberus is the fearsome three-headed hound of the Underworld, offspring of the primordial serpent-giant Typhon and the half-dragon creature Echidna.

† Tasked with guarding the gates of Hades, Cerberus allows the dead to enter but never to leave—a living embodiment of the boundary between life and death.

† Each of his three heads is said to embody a different aspect of mortality—the past, the present, and the inevitable future—while his serpent's tail and mane of snakes remind mortals of death's inescapable grasp.

† Even heroes trembled before him—Heracles himself had to wrestle Cerberus into submission as one of his Twelve Labors—and poets warned that no mortal could slip past his watchful eyes unscathed.

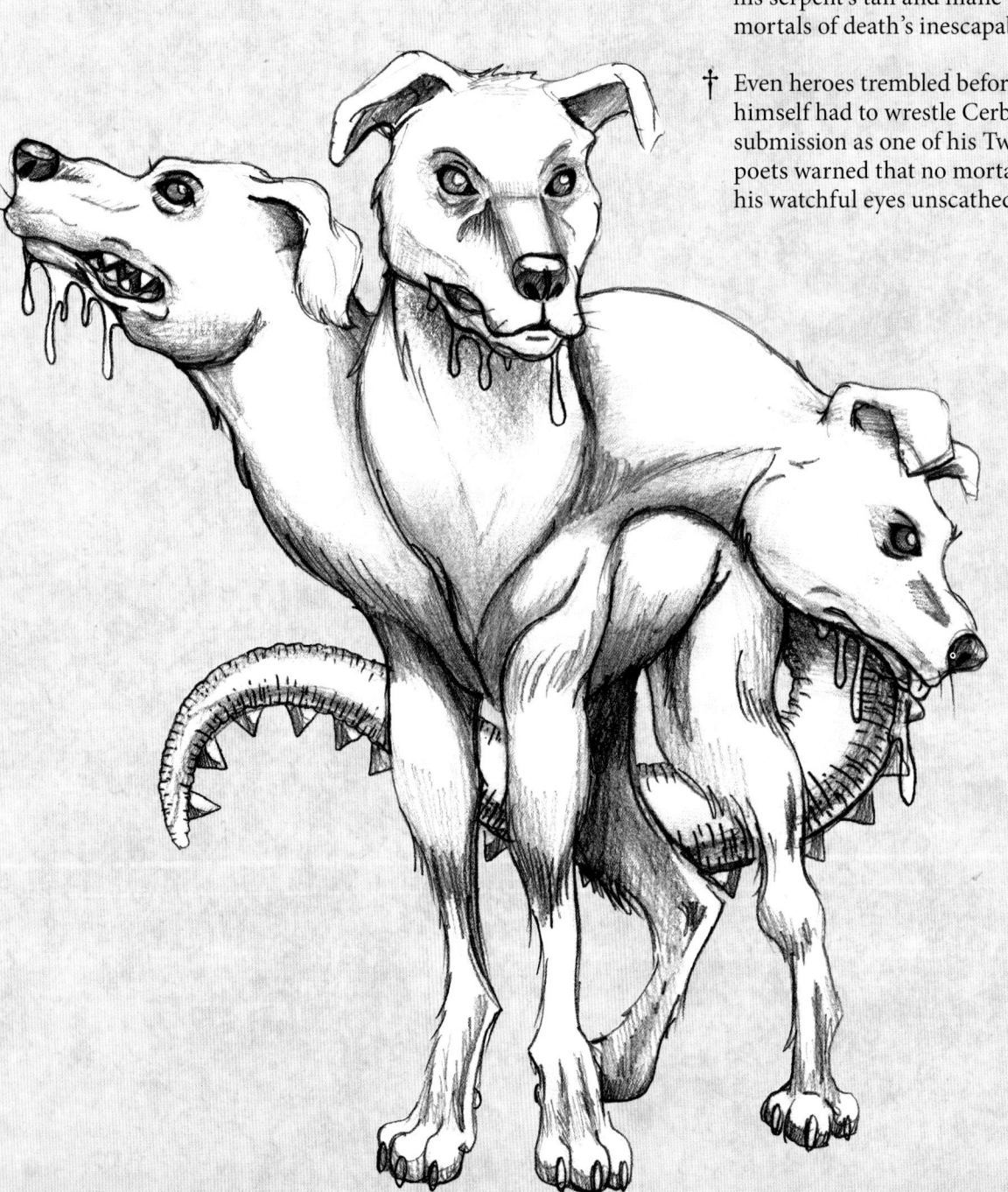

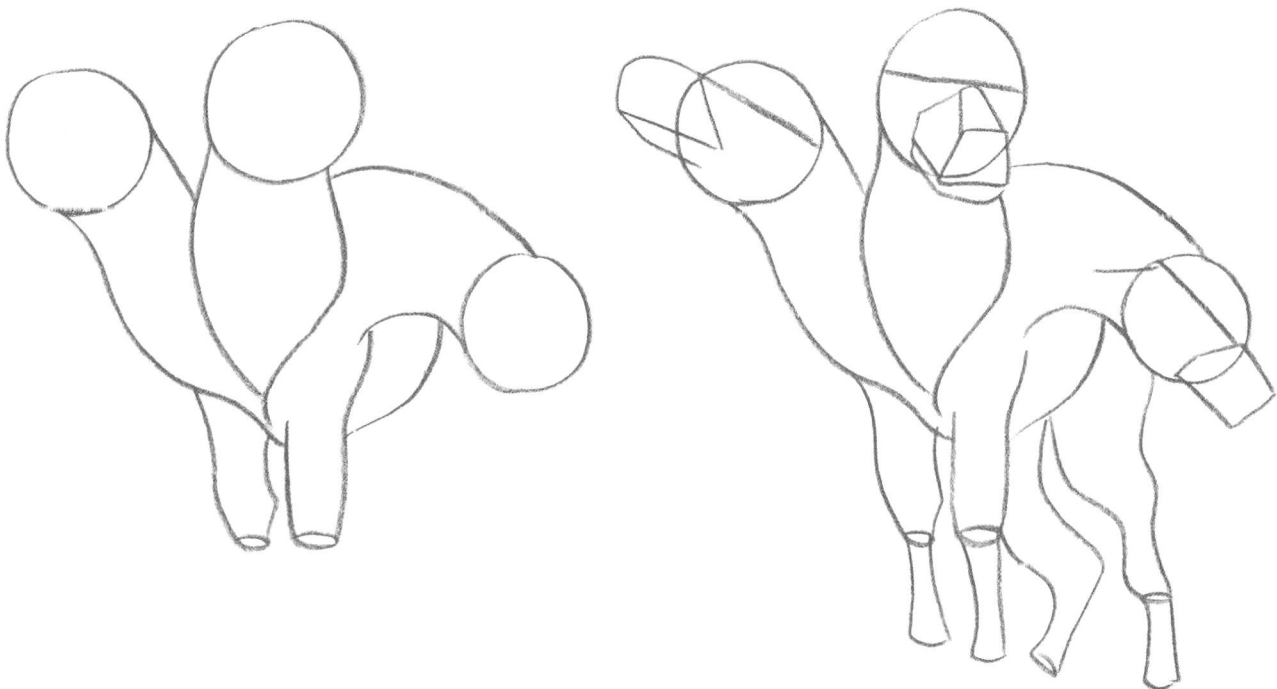

1. Use a 2H pencil to lay in the basic shapes of the creature, indicating how the three heads will emerge from one torso. It's easier to plan out a drawing using simple shapes like these.

2. Add boxy muzzles to all three heads and construct the legs with simple cylinders. Make sure you're happy with the proportions before adding anything else.

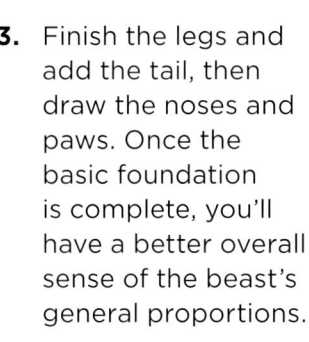

3. Finish the legs and add the tail, then draw the noses and paws. Once the basic foundation is complete, you'll have a better overall sense of the beast's general proportions.

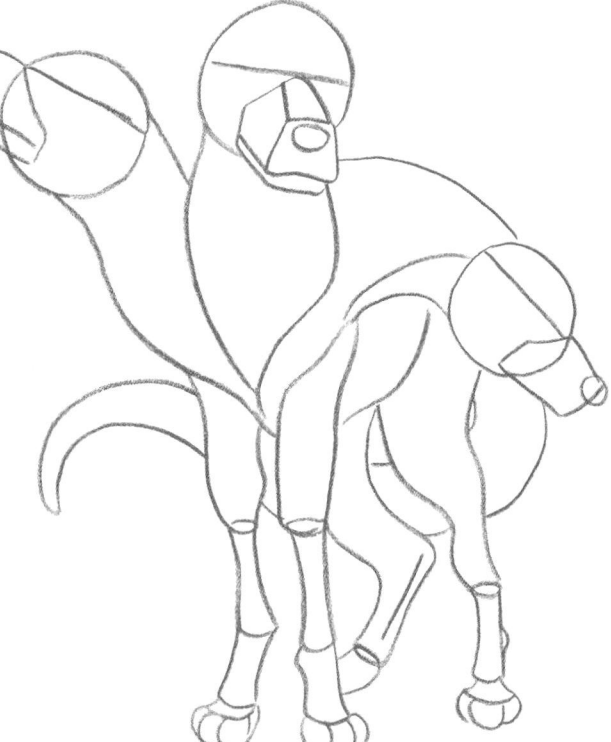

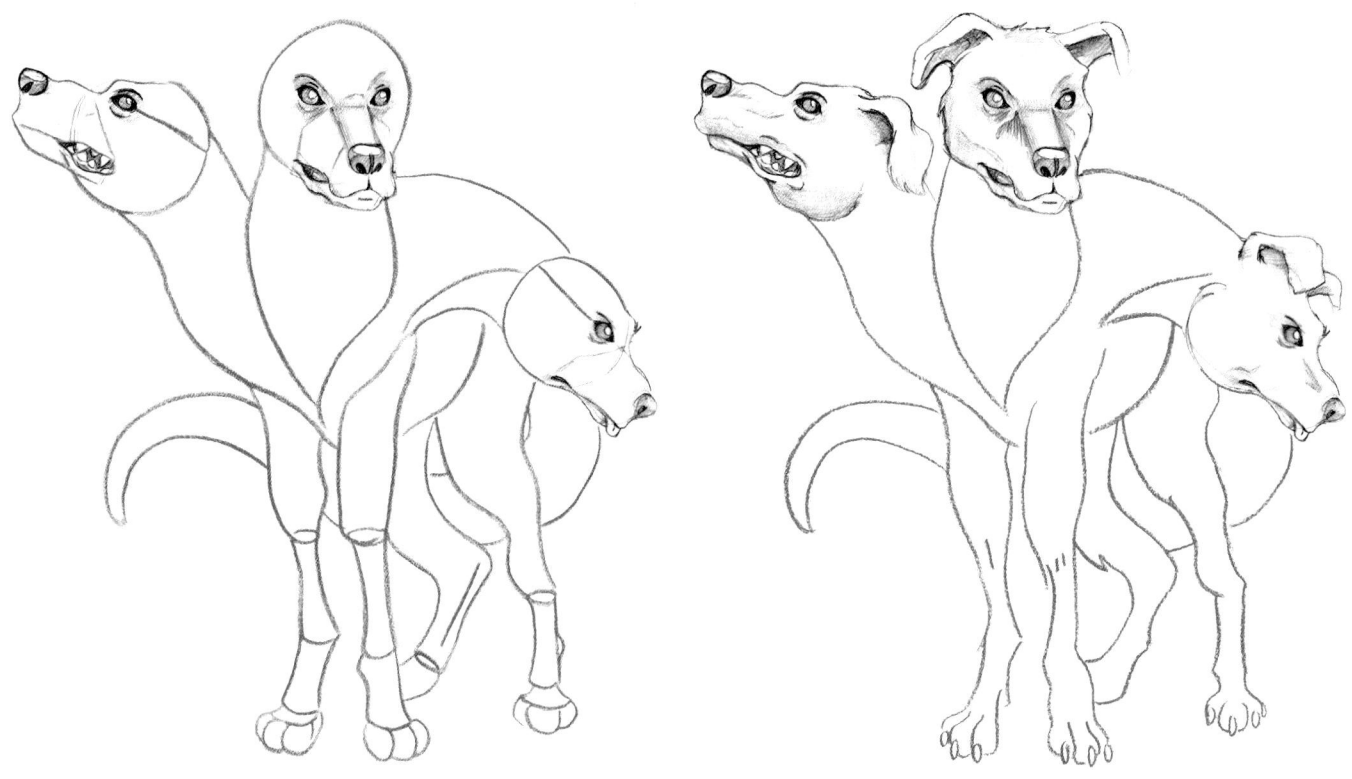

4. Using a 2B pencil, add the facial features. To give each head a different personality, vary the features a bit. The head on the left is baring its teeth, the head in the middle appears to be growling, and the head on the right has its tongue sticking out a bit. Shade the eyes, noses, and mouths, making the area around the eyes intensely dark.

5. Still using a 2B pencil, continue shading the heads, adding the ears and making jagged lines around the heads to create fur. Then refine the legs, adding claws on the toes and more fur around the knees.

6. Carry the shading down the necks and onto the body. To enhance the illusion of depth and form, place more pressure on the pencil to make the outlines and shadows heavier and blacker.

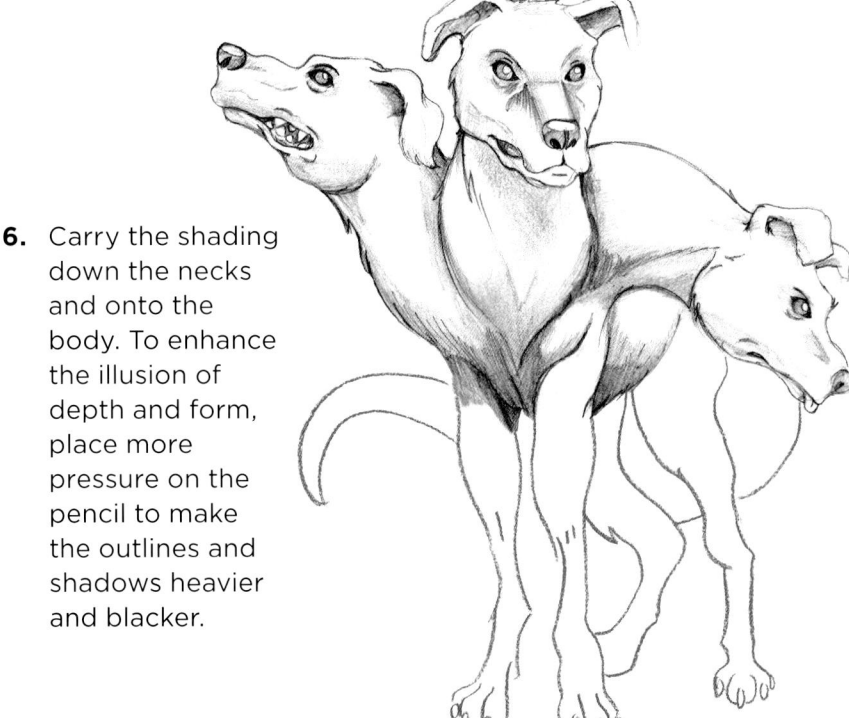

7. Add a liberal dose of drool to each head. Then focus on the tail, which is scaly, using a sharpened 2B and short, uneven strokes to draw a scaly pattern along its edges. Note how hard these lines are compared with the wispier strokes in the fur.

To finish, shade the legs, then darken the claws and add sharp spikes to the tail. Touch up the faces, adding darker tones where needed. Finally, add a few whiskers to each head.

See page 78 for the finished drawing.

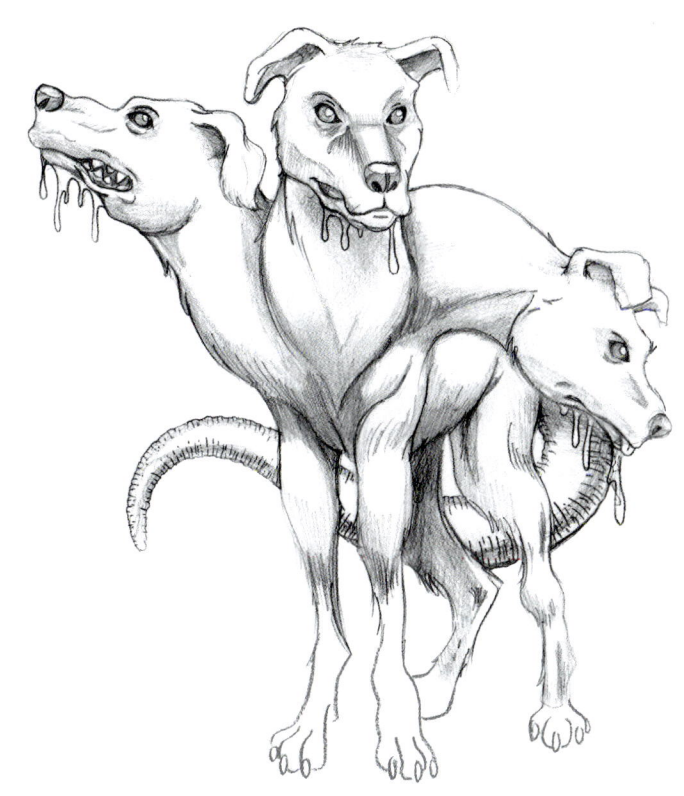

Cerberus: Variation

The heads and body of this Cerberus are large and powerful.

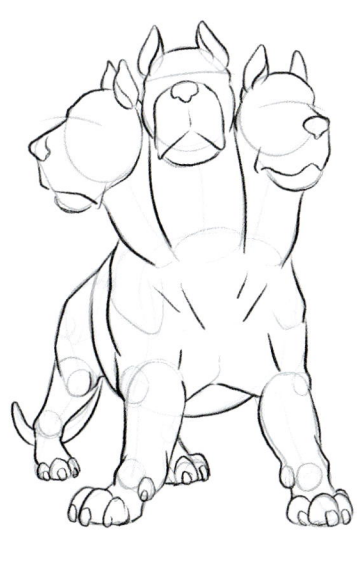

Kraken

LORE & LEGENDS

† Rising from the cold, uncharted depths of Norse legend, the kraken is a colossal sea monster said to possess the tentacled power of an octopus, the armored strength of a crab, or the vast reach of a giant squid—depending on the tale told.

† So immense it is often mistaken for an island, the kraken can sink ships without striking a blow: By merely submerging, it creates a monstrous whirlpool that swallows vessels whole.

† In the original Norse sagas, this terror of the deep was never named, yet its legend endured—an embodiment of the sea's untamed and unknowable might.

† Schools of fish are said to swarm around the creature, luring unwary sailors and fishermen toward their doom, while its very name—derived from the Norwegian *krake*, meaning "something twisted" or "an unhealthy animal"—speaks to its otherworldly nature.

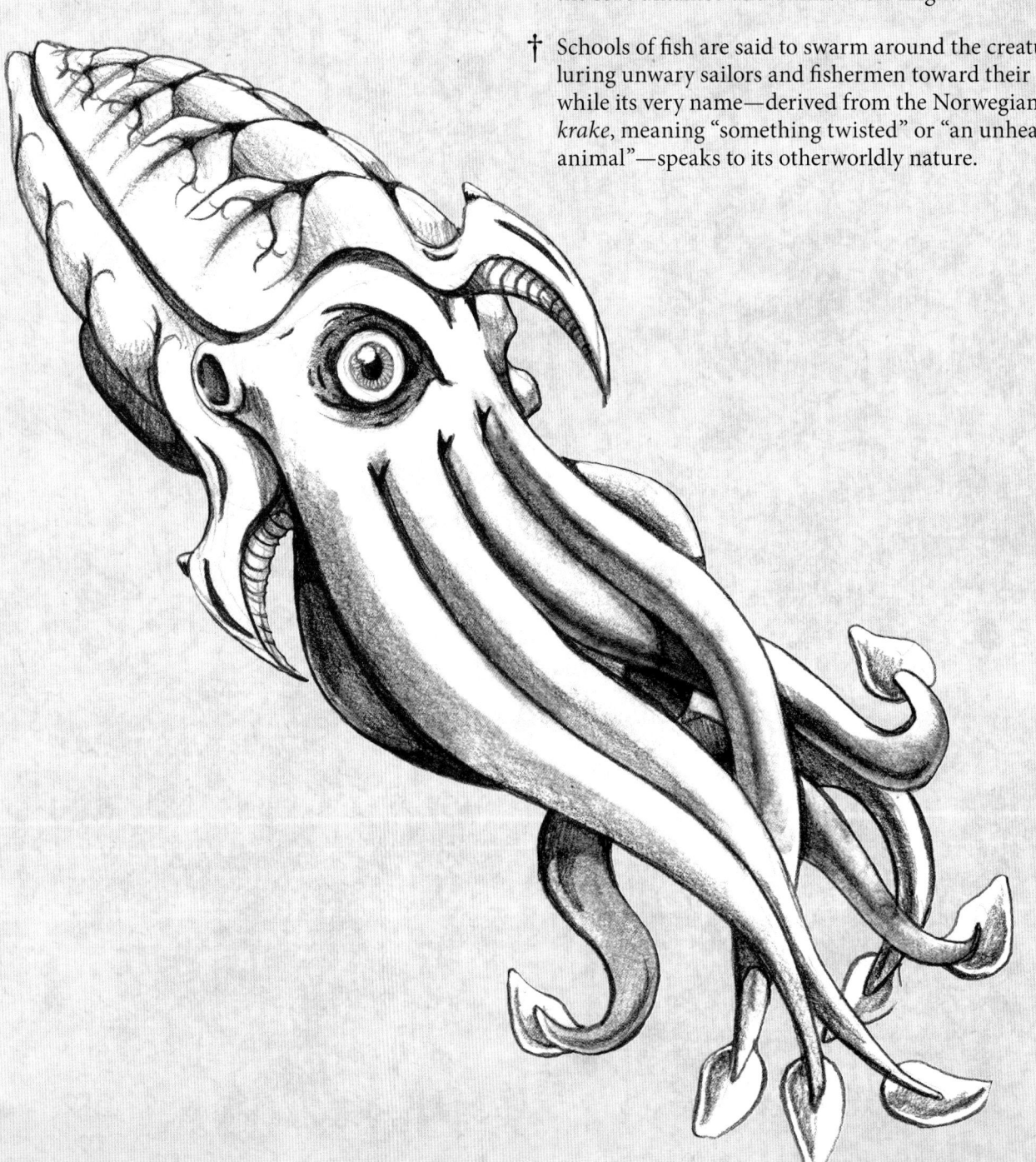

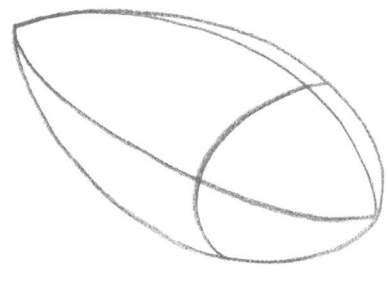

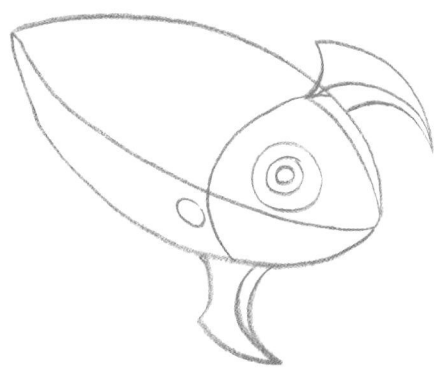

1. With a 2H pencil, draw an almond shape, using construction lines to bisect it vertically and horizontally.

2. Block in the eye, the ear hole, and the two protrusions, picturing the protrusions as can openers.

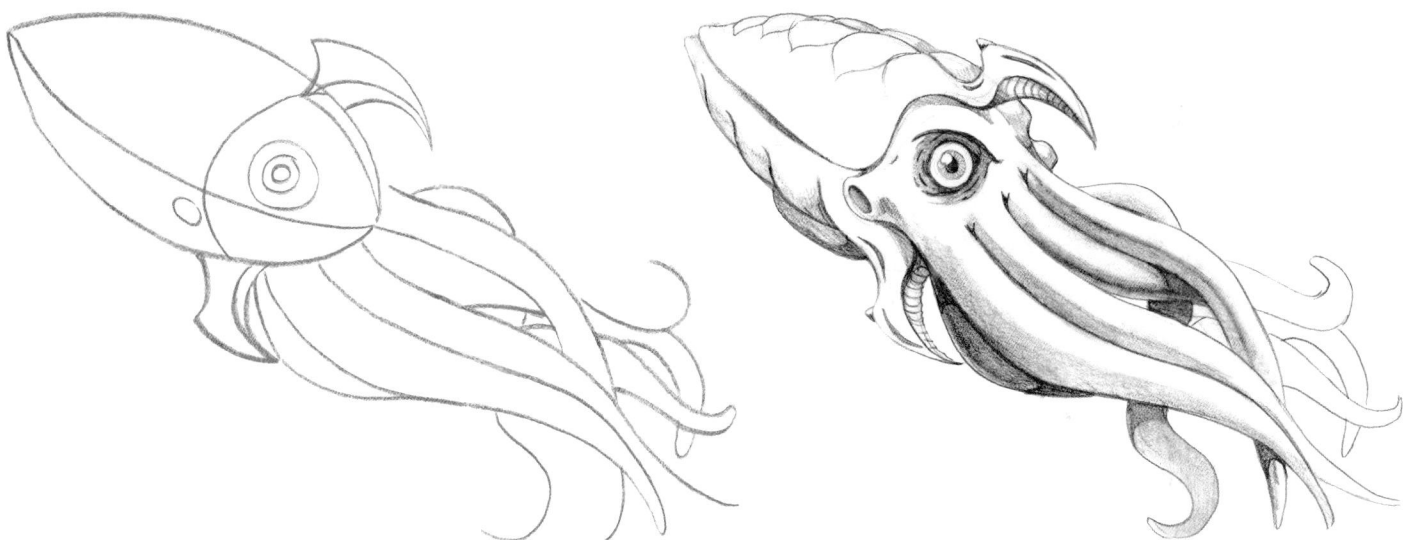

3. Draw the rubbery tentacles, keeping the lines long and flowing.

4. Use a 2B pencil to render the facial details. To make the eye a focal point, create an area of high contrast by placing very dark tones next to a bright white. Add a soft gradation to the underside of the tentacles and give them a sense of depth with cast shadows. As with the eyeball, the shell is a simpler shape that needs extra attention to avoid being overshadowed by the tentacles, so give it an interesting pattern.

To finish, render cracks on the shell to make it appear worn, old, and brainlike. Strengthen the shadowed side of the creature and add leaf shapes at the ends of the tentacles.

See opposite for the finished drawing.

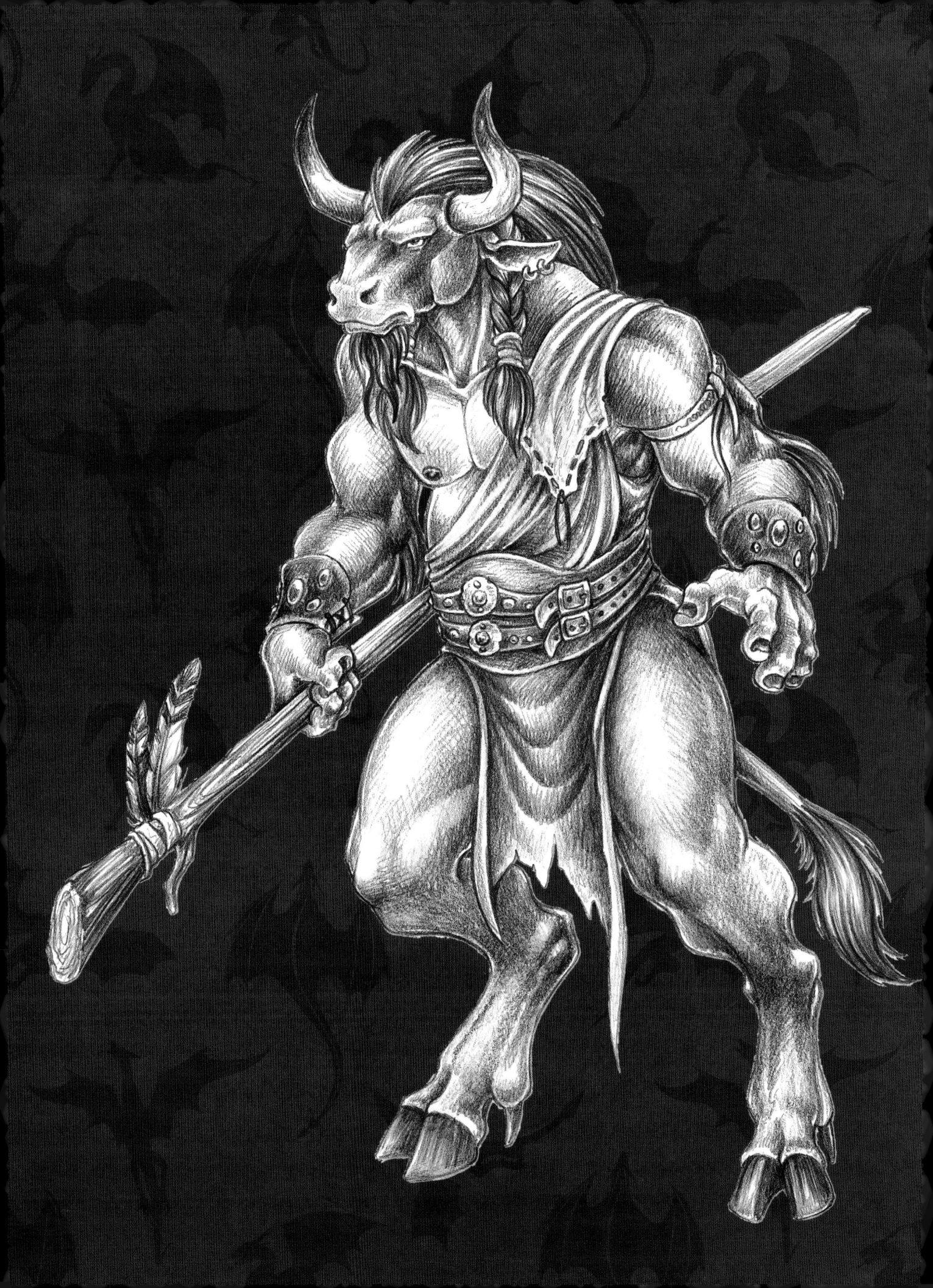

Mythical Beings

Fae

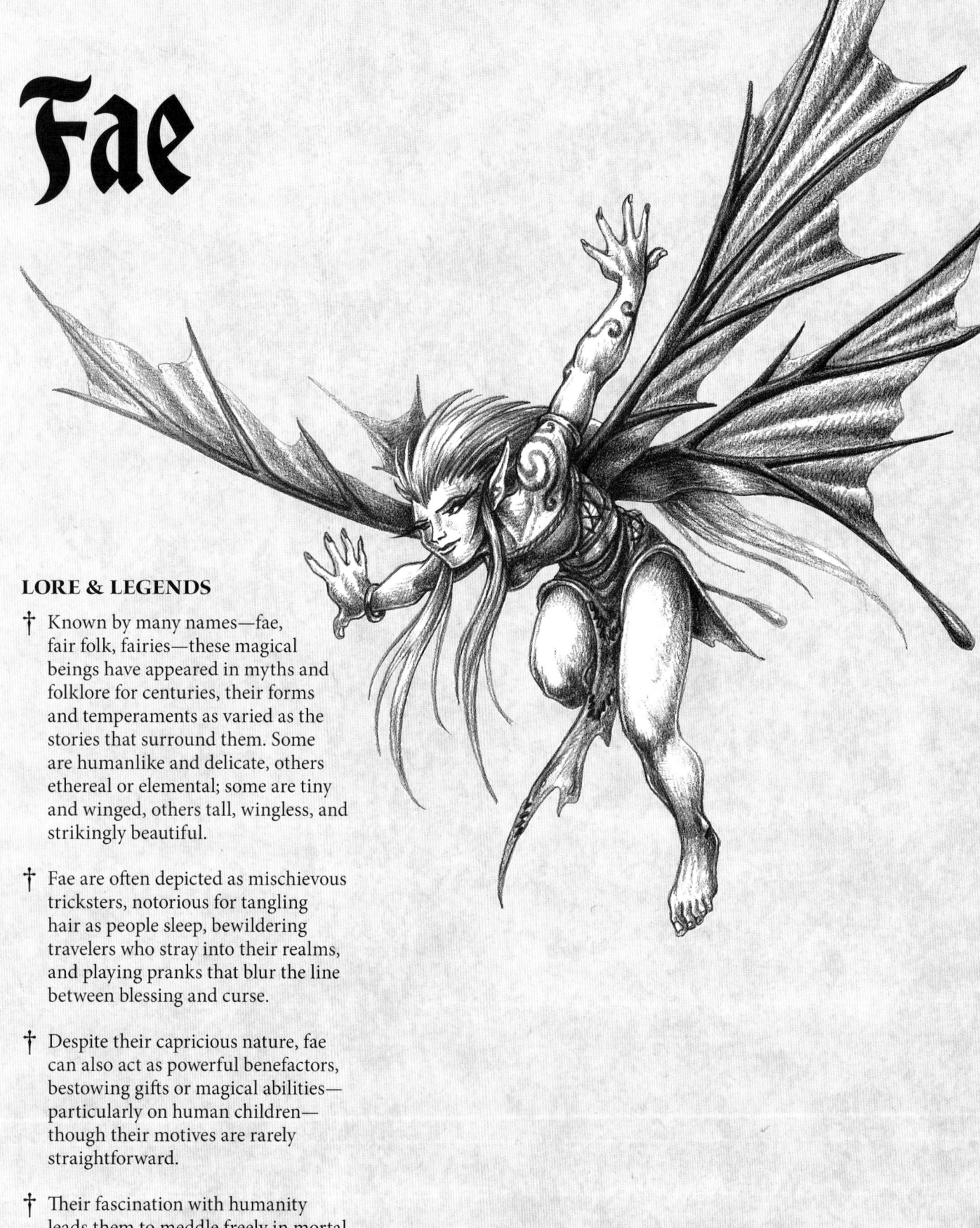

LORE & LEGENDS

† Known by many names—fae, fair folk, fairies—these magical beings have appeared in myths and folklore for centuries, their forms and temperaments as varied as the stories that surround them. Some are humanlike and delicate, others ethereal or elemental; some are tiny and winged, others tall, wingless, and strikingly beautiful.

† Fae are often depicted as mischievous tricksters, notorious for tangling hair as people sleep, bewildering travelers who stray into their realms, and playing pranks that blur the line between blessing and curse.

† Despite their capricious nature, fae can also act as powerful benefactors, bestowing gifts or magical abilities— particularly on human children— though their motives are rarely straightforward.

† Their fascination with humanity leads them to meddle freely in mortal affairs, weaving themselves into human lives in ways both wondrous and dangerous.

FAIRY ATMOSPHERES

Rural, moonlit forest hillsides and "fairy rings"—circles of mushrooms or toadstools like the one pictured here—are common settings in fairy lore.

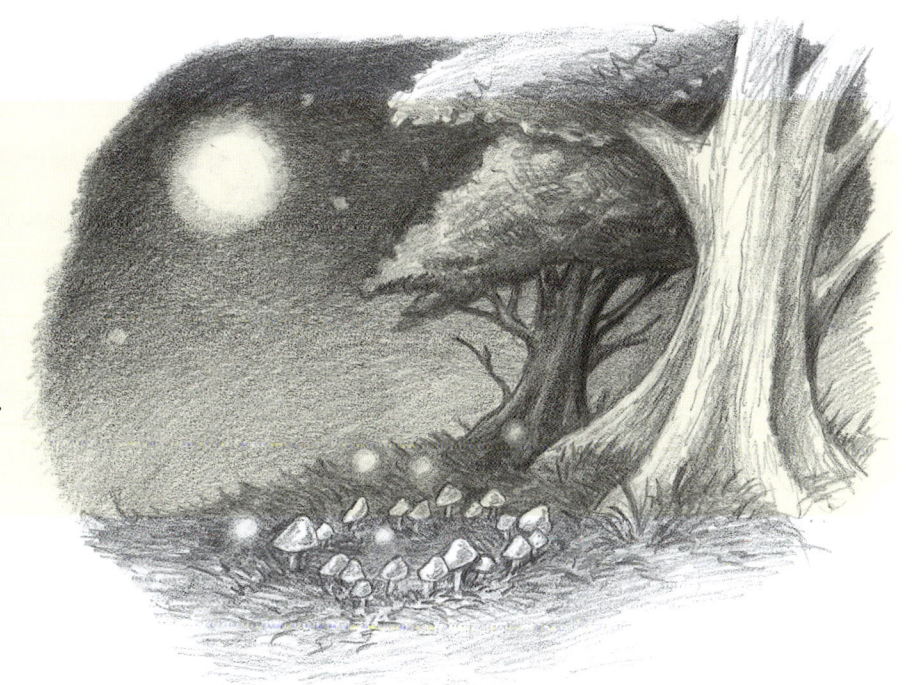

1. Start by drawing the line of action with an HB pencil, and then indicate the rest of the body, including the wings, using basic shapes.

2. Still using the HB pencil, develop the body's form using more basic shapes— circles, ovals, and cylinders. Sketch simple lines to delineate the fingers.

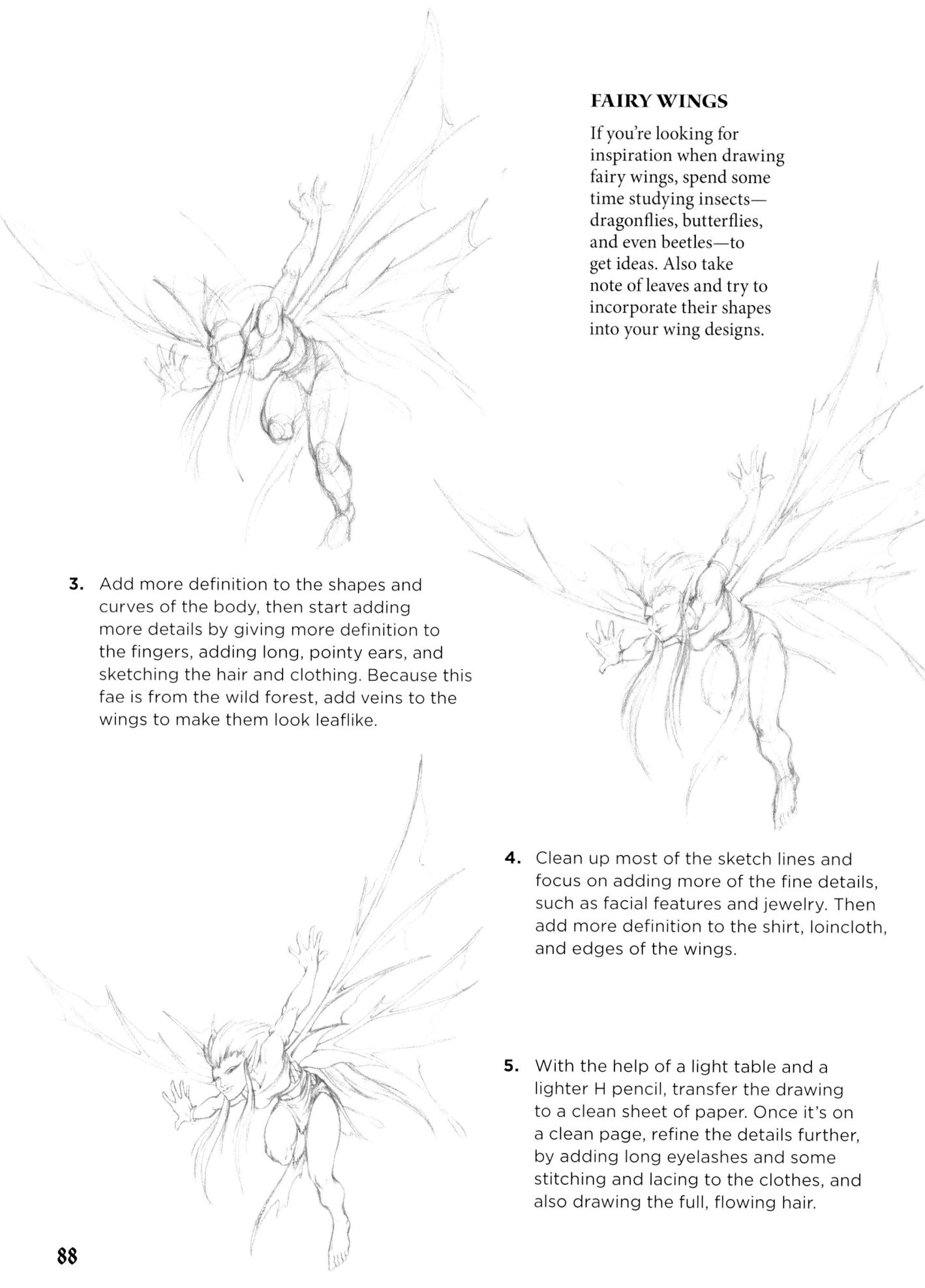

FAIRY WINGS

If you're looking for inspiration when drawing fairy wings, spend some time studying insects—dragonflies, butterflies, and even beetles—to get ideas. Also take note of leaves and try to incorporate their shapes into your wing designs.

3. Add more definition to the shapes and curves of the body, then start adding more details by giving more definition to the fingers, adding long, pointy ears, and sketching the hair and clothing. Because this fae is from the wild forest, add veins to the wings to make them look leaflike.

4. Clean up most of the sketch lines and focus on adding more of the fine details, such as facial features and jewelry. Then add more definition to the shirt, loincloth, and edges of the wings.

5. With the help of a light table and a lighter H pencil, transfer the drawing to a clean sheet of paper. Once it's on a clean page, refine the details further, by adding long eyelashes and some stitching and lacing to the clothes, and also drawing the full, flowing hair.

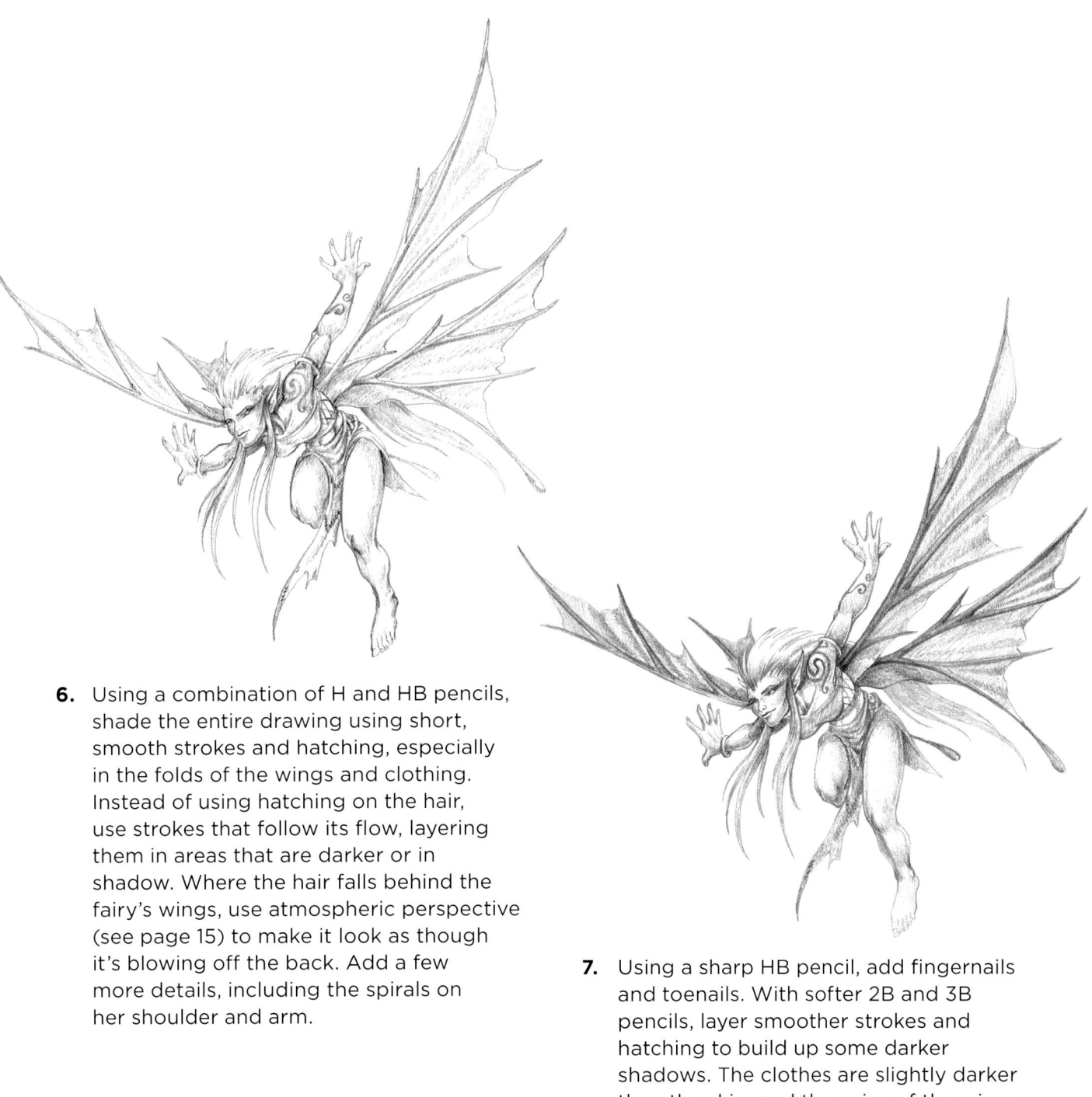

6. Using a combination of H and HB pencils, shade the entire drawing using short, smooth strokes and hatching, especially in the folds of the wings and clothing. Instead of using hatching on the hair, use strokes that follow its flow, layering them in areas that are darker or in shadow. Where the hair falls behind the fairy's wings, use atmospheric perspective (see page 15) to make it look as though it's blowing off the back. Add a few more details, including the spirals on her shoulder and arm.

7. Using a sharp HB pencil, add fingernails and toenails. With softer 2B and 3B pencils, layer smoother strokes and hatching to build up some darker shadows. The clothes are slightly darker than the skin, and the veins of the wings are even darker. Keep the shading on the skin as smooth as possible, and use rough hatching on the wings and clothes to add texture.

To finish, use a 4B pencil to build up and refine the darkest area, then blend as needed with an HB pencil. Use a kneaded eraser to lift out highlights and gradually lighten the wing farthest from the body as well as the areas of the body paint that don't fall into shadow.

See page 86 for the finished drawing.

Gnome

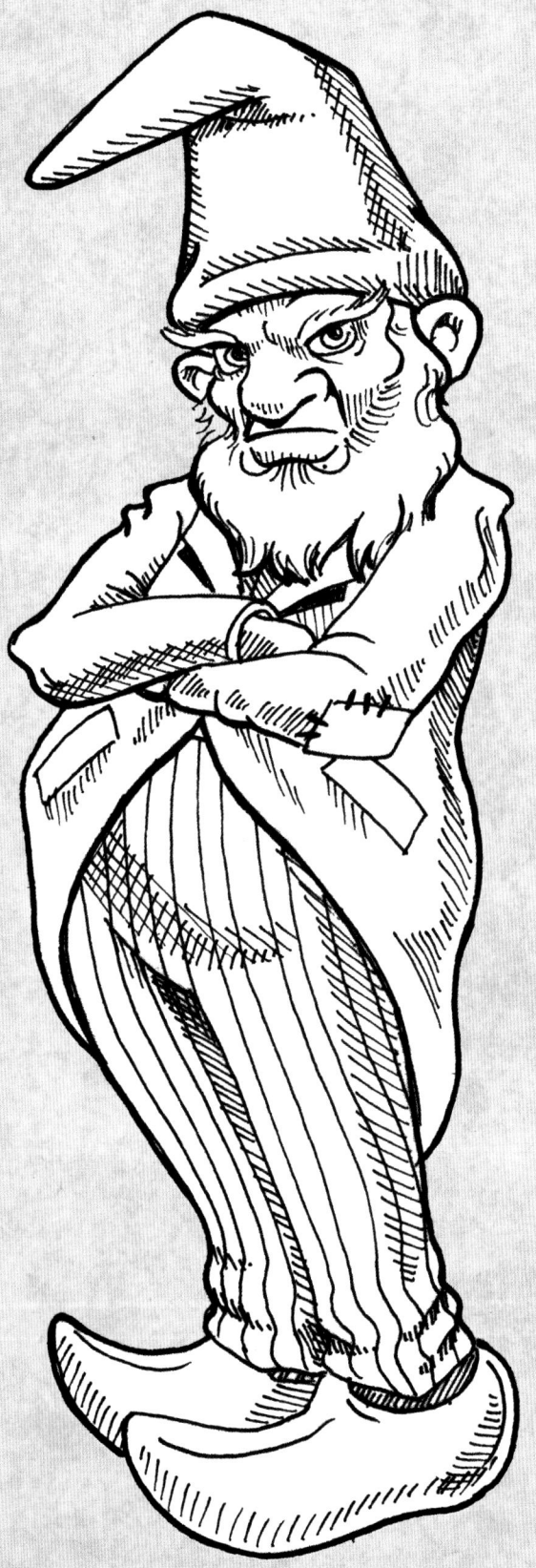

LORE & LEGENDS

† The gnome is a small, dwarflike earth spirit whose name comes from the Greek *gnosis*, meaning "knowledge," reflecting its role as a guardian of hidden wisdom and ancient secrets. Often considered part of the broader fae family—or at least closely related—gnomes embody the deep, grounded magic of the natural world.

† Dwelling deep underground, they are devoted protectors of buried treasures, minerals, and sacred knowledge—and are renowned for their exceptional vigilance.

† According to legend, exposure to daylight turns a gnome to stone, a detail that likely inspired the widespread tradition of placing garden gnome statues as protective sentinels over home and land.

† Gnomes are also beloved as caretakers of animals and wildlife, tending to forest creatures and maintaining the natural balance of their subterranean realms.

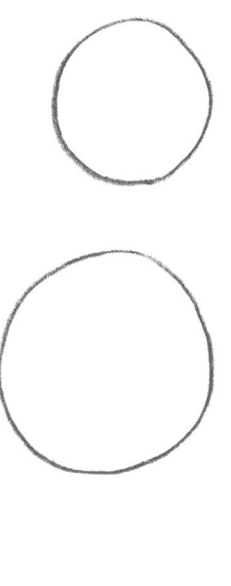

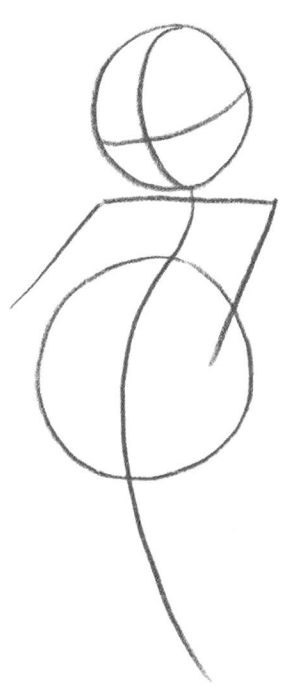

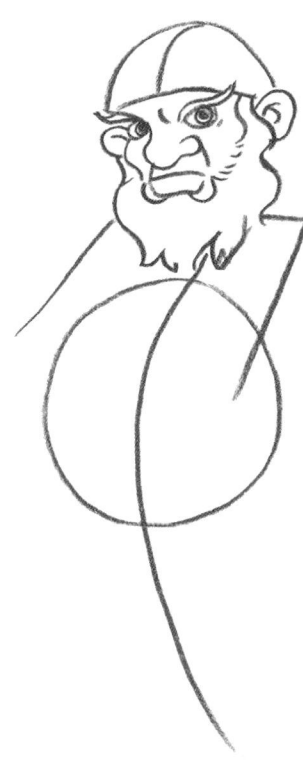

1. Using a 2H pencil, draw two circles for the head and torso of the gnome.

2. Indicate the facial guidelines and draw a line through the body to suggest its curvature. Draw a few more lines to set the position of the arms and shoulders.

3. Building on the guidelines, add the round eyes, wide nose, and slightly frowning mouth. Then draw the small ears and the full beard, breaking up the line along the gnome's left cheek. Draw thick eyebrows and indicate the line of the hat across the forehead, and add very faint hatch marks above the line of the hat and along the edge of the beard for subtle shadows.

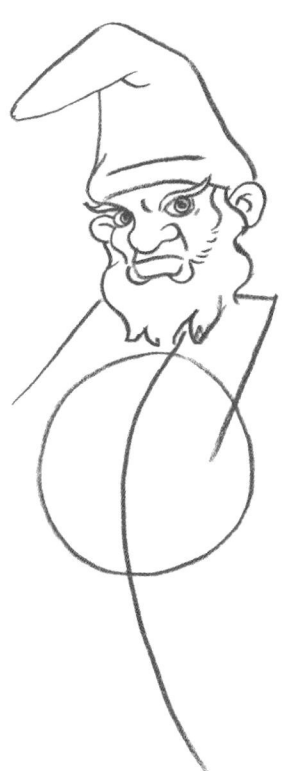

4. Draw the conical hat so it flops over at the top. Make the base of the hat rounded to indicate the shape of the head underneath.

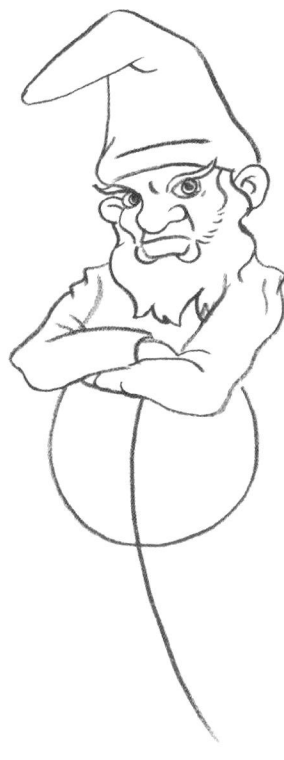

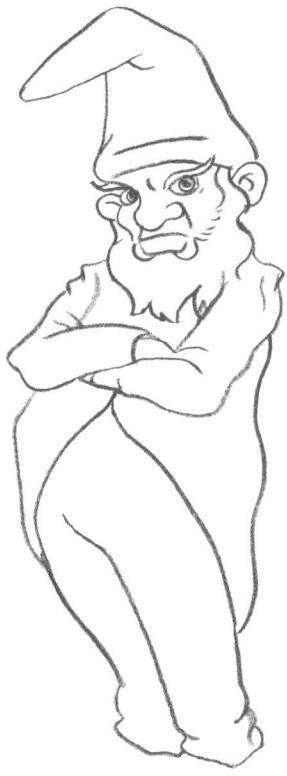

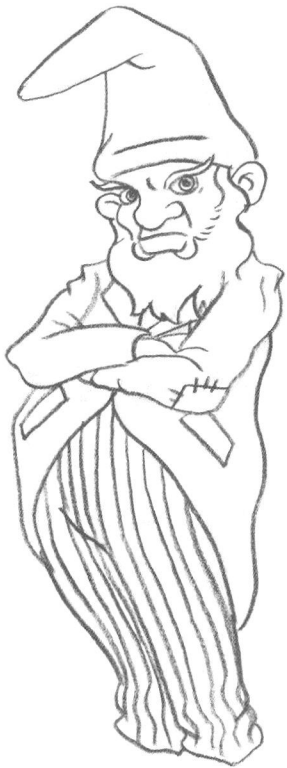

5. Following the guidelines, draw the gnome's shoulders and crossed arms.

6. Extend the coat down the hips and toward the legs, curving the lines to follow the gnome's bulging contours. Then draw the legs, adding lines near the ankles to indicate creases in the bunched fabric.

7. After lightly hatching the hat, arms, jacket, and pants, add pinstripes to the pants and draw pockets, an elbow patch, and lapels on the jacket. The pinstripes curve where the pants gather at the ankle.

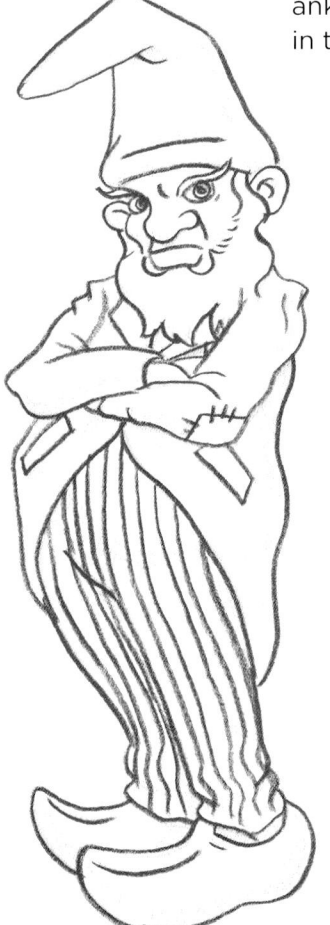

8. Add a pair of oversized wooden clogs to complete the gnome's ensemble, using light hatch marks to define the form.

To finish, use a .2 mm ink pen to trace over all the pencil lines. When the ink has dried, go over the drawing with an art gum eraser, then use a .5 mm pen to retrace the exterior contour lines of the character and the hatch marks to give the gnome a more dynamic appearance. Erase the pencil lines when the ink is dry.

See page 90 for the finished drawing.

Gnome: Variations

A gnome on the run.

A fully armed gnome dragon slayer.

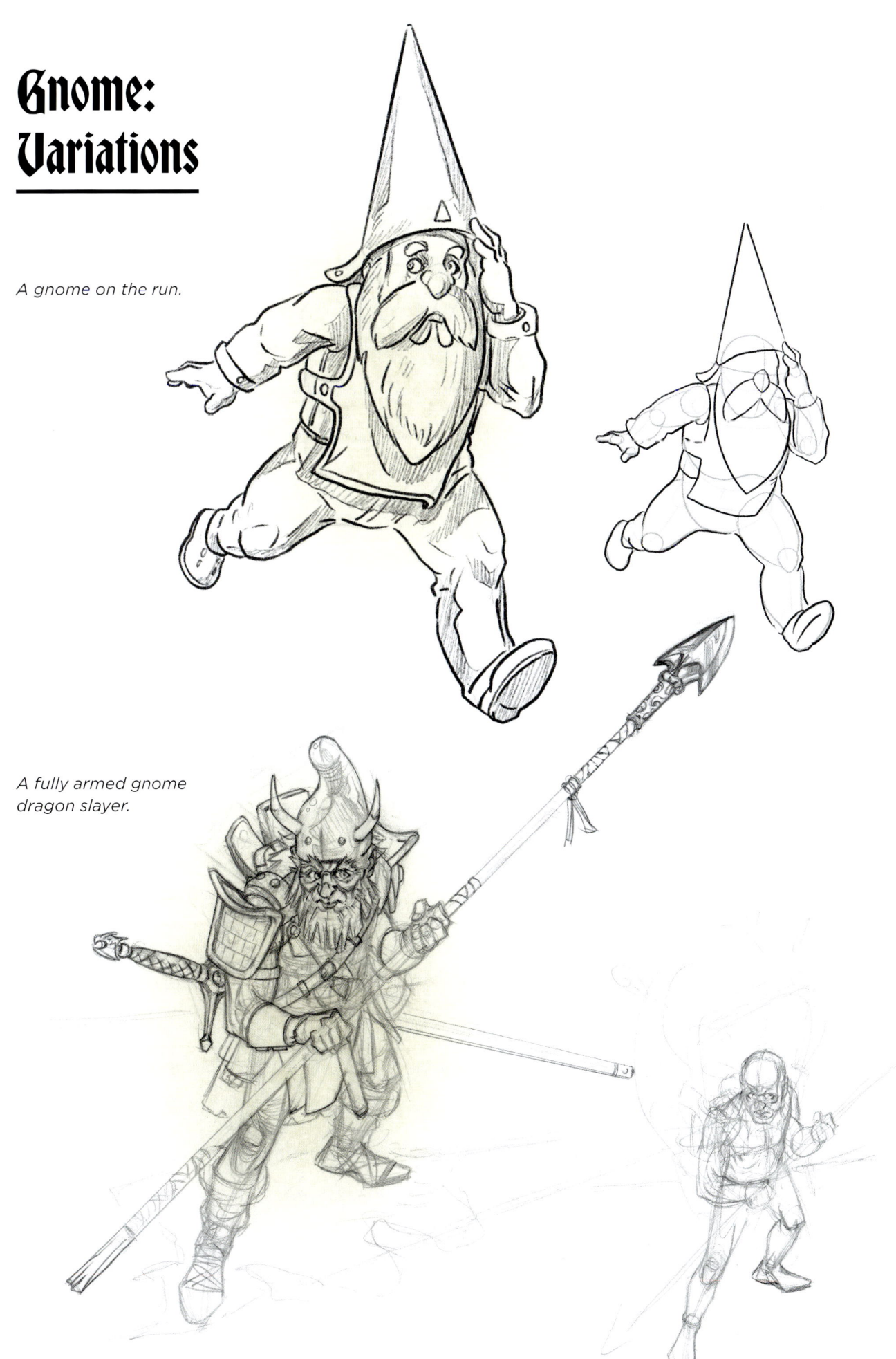

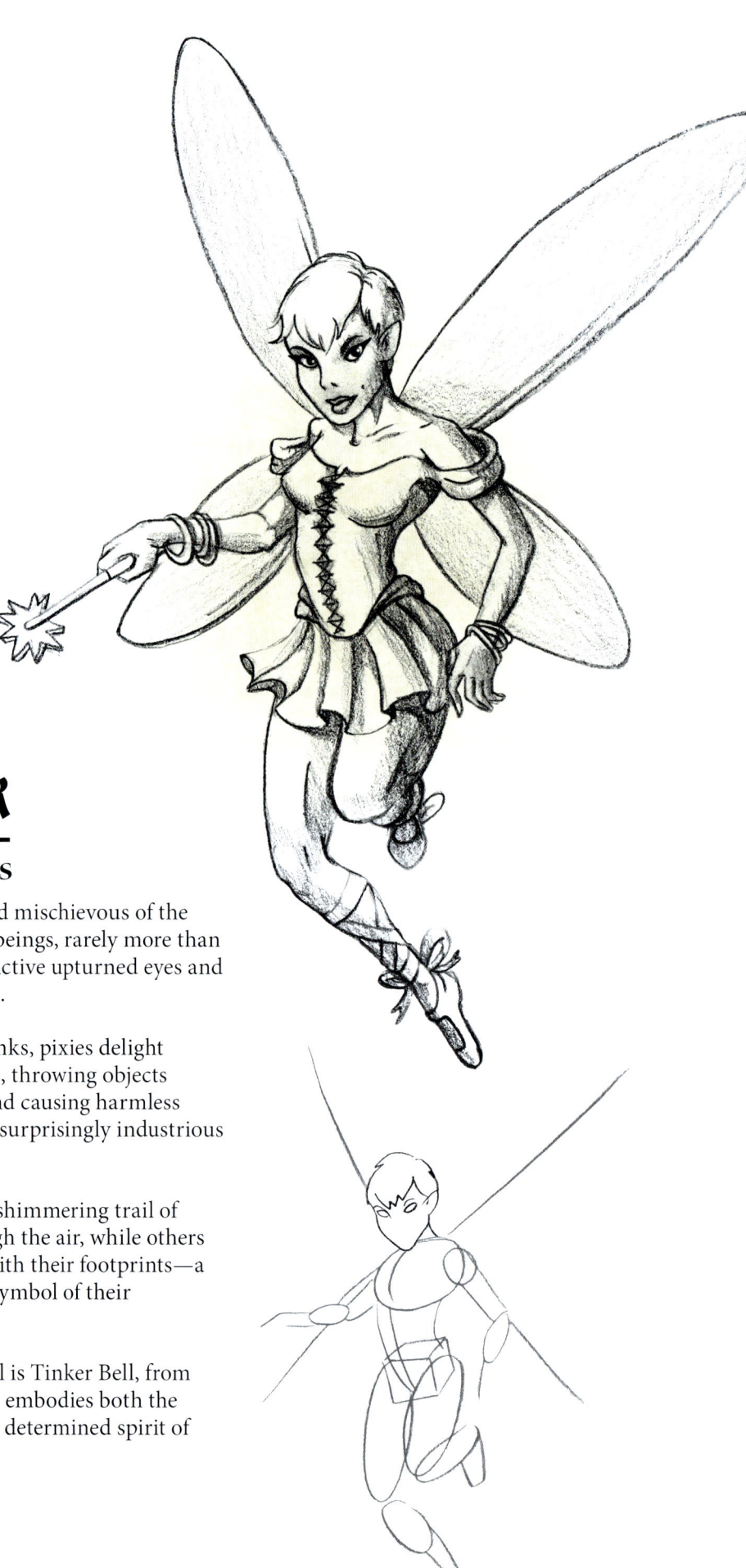

Other Fae Folk

PIXIE: LORE & LEGENDS

† Among the most playful and mischievous of the fae, pixies are tiny magical beings, rarely more than a few inches tall, with distinctive upturned eyes and an irrepressible sense of fun.

† Known for their love of pranks, pixies delight in stealing small belongings, throwing objects at unsuspecting humans, and causing harmless chaos—though they can be surprisingly industrious when a reward is offered.

† Some pixies leave behind a shimmering trail of pixie dust as they flit through the air, while others sprinkle the magical dust with their footprints—a sign of their passing and a symbol of their enchantment.

† The most famous pixie of all is Tinker Bell, from J.M. Barrie's *Peter Pan*, who embodies both the mischievous charm and the determined spirit of these beloved fairyfolk.

BROWNIE: LORE & LEGENDS

† Originating in Celtic and Scottish folklore, brownies are gentle, helpful household spirits often considered part of the fae realm, closely tied to the magic of hearth and home.

† They are known for secretly performing chores during the night while humans sleep—sweeping floors, mending clothes, or tending to livestock.

† They ask for very little in return, often just a bowl of cream, a crust of bread, or a small offering of thanks. However, if they are insulted, mistreated, or offered direct payment, they will disappear forever, never to return.

† As guardians of hearth and home, brownies embody the idea that kindness, gratitude, and humility invite fae magic into everyday life.

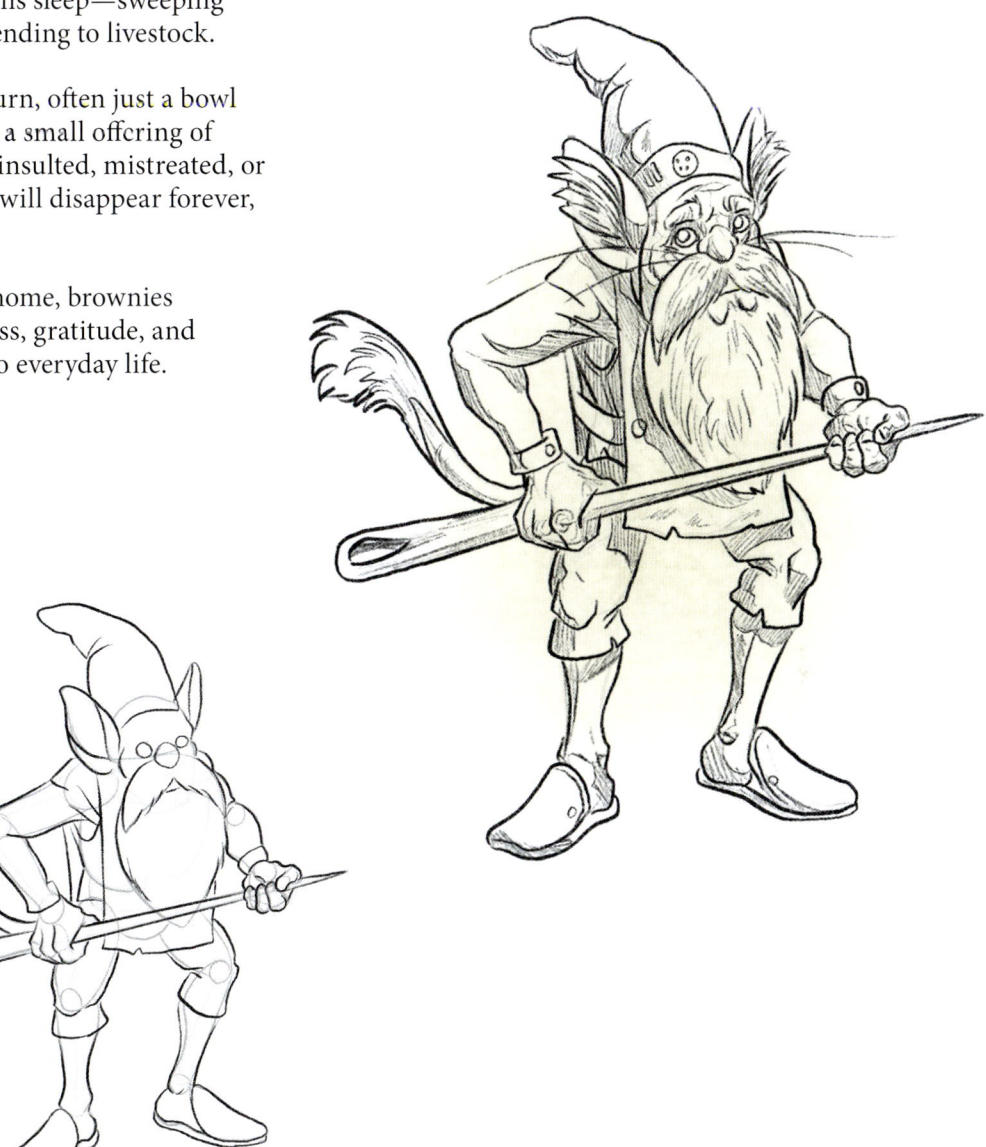

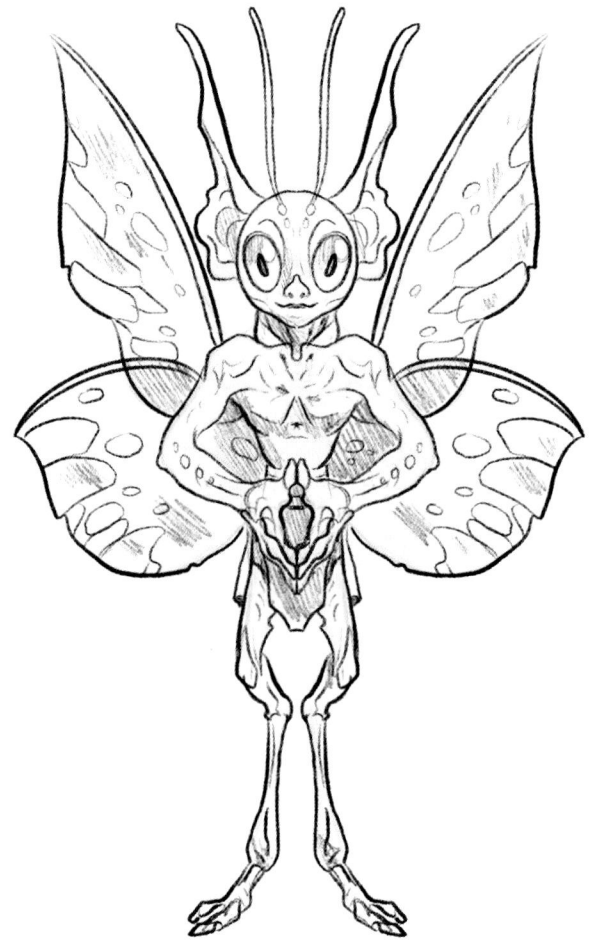

SPRITE: LORE & LEGENDS

† Sprites are tiny, radiant elemental beings said to be born from sunlight, dew, or blossoms, embodying the delicate and fleeting beauty of the natural world.

† As guardians of nature's smallest wonders, they tend to flowers, streams, and forest glades, ensuring that even the most overlooked corners of the earth flourish with life.

† With their dazzling, iridescent wings and quicksilver speed, sprites often serve as messengers between the mortal and fae realms, darting unseen through sunbeams and shadows alike.

† Mischievous by nature, they are playful tricksters—rewarding those who honor and protect nature with blessings, while leading the careless and disrespectful astray.

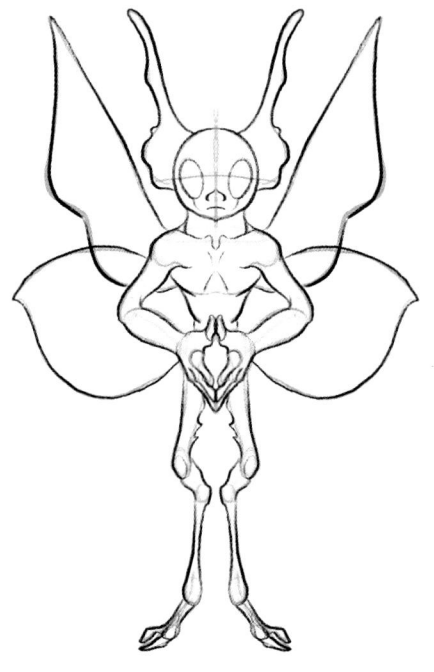

WOOD NYMPH: LORE & LEGENDS

† Wood nymphs are graceful nature spirits deeply connected to the forests, groves, and ancient trees they inhabit. They embody the spirit of the wild wood—timeless, elusive, and eternally bound to the life force of the earth.

† Often appearing as beautiful, ethereal maidens, wood nymphs are protectors of their woodland realms, nurturing plant life and safeguarding the delicate balance of the forest ecosystem.

† They are known to be shy and elusive, vanishing into bark or mist when approached, yet they sometimes reveal themselves to those who show respect and reverence for nature.

† Playful but powerful, wood nymphs can bless those who honor the forest with good fortune and guidance—or curse those who harm it with misfortune and confusion.

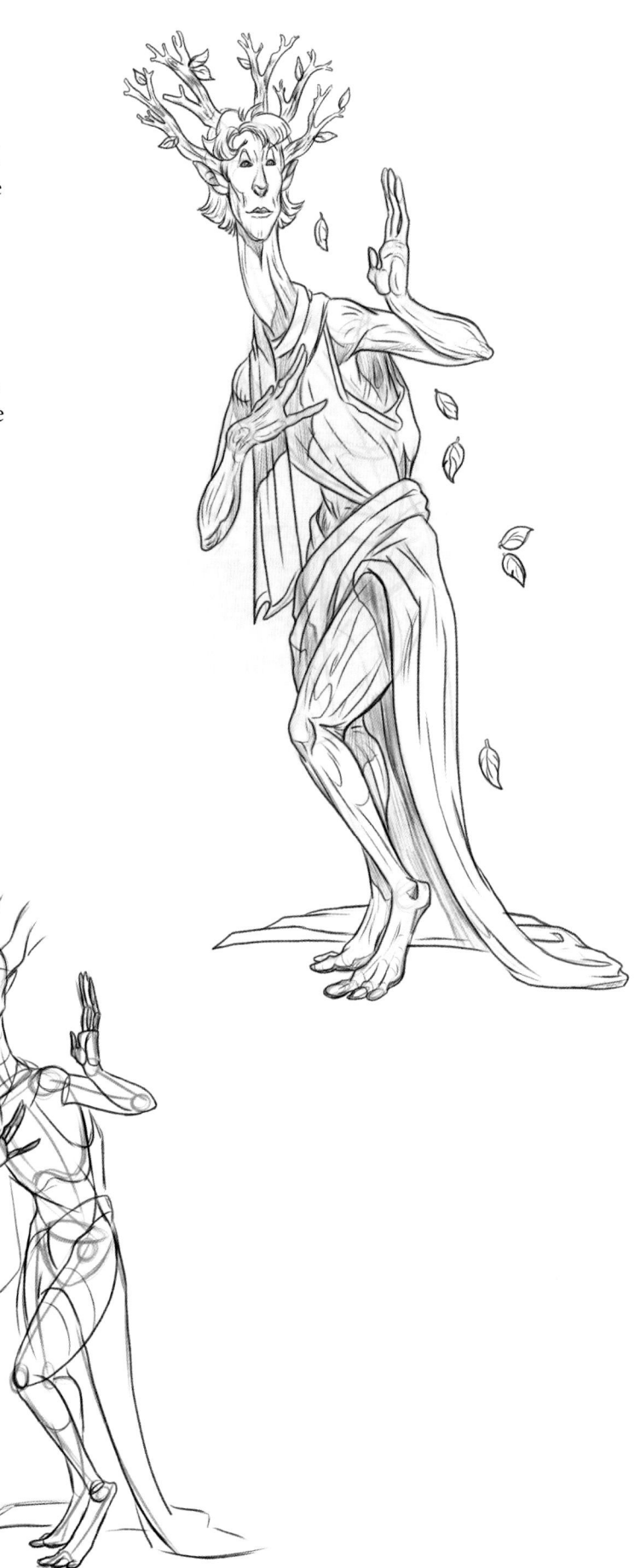

Centaur

LORE & LEGENDS

† In Greek mythology, centaurs embody the duality of human nature—representing both the noble and the base, the civilized and the wild—as creatures who are half human and half horse.

† Often depicted as boisterous, unruly, and quick-tempered, centaurs are infamous for their rowdy behavior and love of wine, with drunkenness frequently leading to chaos in ancient myths.

† Yet not all centaurs are ruled by impulse. Some are renowned for their wisdom, love of knowledge, music, and healing arts— none more so than Chiron, the wise centaur who mentored many Greek heroes, including Heracles.

† Skilled with the bow and arrow, centaurs are celebrated as master archers and hunters, their dual nature allowing them to move swiftly through wilderness and battlefield alike.

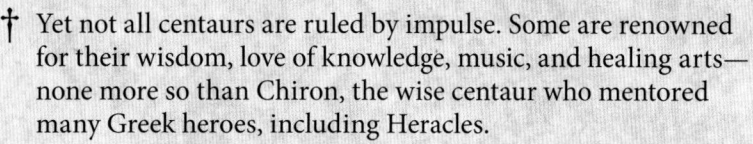

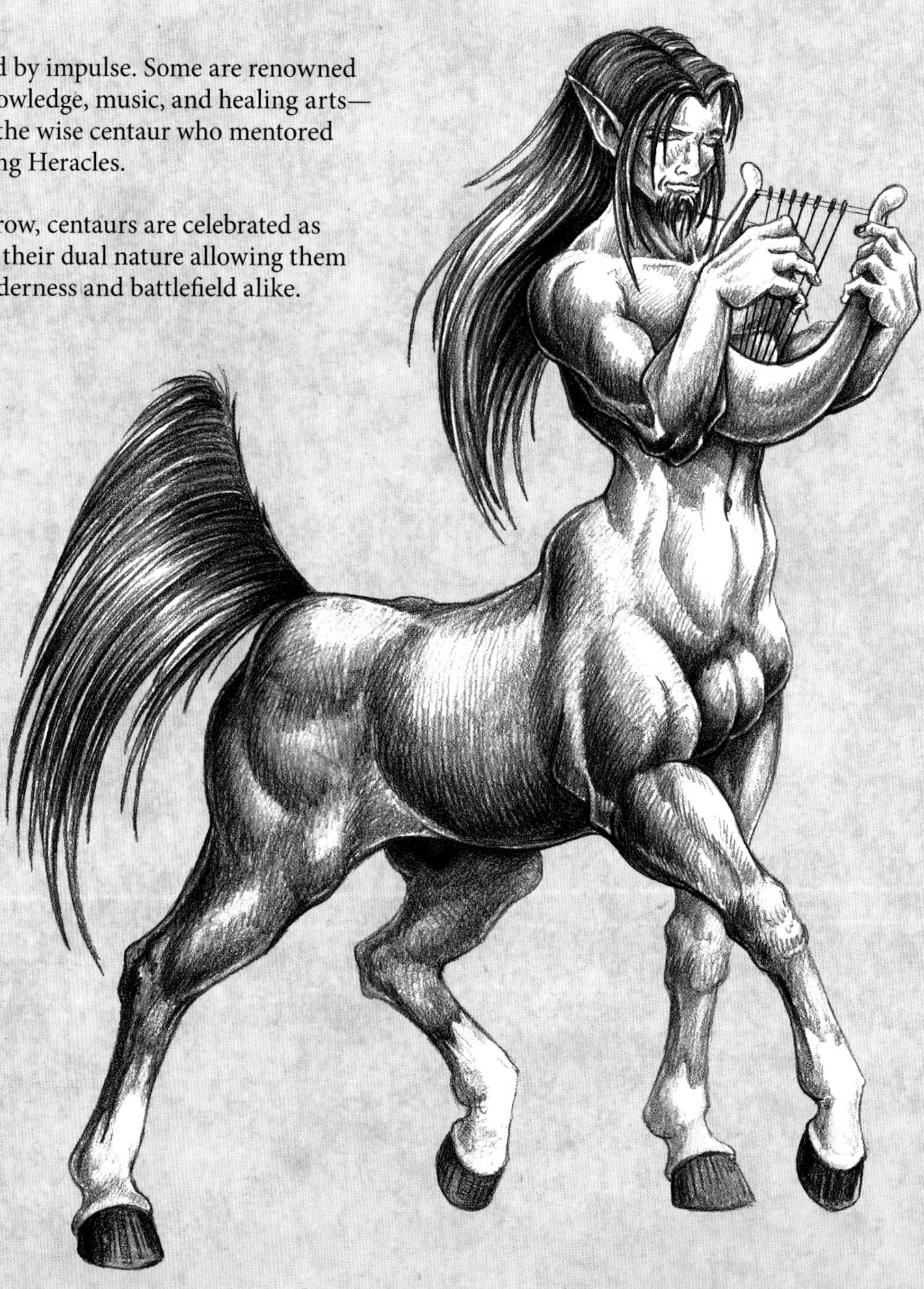

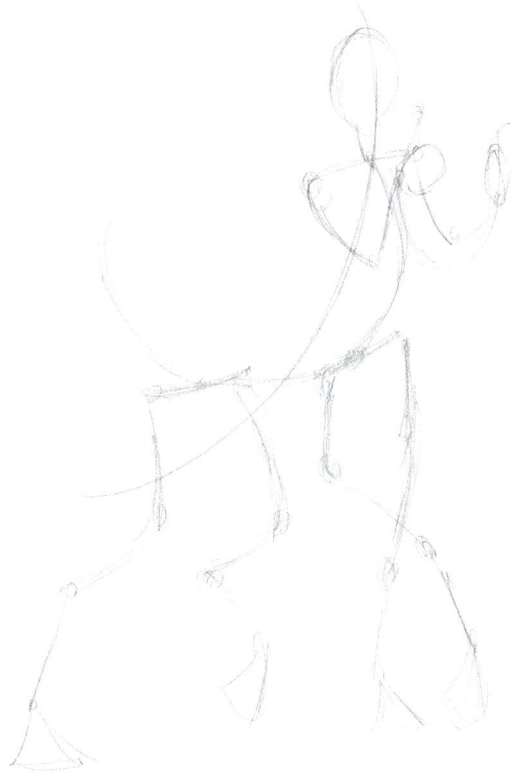

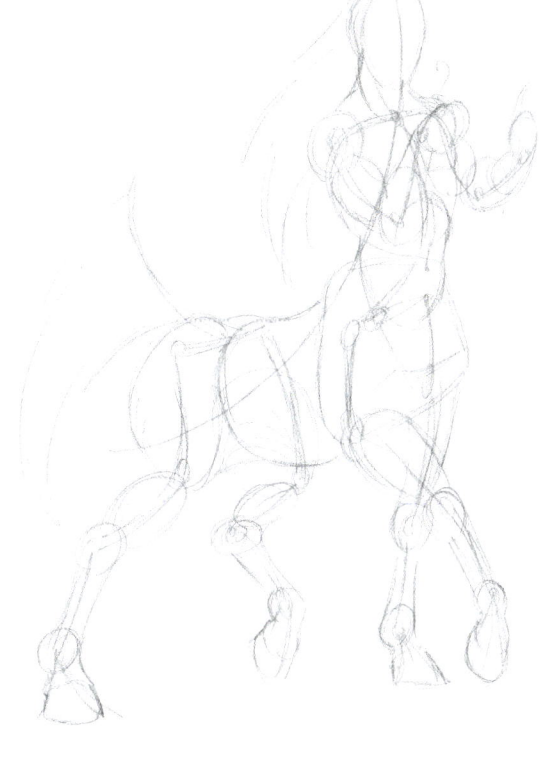

1. Start by drawing the line of action and sketching the basic figure with an HB pencil. Indicate the hands so they're raised in front of the figure, because this centaur will be plucking a lyre. Include the bony length of the tail in the sketch to indicate how the rest of the tail will flow. The base of a horse's tail is actually bone—it's the hair that grows from the tail that makes it look long. The position of the tail can say a lot about a horse's (and thus a centaur's) mood—a raised tail usually means excitement or happiness.

2. Use the HB pencil and simple shapes to develop the forms of the body. Draw the general shapes of the hair and tail.

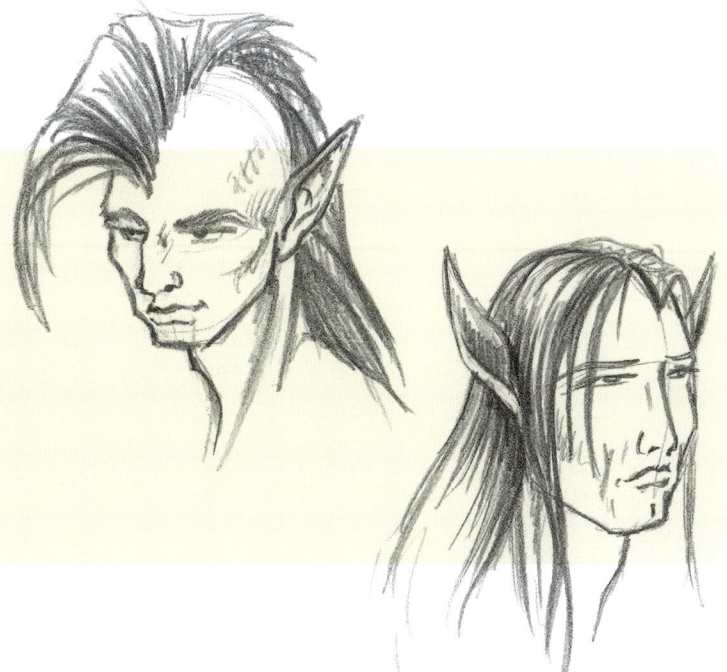

HORSING AROUND

A slightly longer face and nose (far right) will make your centaur appear more horselike. Long hair also looks good on a centaur—the hair could grow in a straight line down the scalp, like a horse's mane (near right). You can also draw horse ears.

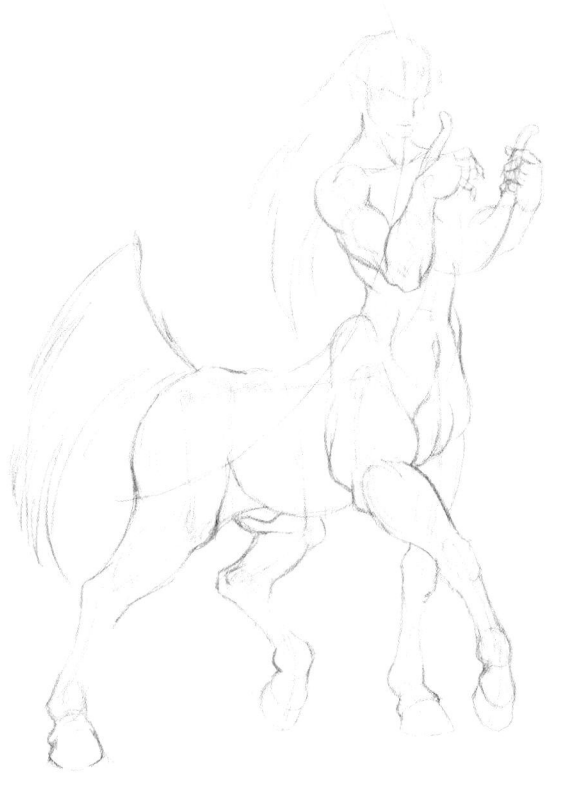

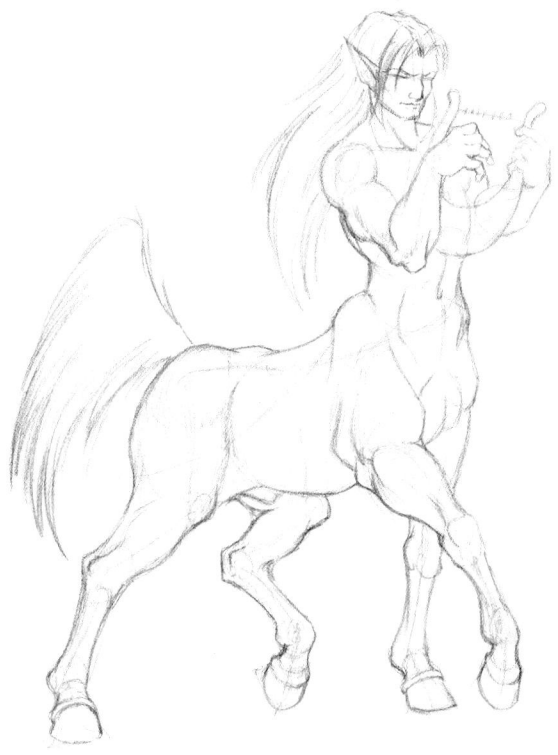

3. Start developing the shapes. Delineate the hooves and fingers and block in the eyebrows, nose, mouth, and pointed ears. Draw the curved lyre between the hands.

4. Create bangs that frame the face, similar to a horse's forelock. Add long strokes to the hair and tail, making them appear wispy, then develop the face, adding the eyes and darkening the brows to make him look thoughtful. Also add the crossbar and harp pins to the lyre.

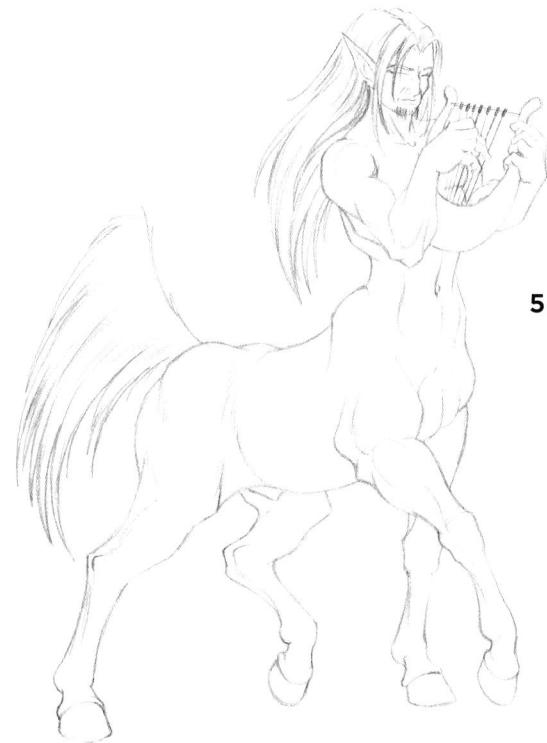

5. Place the sketch on a light table and transfer the drawing to a clean sheet of paper. As you trace the lines, you can make adjustments, such as adding a bit of scruff to the chin so he looks a bit more untamed. Also add strings to the lyre.

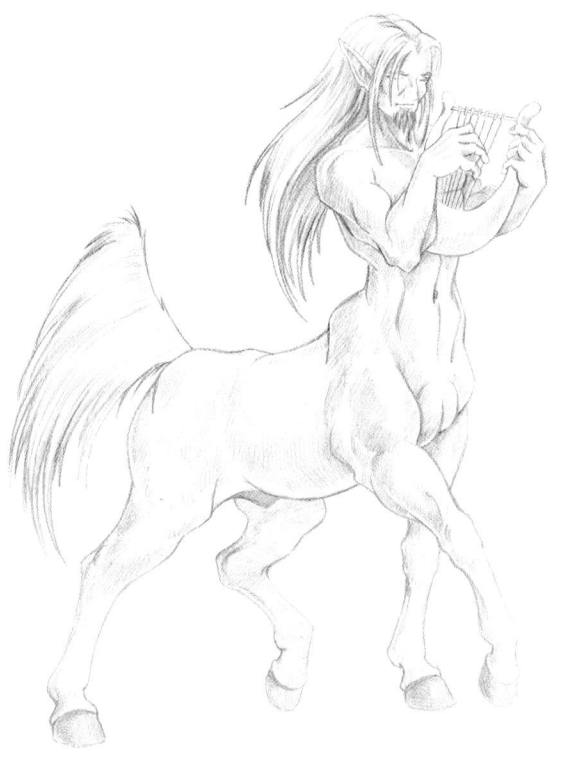

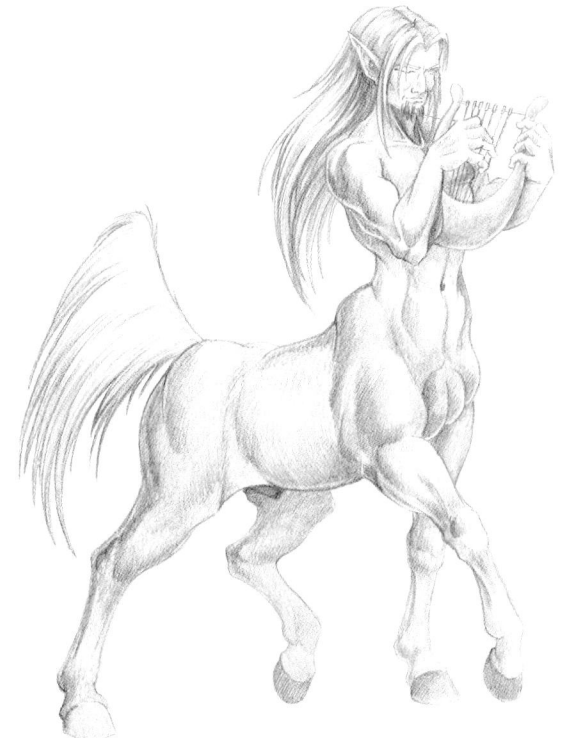

6. Still using the HB pencil, begin to shade areas of the centaur with light hatch marks. Add more strokes in the hair and tail, following the direction of hair growth so the hair looks smooth and shiny. Hatching across long hair tends to make it look dull; this is fine for hair that's in shadow, such as the hair behind the centaur's shoulders.

7. With a 2B pencil, deepen areas of shadow with more hatching and crosshatching, switching to an HB pencil to blend the darker areas into the surrounding lighter ones. When hatching across a large area like the horse's barrel, make sure your strokes run crosswise across the form, changing the angle as the form curves to give it depth. Conversely, keep the shading of the rear leg on the left very flat to suggest distance. Use a ruler to draw the strings of the lyre.

To finish, use a soft 4B pencil to push the darkest areas, and the 2B and HB to blend the dark shadows into the lighter areas. You don't want too much detail in the short, smooth coat, but you also don't want the body to look as if it were carved from stone, so add a bit of hatching and crosshatching to imply the coat's texture. To make the dark hooves look shiny, use the HB to blend them until they look smooth, then lift out some vertical highlights with a kneaded eraser. Also use the eraser to lift out some tone on the fetlocks, defining the edges of these light areas with the HB. With the 4B, add darks to the hair and tail, lifting out highlights with the kneaded eraser. Then add some darker shadows to the hind legs and the lyre.

See page 98 for the finished drawing.

Other Mythic Hybrids

Not all human–animal hybrids are guardians or guides—some embody humanity's most primal instincts. The Satyr and the Minotaur reveal the dual nature of mythic hybrids: both joyful and savage, chaotic and powerful.

SATYR: LORE & LEGENDS

† Satyrs are half human and half goat, known in Greek mythology for their wild, carefree nature and their deep connection to the untamed forces of pleasure, music, and celebration.

† They are most often depicted as companions of Dionysus, the god of wine, and are notorious for their love of drink and revelry, often seen dancing, feasting, or causing mischief in a state of joyful abandon.

† True to their hedonistic spirit, Satyrs are frequently shown playing musical instruments, especially the panpipe, which symbolizes their connection to nature and their patron, Pan—the most famous Satyr-like god.

† Almost always portrayed as male, Satyrs traditionally sport short, curved caprine horns—sometimes called "Pan horns"—that emerge from their heads, emphasizing their goat-like heritage and primal energy.

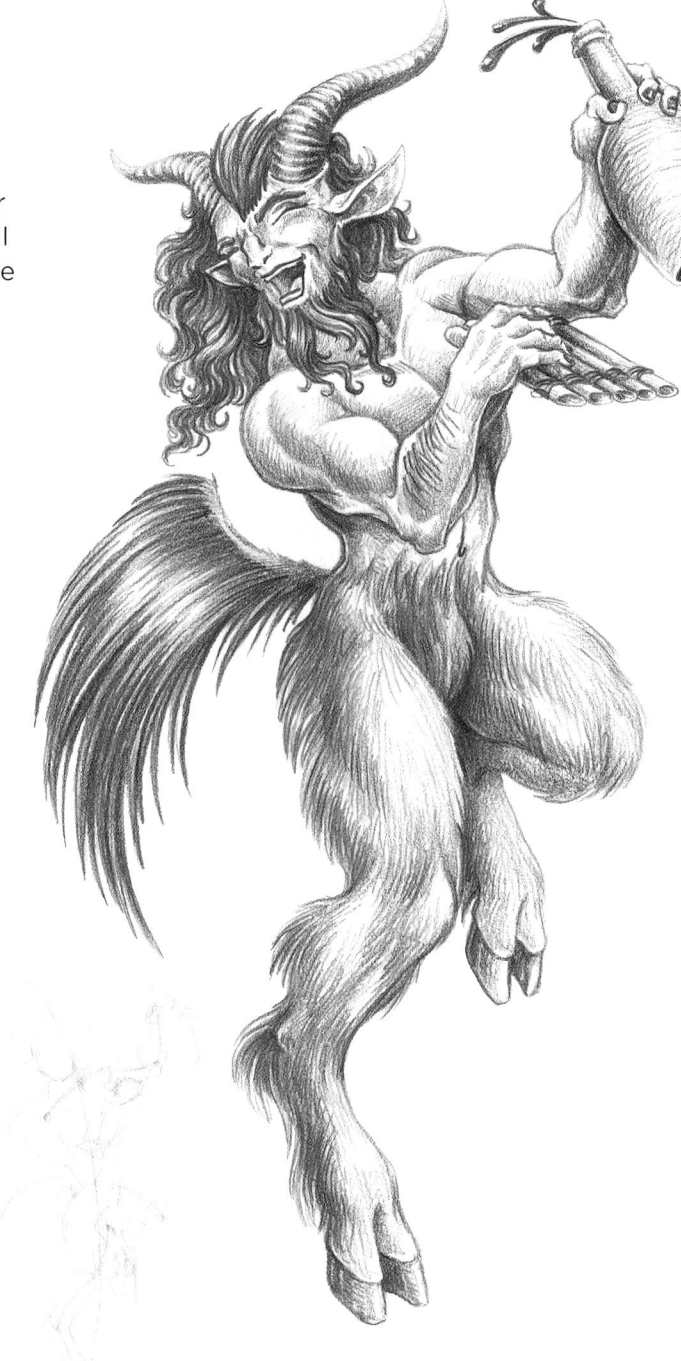

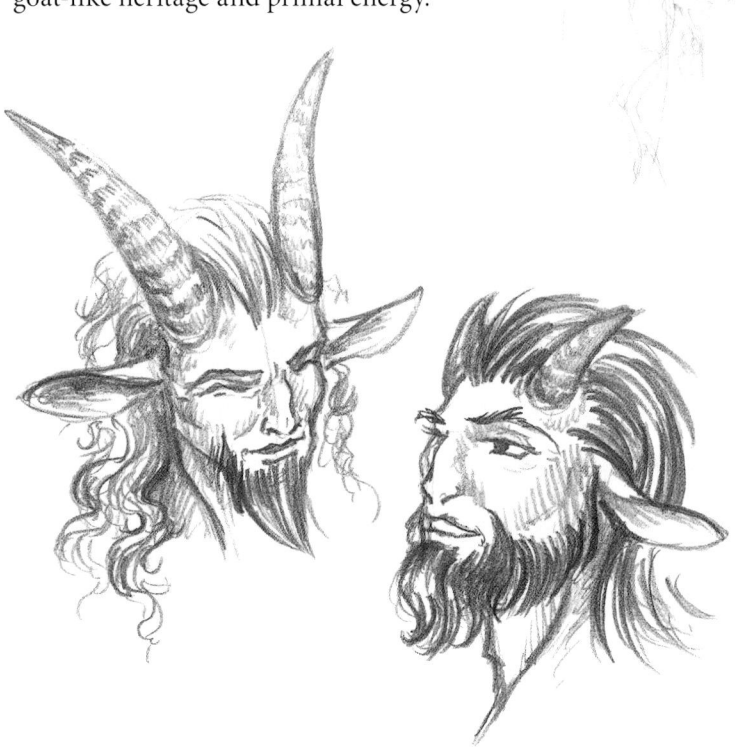

PAN HORNS

Pan horns are wonderfully varied. Research ideas for different horns for your Satyr; you might even want to try combining two types to make your character truly unique.

MINOTAUR: LORE & LEGENDS

† A creature of brutal strength and primal fury, the Minotaur is a half-man, half-bull monster born from the union of King Minos's wife and a sacred bull—a punishment inflicted by Poseidon after Minos defied the sea god by stealing the animal.

† Savage and carnivorous, the Minotaur terrorized the island of Crete, leaving a trail of destruction so great that Minos ordered the master inventor Daedalus to construct an elaborate labyrinth to contain him.

† Within that maze of twisting corridors, the beast devoured sacrificial victims until he was finally slain by the hero Theseus, who used wit and courage to end the Minotaur's reign of terror.

† In contemporary fiction and games, Minotaurs often appear as formidable villains—embodiments of rage, power, and physical dominance—yet they are also sometimes portrayed as intelligent and noble, even stepping into the role of the hero.

BLENDING THE FEATURES

Because a Minotaur is half bull and half man, it's important that the different features blend cohesively. One trick is to place the eyes closer together on the head (instead of placing them far apart as you'd see on a cow), which makes the face appear more human. Another trick is to draw the lips so they're fuller and fleshier, making them look capable of speech and expression. Adding long hair on the head can help too.

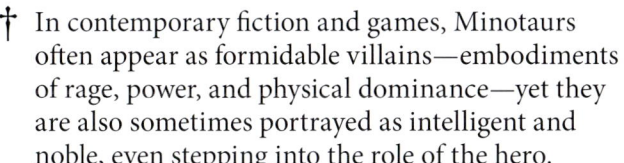

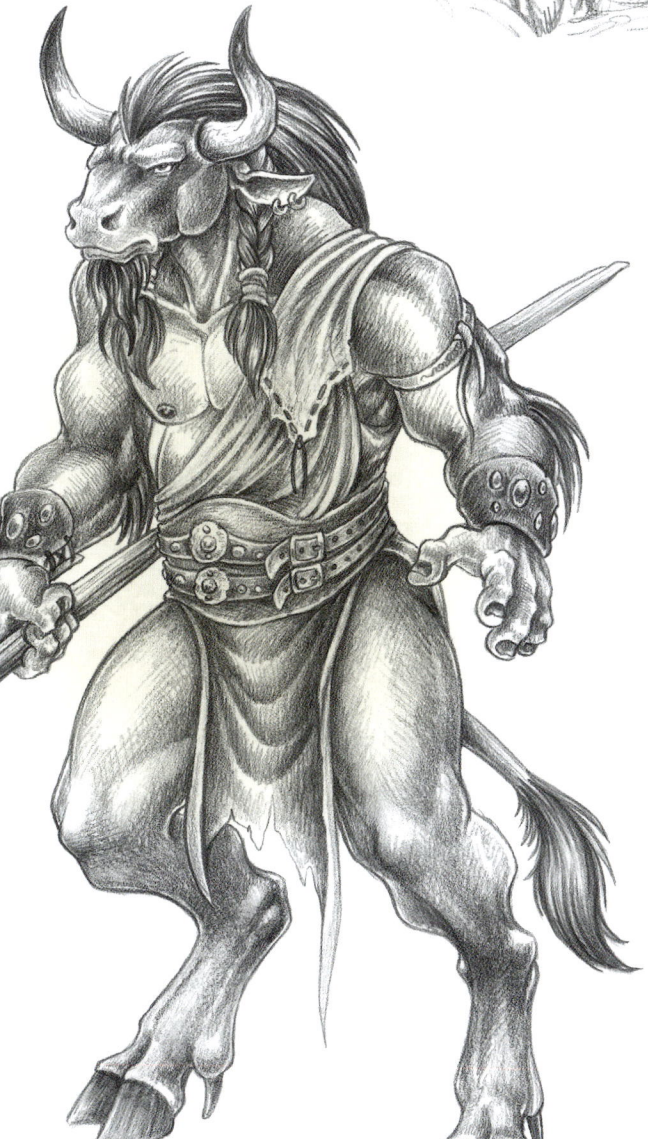

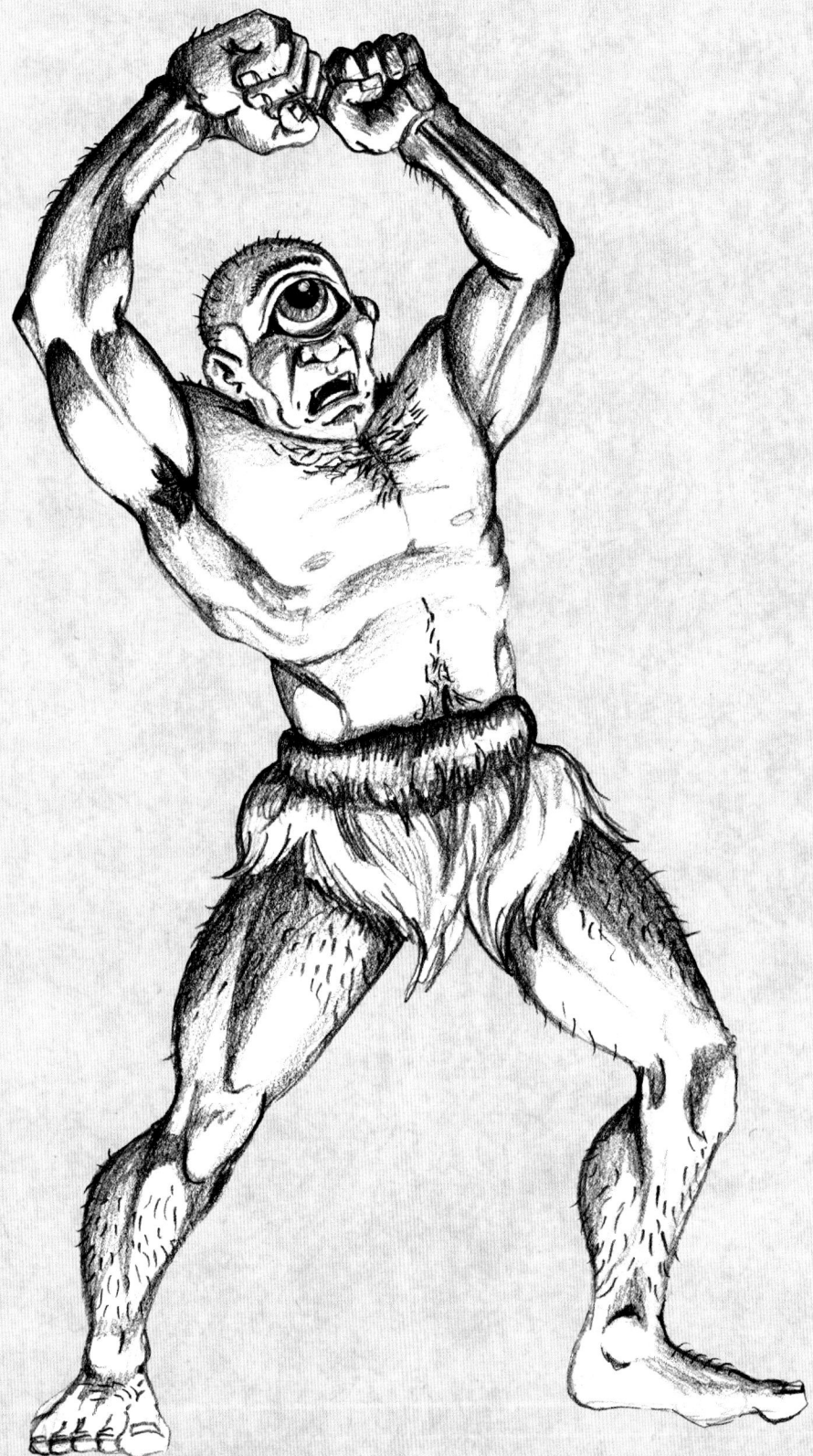

Cyclops

LORE & LEGENDS

† The Cyclops—a towering giant with a single eye set in the center of its forehead—originates from Greek mythology and remains one of the most recognizable figures in ancient legend.

† According to Homer's *Odyssey*, the cyclopes (plural) lived as a community of shepherds and blacksmiths in what is now Sicily, dwelling apart from humans and following their own primal laws.

† Greek myth tells of two races of cyclopes: one residing in the heavens as divine craftsmen, and another living on Earth on the Isle of Cyclops, where the Greek hero Odysseus famously encountered Polyphemus during his return from the Trojan War.

† Renowned for their mastery of metalwork, the cyclopes forged many of the gods' most powerful weapons and artifacts—including Zeus's thunderbolts, Artemis's bow, Poseidon's trident, and Perseus's helmet of invisibility.

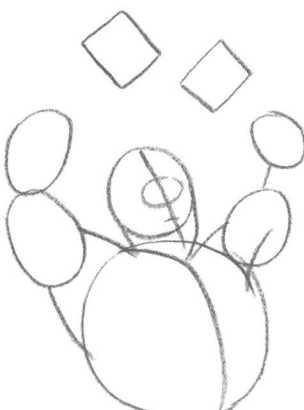

1. With a 2H pencil, draw the basic shapes of the figure's torso, head, and arms, which are raised above the head.

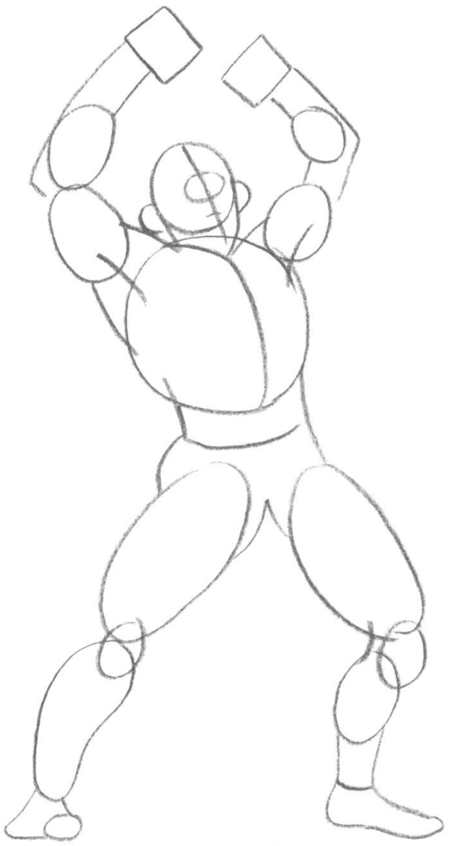

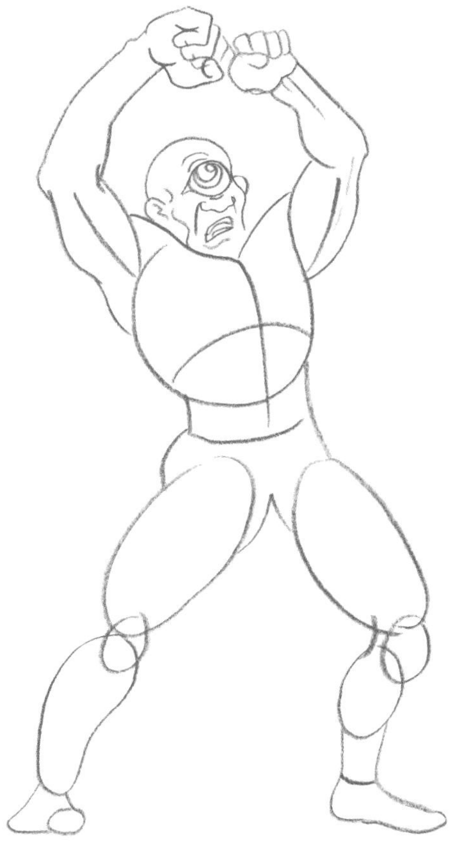

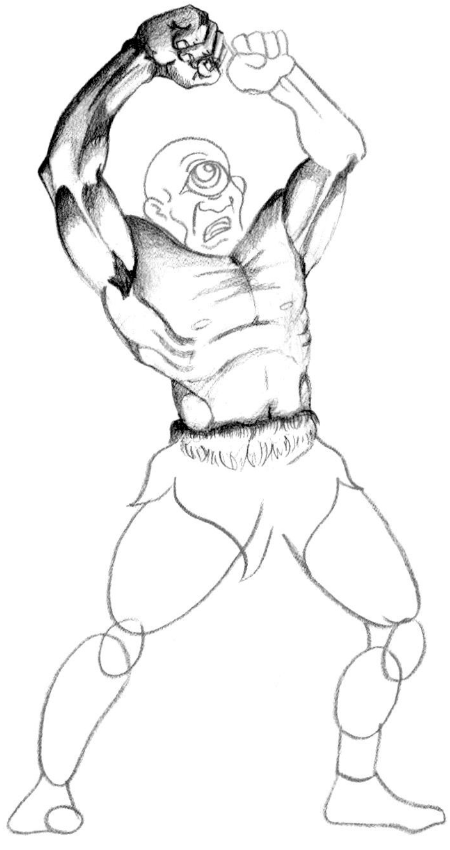

2. To convey a sense of power, block in the legs with a wide stance.

3. Add a guideline across the chest to suggest curvature. Then refine the arms and hands, making them large and beefy. Switch to a softer HB pencil to add the facial features. Make the nose extra wide to balance the oversized eye.

4. Still working with an HB pencil, draw the outline of the loincloth, which barely covers the muscular thighs. Add the furry band at the top, using short, curved strokes. Shade the upper portion of the Cyclops with a 2B pencil. Define the muscle groups of the beast's right arm, shading them so they appear to be lit from below. In the torso, keep the darker tones in the upper portions of each interior body shape.

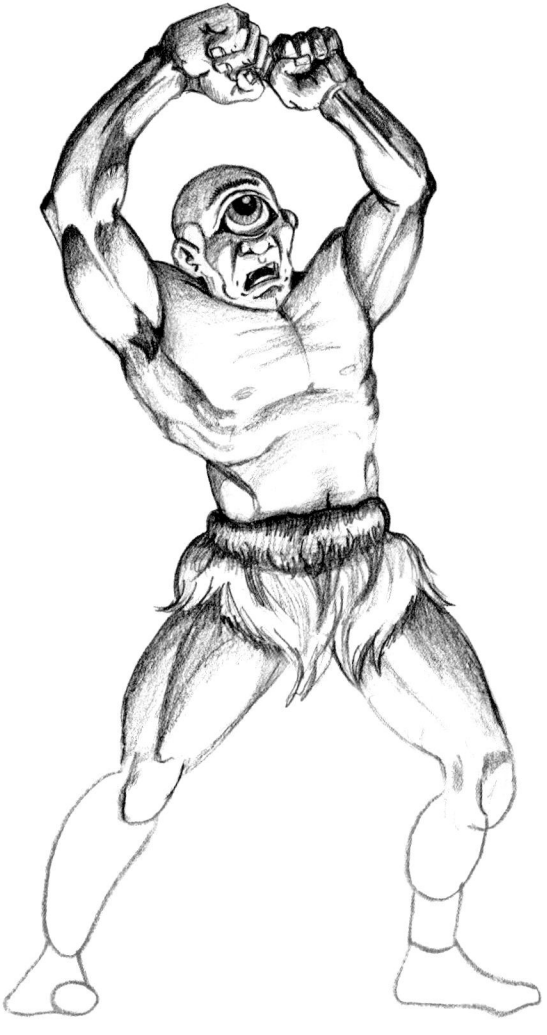
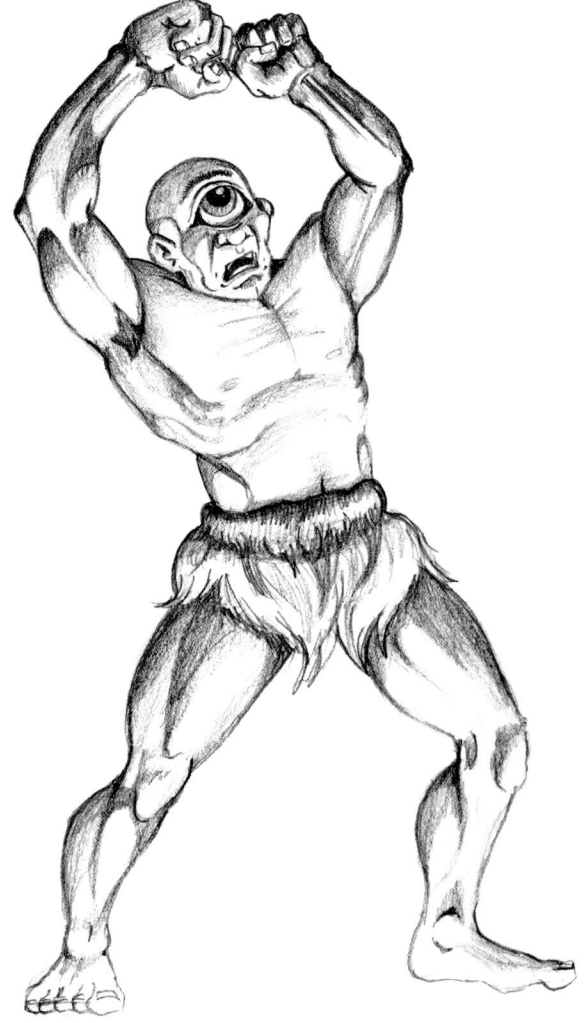

5. With the 2B pencil, shade and detail the face, saving the darkest values for the curving eyebrow and the large pupil. Then continue to add tone to the rest of the body. Make the shadows on the upper body darker than those on the lower body, which is closer to the light source. Using a very sharp point, render long, wispy hair on the loincloth, curving around the thighs.

6. Refine the bottoms of the legs and the feet, separating the toes and drawing large toenails. Add curved shadows on the calves to make them bulge. Then add tone to the tops of the feet.

To finish, use a sharpened 2B and add patches of hair to the arms, the top of the head, the chest, the torso, and the legs. You can even add some stubble to the tops of the feet!

See page 104 for the finished drawing.

Gargoyle: Another Nonhuman Being

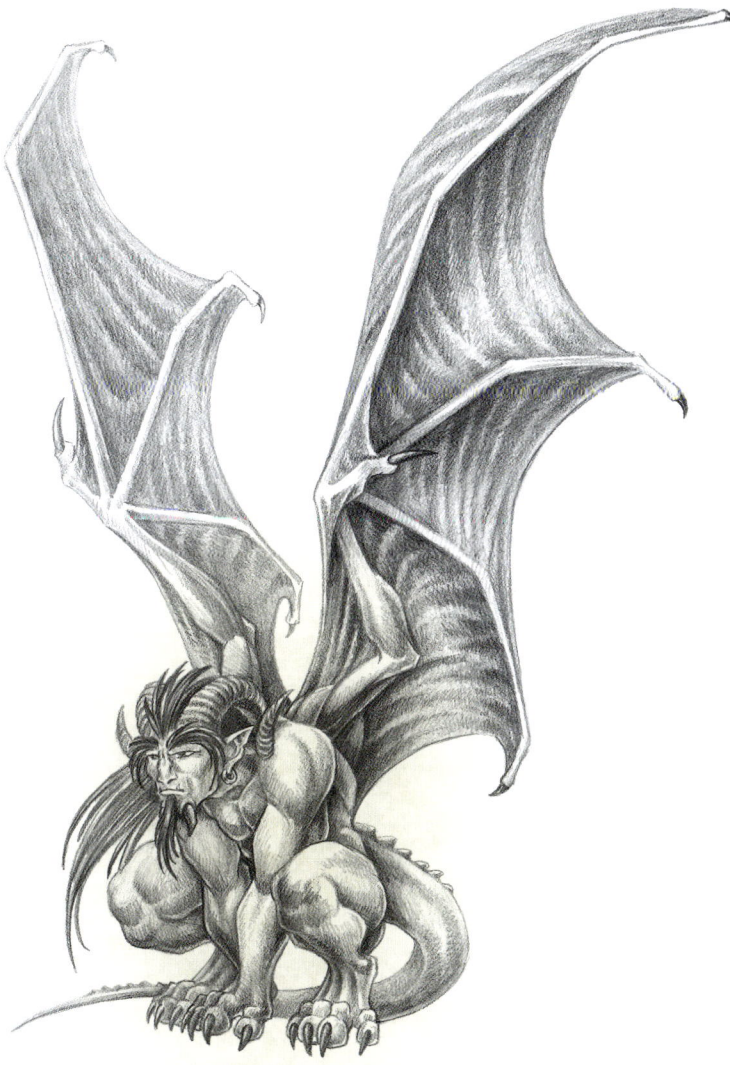

LORE & LEGENDS

† Perched high on rooftops and cornices, gargoyles silently watch over the world below, their grotesque faces and fearsome forms believed to ward off evil spirits and protect the buildings they inhabit.

† Despite their monstrous appearance—which often leads them to be misunderstood as sinister beings—gargoyles are, in fact, staunch guardians, created to defend sacred and important places from malevolent forces.

† In mythology, gargoyles are said to turn to stone during the day, either by choice or by magical compulsion, and come alive at night, when they prowl rooftops and ramparts to keep watch.

† The tradition of gargoyles dates back to the ancient world—in Egypt, gargoyle-like spouts were used to eject water from temple rooftops after ritual washings of sacred vessels.

† The name itself comes from the French word *gargouille*, meaning "throat," a nod to their original purpose as decorative rainspouts channeling water away from buildings. Similar statues that serve no drainage function are known as "grotesques."

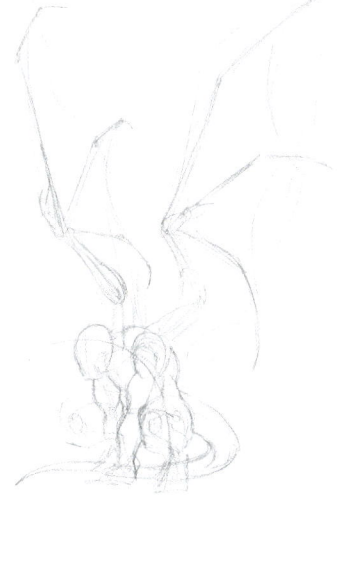

ARCHITECTURAL DIFFERENCES

In architecture, the term "gargoyle" refers to carved waterspouts that direct excess water off rooftops (far left). Nonfunctional statues of these beasts are called "grotesques" (near left). Try your hand at drawing both!

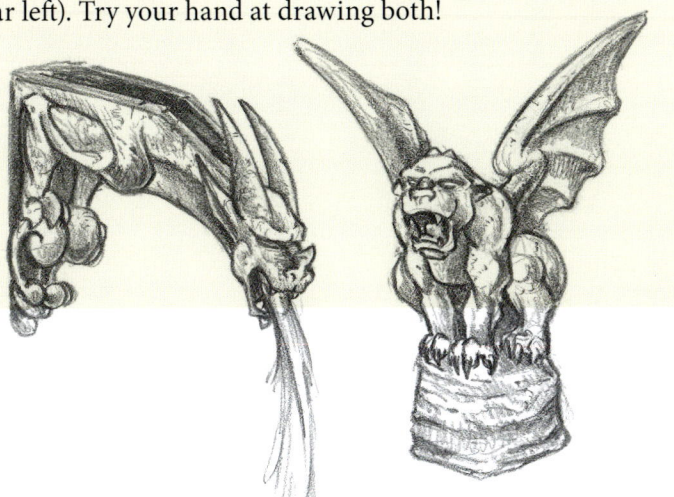

Sorcerer

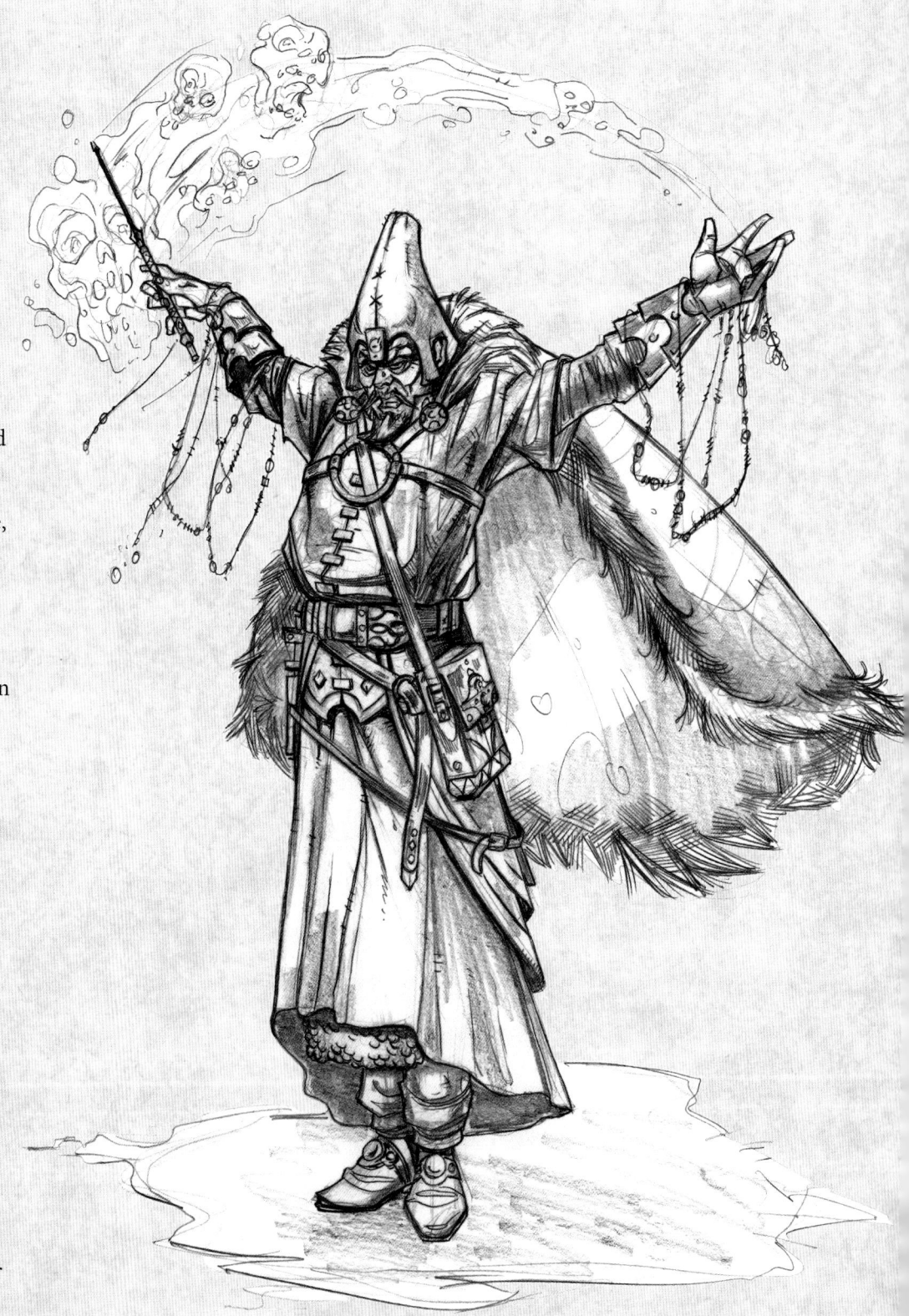

LORE & LEGENDS

† Magic users have appeared in myths and stories across cultures under many names— wizard, warlock, mage, and sorcerer among them—each wielding powers that transcend the natural world.

† A sorcerer may be born with innate magical talent or gain their abilities through years of study in arcane or occult lore, mastering the forces that allow them to bend reality, summon elements, or reshape fate.

† Because their strength lies in knowledge and supernatural skill, sorcerers rarely rely on physical might. Instead, they are often depicted with wands, staffs, enchanted books, elaborate robes, and dramatic hats—symbols of their mastery and focus.

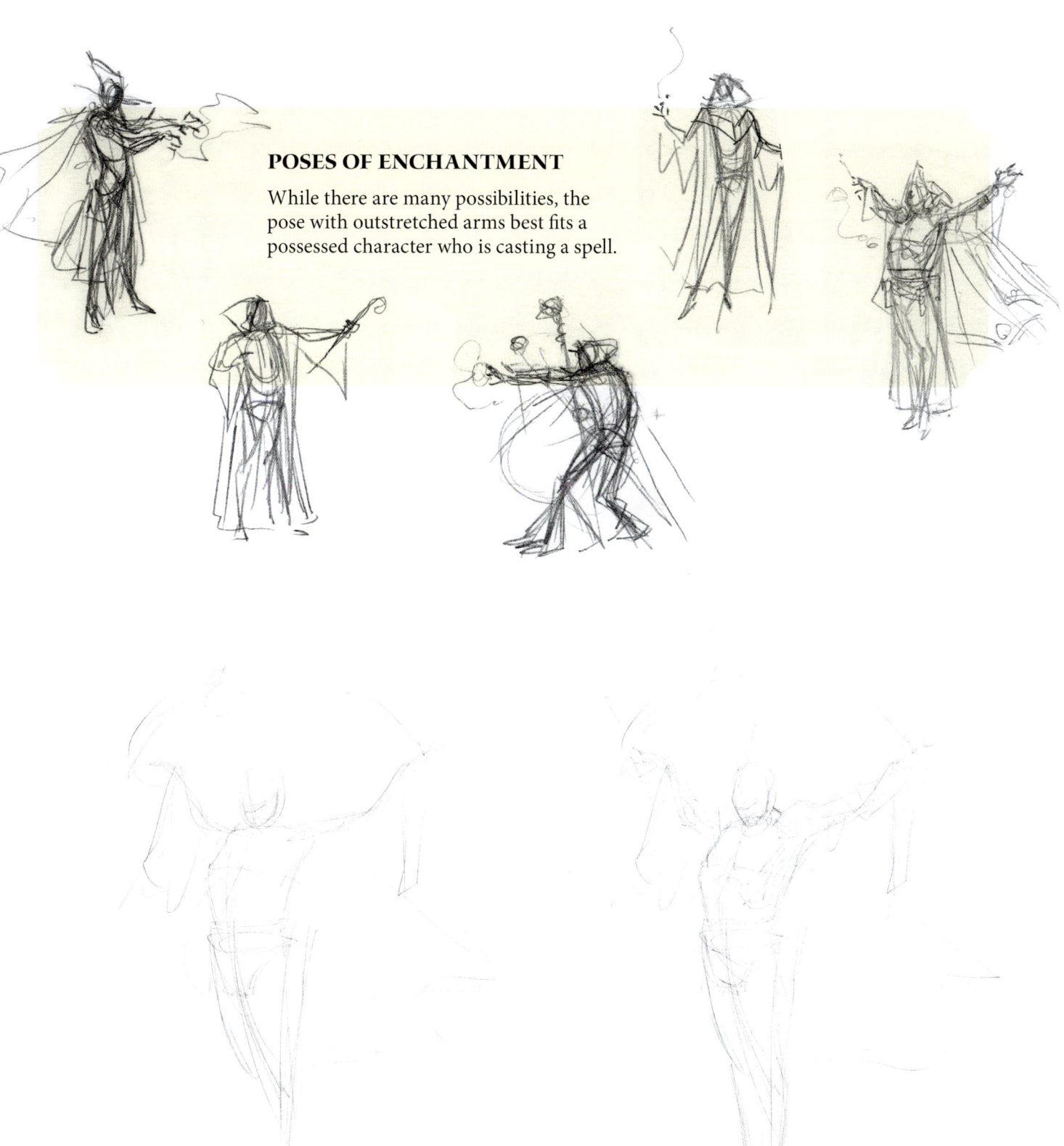

POSES OF ENCHANTMENT

While there are many possibilities, the pose with outstretched arms best fits a possessed character who is casting a spell.

1. Develop the thumbnail sketch with a 2H pencil, indicating the major shapes of the pose. Indicate the ellipses of the torso and the placement of the wand effect over his head.

2. Work lightly over the sketch to indicate the solid forms of the arms and legs and some other anatomy, to get a better idea of how the pose is working and how the proportions look.

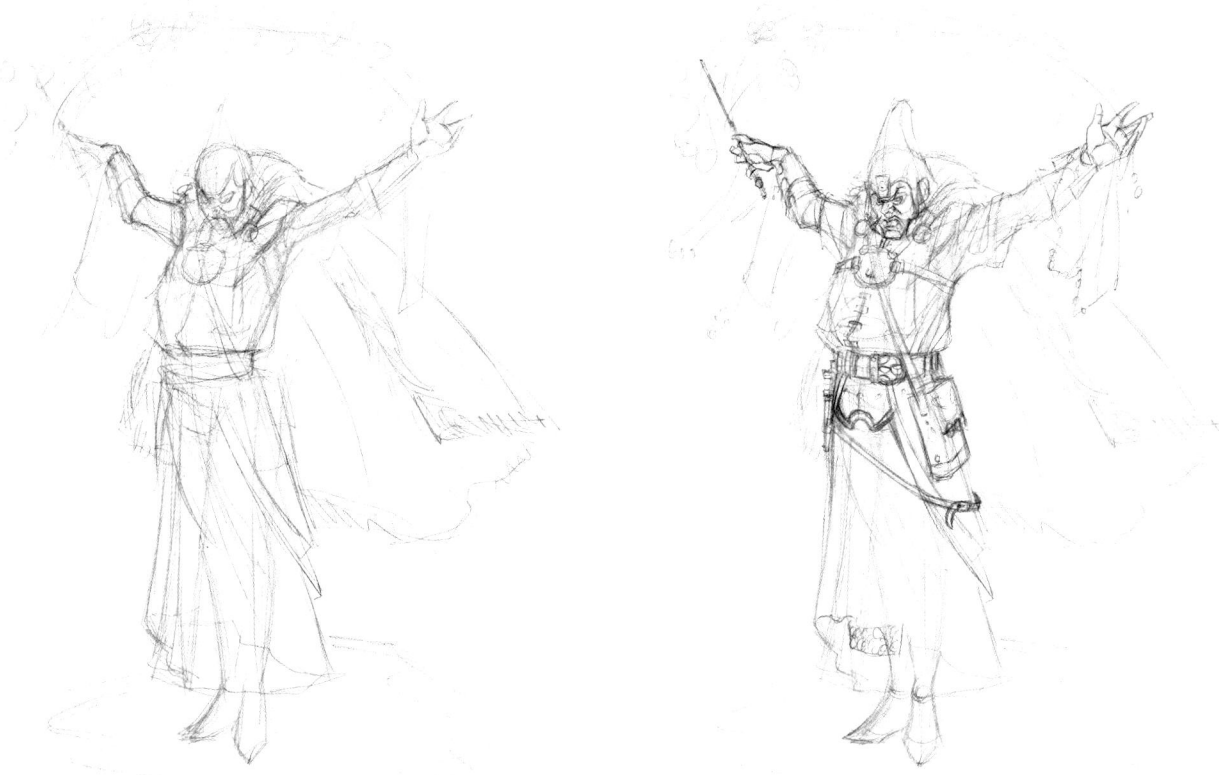

3. Create the structure of the skull and some more anatomy, especially in the shoulders and arms. Then use the side of the 2H to sketch the main areas of the costume. "Draw through" the forms of the body, making sure the costume wraps around them.

4. Pressing harder on the pencil, get more specific with the costume details and the visible anatomy. Then work on the facial expression, making it more sinister. Notice the ellipses around his arms (sleeves and bracers) and how they differ on each side of the body. Indicate a bunch of strung-together beads that may be part of the ritual.

5. Use the 2B pencil to lay in final lines. Starting with the feet, outline form, find plane breaks, indicate texture, and fill in smaller areas of shadow. Switch to the side of the 2H to fill in the shadow under the robe. The shapes around the wand effect look like skulls, so add some more lines to define them.

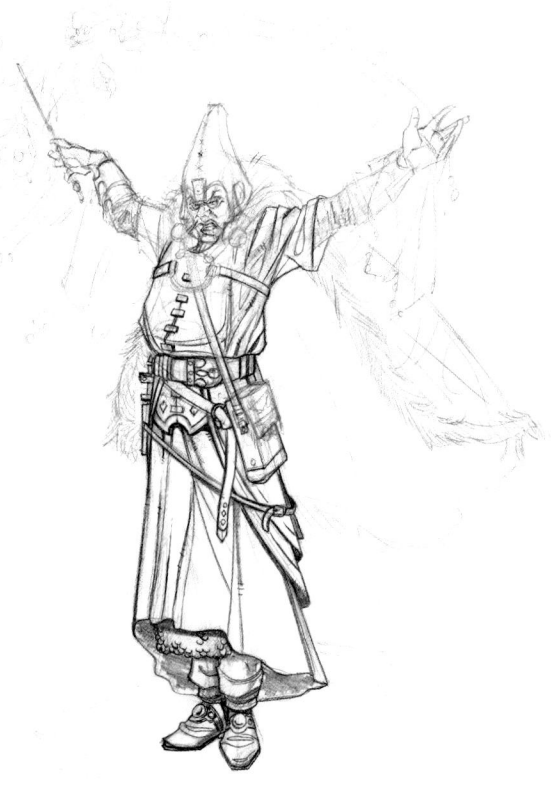

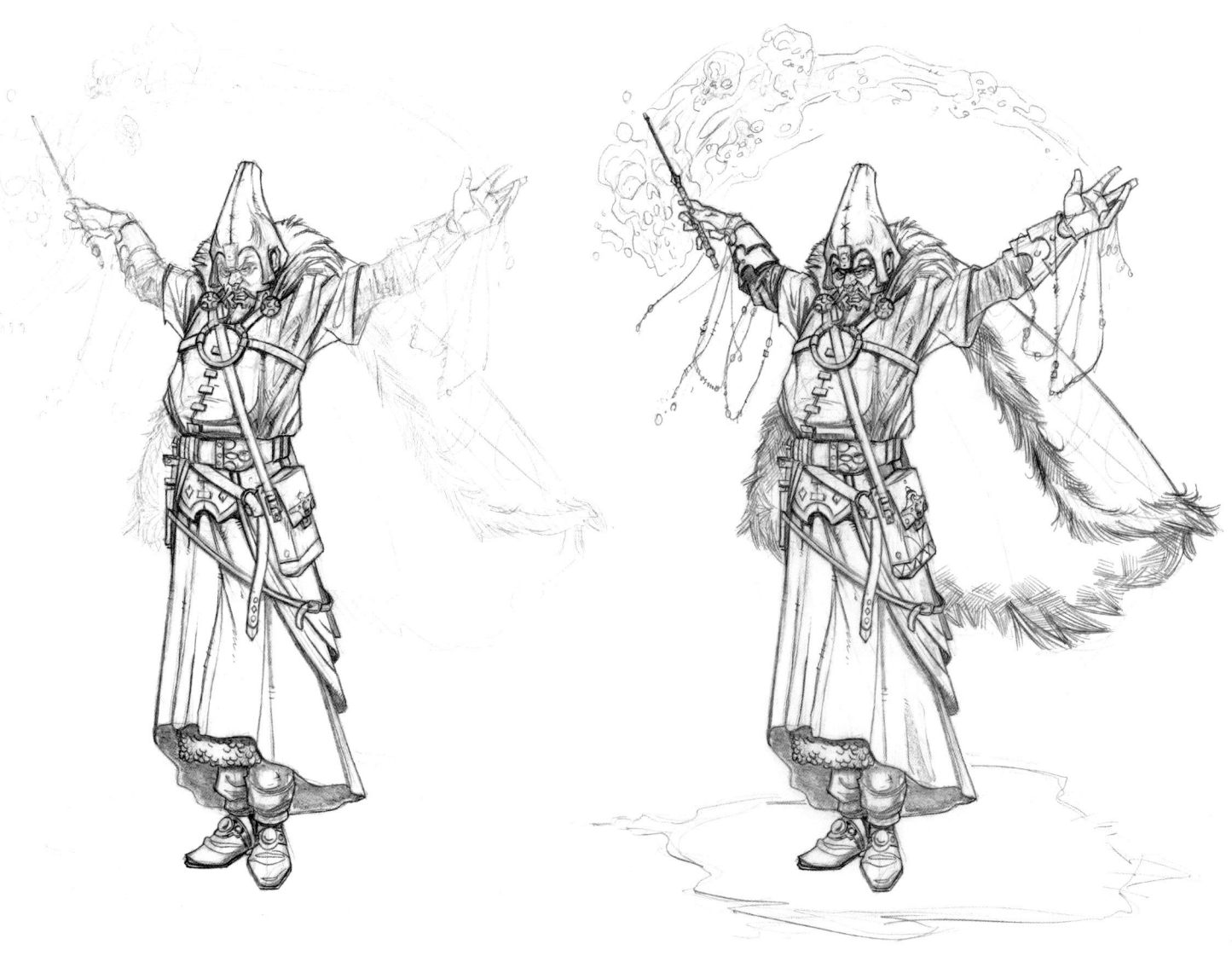

6. Working up toward the head, continue adding final lines to the details of the costume, including the bag that holds the spell book and the hat.

7. Finish outlining the figure, then use hatching to indicate the fur trim on the cape. Use a pencil with a very sharp point to darken the lines of the wand effect, which should be nice and thin.

To finish, use the side of the 2H to lay in some midtones and large shadow areas.

See page 108 for the finished drawing.

Vampire

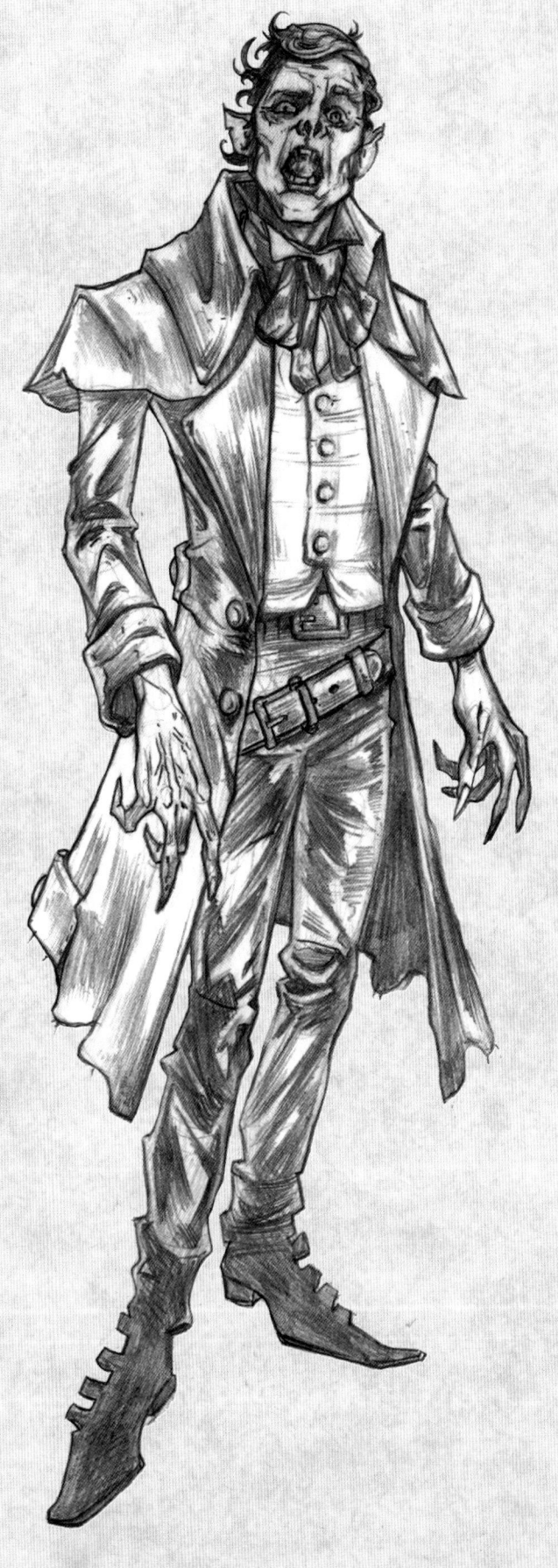

LORE & LEGENDS

✝ Vampires are the risen dead who have been cursed by the bite of another vampire (or other means) and can only derive sustenance from the blood of the living.

✝ Modern Western folklore holds that most vampires are charming and elegant with an air of decrepit age and ancient evil. At their best, vampires are able to attract and repulse victims at the same time.

✝ Depictions of vampires greatly vary in popular culture, and the bloodsucking undead are used as analogies for all sorts of human behavior. As story elements, they possess a seemingly endless well of melodrama built into the conflict between their once human existence and their true vampire nature.

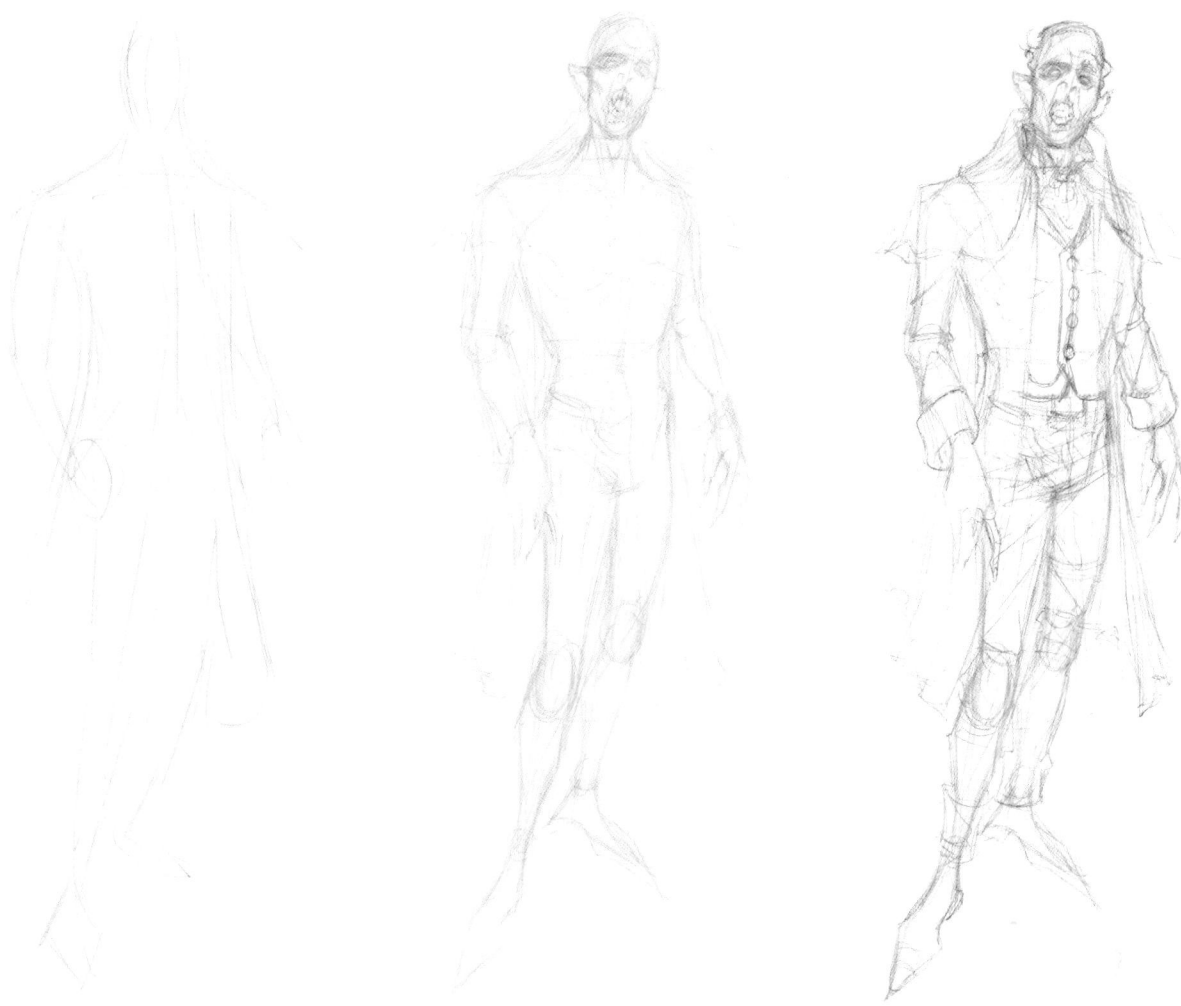

1. Lightly sketch the pose with a 2H pencil, starting with the centerline (or line of action) and a few lines to define the torso, legs, and arms. Aim for a general idea of the figure's proportions and position, without worrying about being too exact because things may move around a bit as you develop the character.

2. Adjust the angle of the head as needed, then start defining major areas of the figure, including the coat. This vampire character has a sinuous body with signs of age and atrophy, so the joints and bone structure are exaggerated, especially in the hands, feet, and face.

3. This vampire is wearing a coat from the Edwardian/Victorian era, with some details reminiscent of armor. The clothing should have a dapper and aged look. Start to develop the vampire's hair and facial expression.

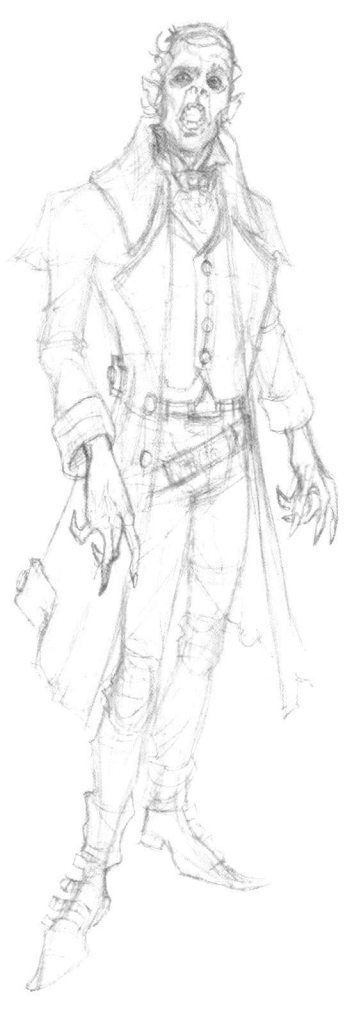
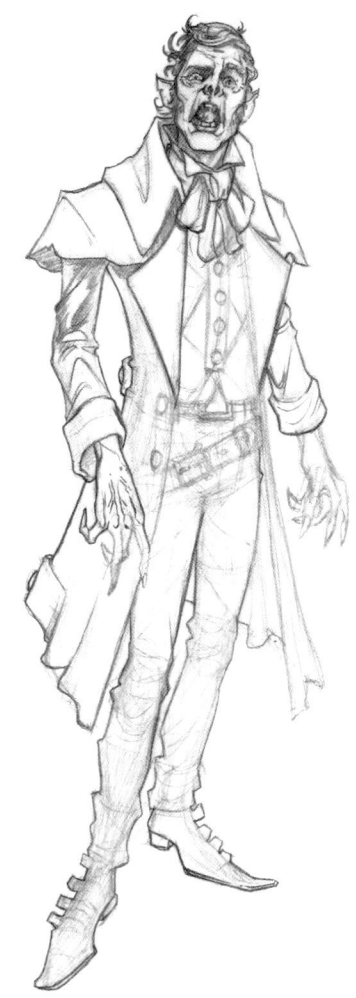
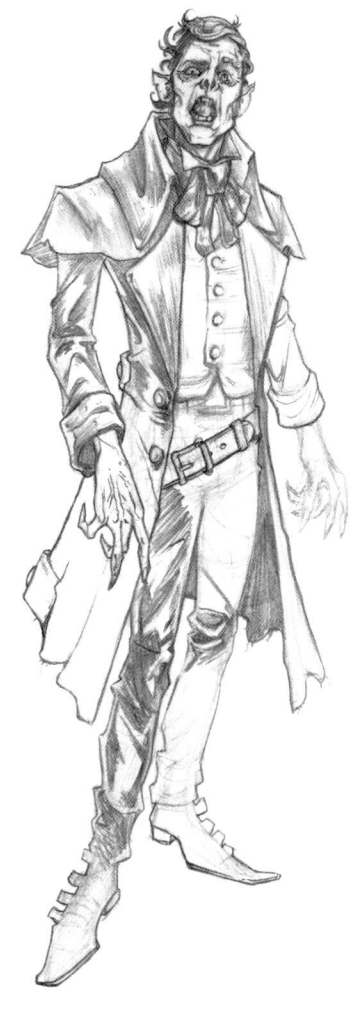

4. Use a 2H to develop the costume and figure. Focus on the facial expression and textures before placing final lines, as they'll be harder to erase. This vampire's hands should look aged and powerful, so the knuckles should be large, the veins prominent, and the fingers sharp. Then add details to the coat, pants, and shoes.

5. Switch to a 2B to start darkening lines and adding shadows, erasing construction lines as you go. Add curving lines to the hair to show motion. Try adding a check pattern to the vest, then adjust the shape and size of the bow at the neck.

6. Continue working up shadows and filling in dark areas of the clothing, leaving white areas for highlights. Add frayed edges to the coat to show age. If you decide you don't like the check pattern on the vest, remove it with a kneaded eraser (as shown here).

To finish, add details and refine the figure, making the vampire's fangs more prominent and the hands look especially veiny and ancient, with long, sharp nails. Use a plastic eraser to clean up edges and create more areas of highlights.

See page 112 for the finished drawing.

Vampire: Variation

A cloaked vampire inspired by the 1927 film Nosferatu.

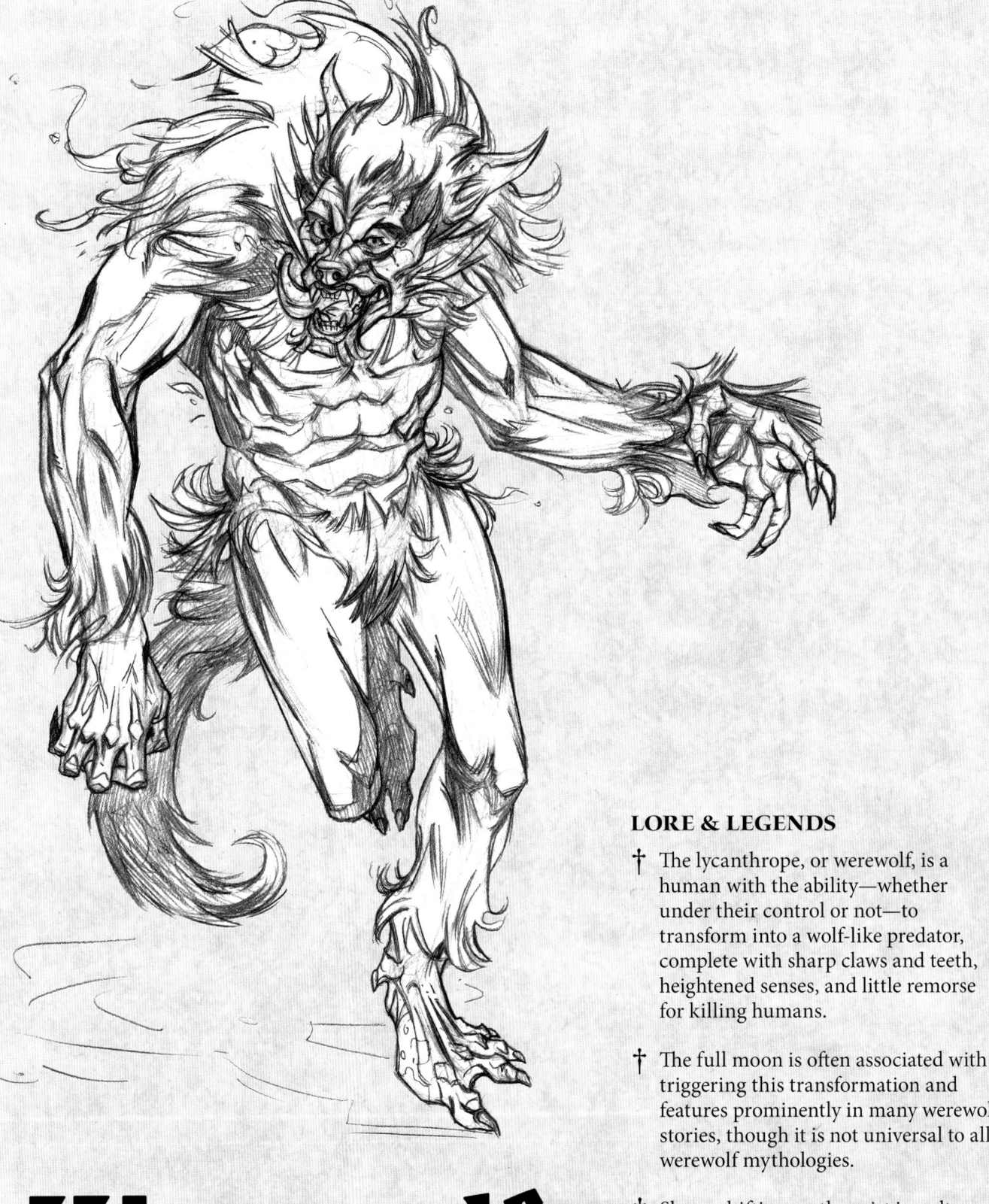

Werewolf

LORE & LEGENDS

† The lycanthrope, or werewolf, is a human with the ability—whether under their control or not—to transform into a wolf-like predator, complete with sharp claws and teeth, heightened senses, and little remorse for killing humans.

† The full moon is often associated with triggering this transformation and features prominently in many werewolf stories, though it is not universal to all werewolf mythologies.

† Shape-shifting myths exist in cultures around the world, depicting humans transforming into a variety of animal forms—wolves being among the most feared and enduring.

GESTURE SKETCHES

The loping run pose is deceptively casual yet threatening.

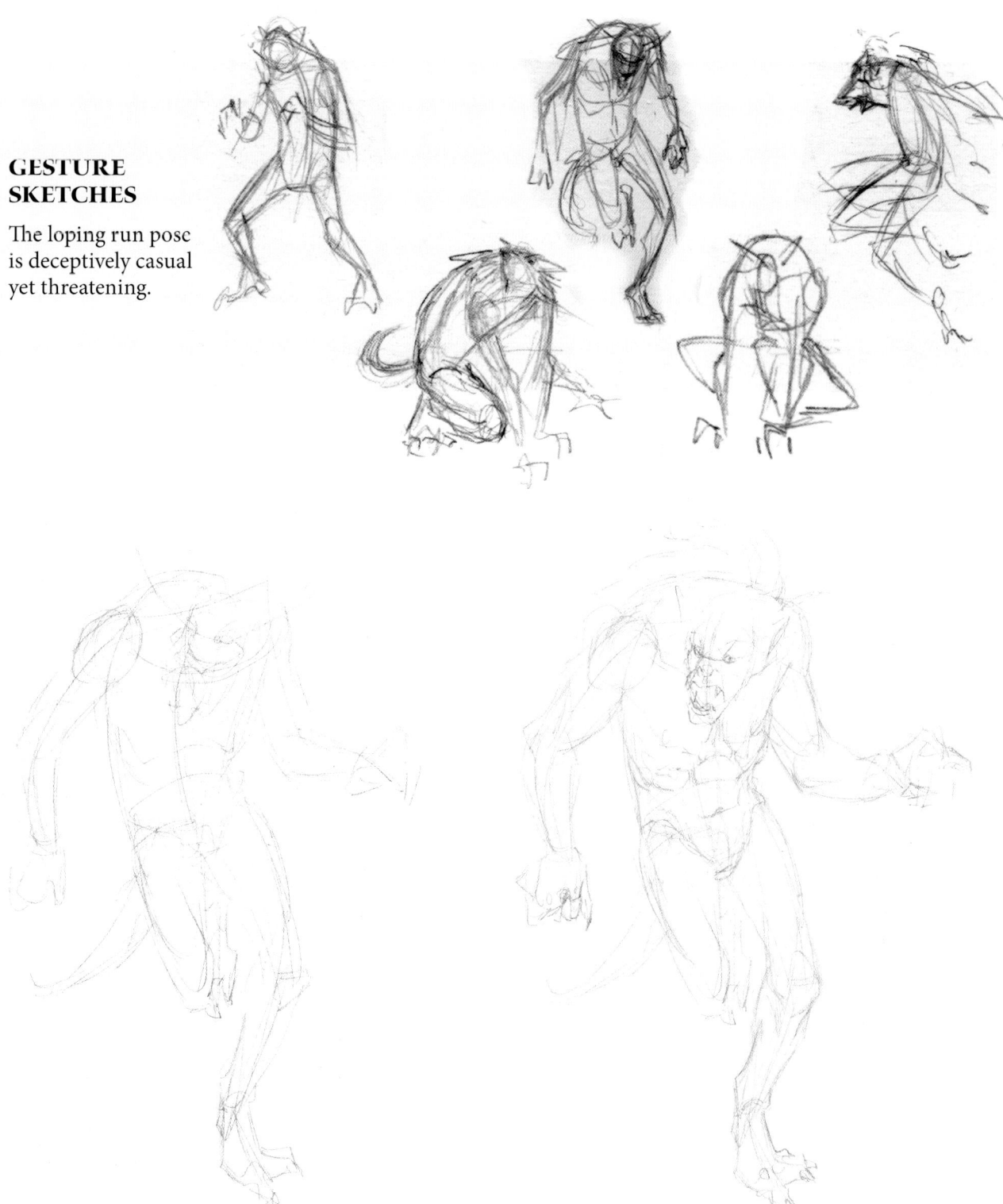

1. Trace the thumbnail shown (top, center), noting the movement of the spine, the relation of the hips to the shoulders, the placement of the limbs, and the distribution of the weight. With the 2H, start lightly drawing the major forms. In the featured thumbnail, the figure is running with his hands clawing through the air. The major forms of the head should indicate direction as well as expression.

2. Focus on the specific details, noting major muscles and anatomy, and begin to draw some of the surface anatomy. This character will be covered in fur, but make sure the underlying anatomy is solid before you start laying in fur patterns.

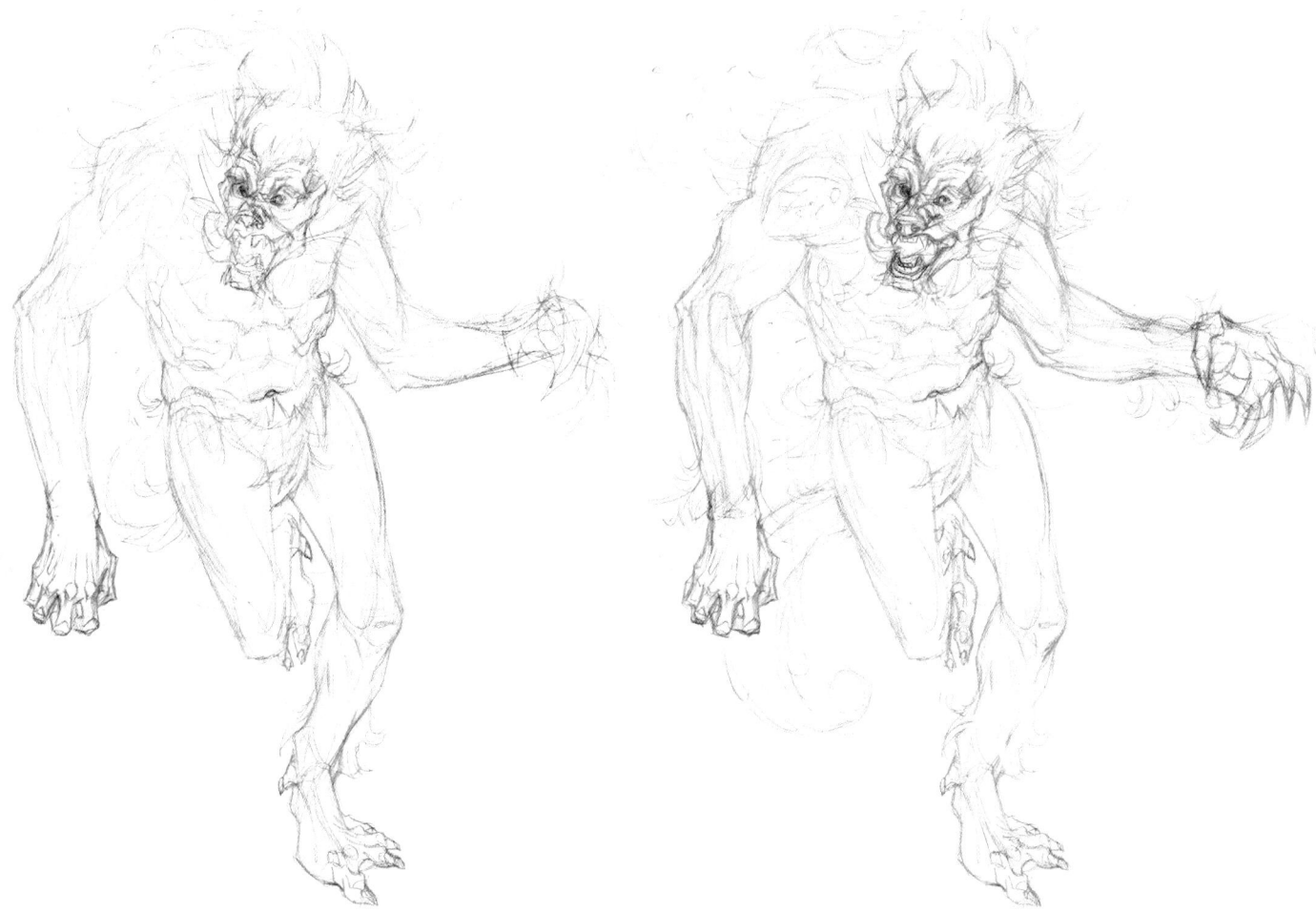

3. Starting with the face, go a step darker with the 2H, figuring out the personality of the beast. Begin to sketch the hair on the head and body. You can get a bit detailed here, placing the forms of the rib cage and surface muscles. The hands are important, as they convey the movement of the body.

4. Go back into the face, making it a bit more wolf-like by extending the muzzle and adding more details. Get more specific about the movement and placement of the longer hair. Add some flying bits of detritus to communicate movement, and reposition the tail to add to the flow of the figure. Make the raised hand a bit relaxed; he's not attacking now, but he could at any moment.

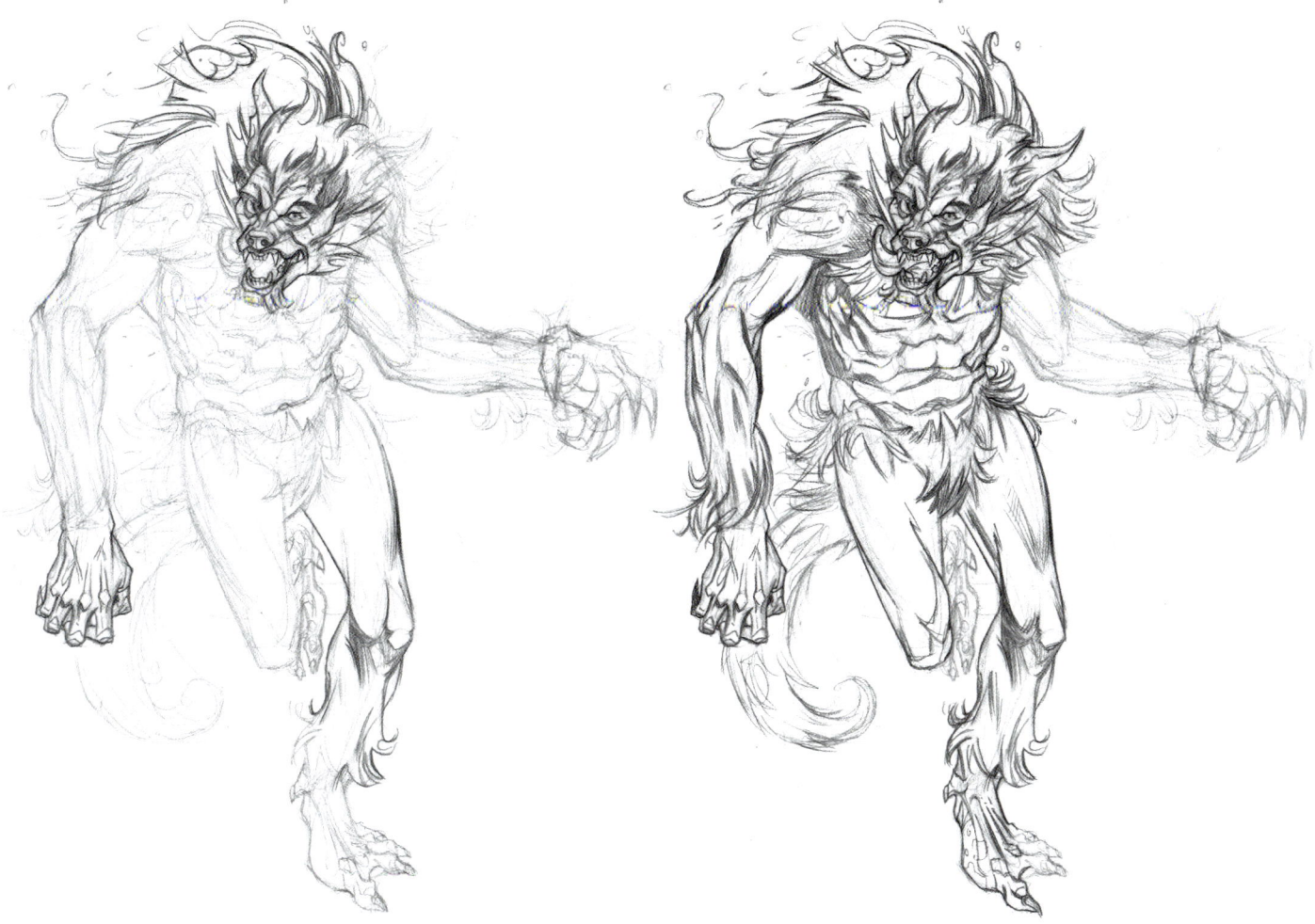

5. Start making your final lines with the 2B, beginning with the face and back and shoulder fur. Use the fur texture to accentuate the form, and make many sharp shapes in the fur to mimic the claws and teeth. Continue refining details, outlining edges and filling in shadows as needed.

6. In this step, focus on how the figure is lit (from above). Accentuate the powerful muscles, making the forearms a bit long to give the impression that the werewolf can run on all fours in a semi-upright position. Enhance the contrast of the flowing hair fur and the hard muscle forms by making interesting shapes in the hair.

Complete the rest of the figure and then go back to darken forms that recede, create cast shadows, and erase planes that face up and forward. Finally, place a few lines on the ground to indicate a cast shadow and some ground texture.

See page 116 for the finished drawing.

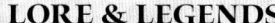

LORE & LEGENDS

† Mermaids, half human and half fish, are among the most enduring mythical beings in folklore, often dwelling in vast underwater kingdoms hidden beneath the waves.

† Both enchanting and perilous, they are known for luring sailors with their beauty and song, sometimes causing shipwrecks and accidents— or even squeezing the life from men in misguided attempts to "rescue" them.

† In other tales, mermaids are portrayed as naive and curious, forgetting that humans cannot breathe underwater and inadvertently bringing about their doom.

† Across cultures, mermaids embody the mystery and duality of the sea— beautiful yet deadly, compassionate yet indifferent, protectors of the ocean and symbols of its unpredictable power.

Mermaid

CHANGING TAILS

Most merfolk are given tails with horizontally oriented flukes that resemble a dolphin's tail in shape and size. However, that doesn't preclude the possibility of giving your merfolk other types of tails, such as shark, eel, octopus, and squid tails. Note that in the examples at right the mermaid with the fish tail looks smoother and more fluid than the merman with the shark tail does, but the shark tail is still visually interesting.

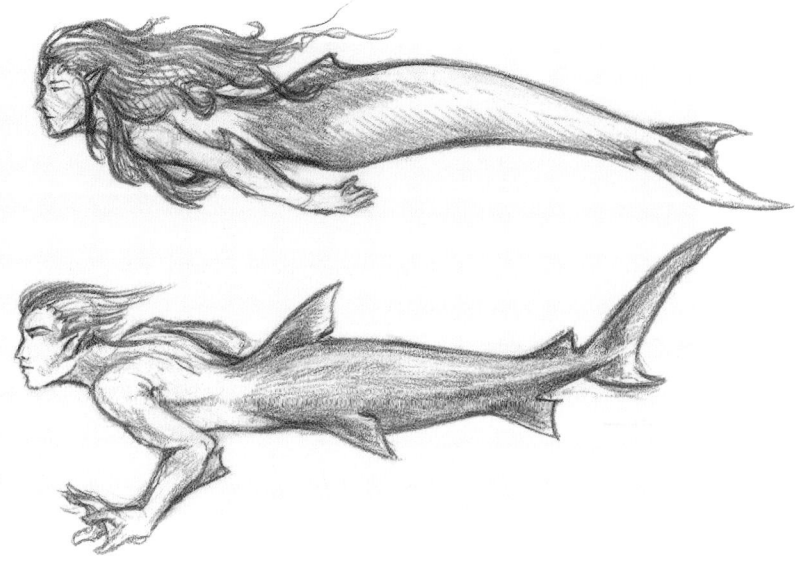

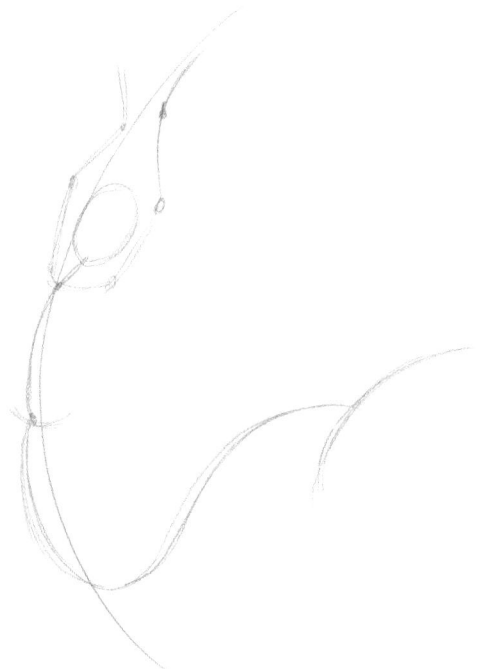

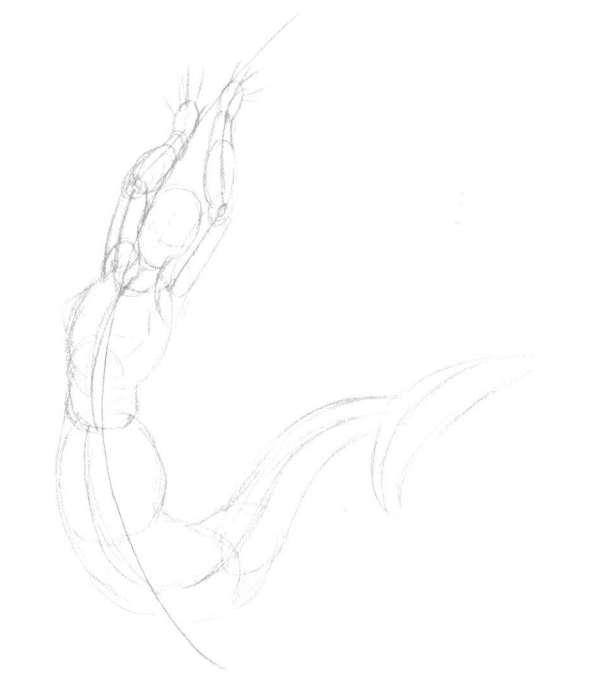

1. Start by drawing a curved line of action to show the mermaid's arched pose, then build the rough stick figure over it, drawing the arms so that they're raised above the head. Draw a curved line to suggest the length and motion of the tail; the perpendicular line at the end of the tail shows where the tail ends and roughly indicates the angle of the flukes. Note the length of the tail: In terms of proportion, her tail would be at least as long, if not longer, than her legs would be if she were human. Keep this in mind so that your merfolk appear to have sufficient strength and power in their anatomy to propel them through the water.

2. With an HB pencil and basic shapes, sketch the mermaid's form over the stick figure, using large forms to indicate areas of muscle mass. Avoid making any angles or sharp bends in her tail; its bones are most likely a continuation of her spine, so a sharp, angular bend in the tail would look unnatural—like a human wearing a mermaid costume. Keeping the curves of the tail smooth visually drives home the point that a mermaid is anatomically different from a land-dwelling human.

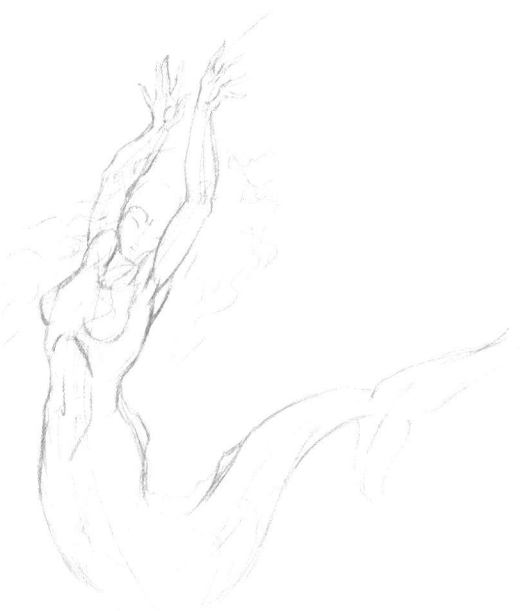

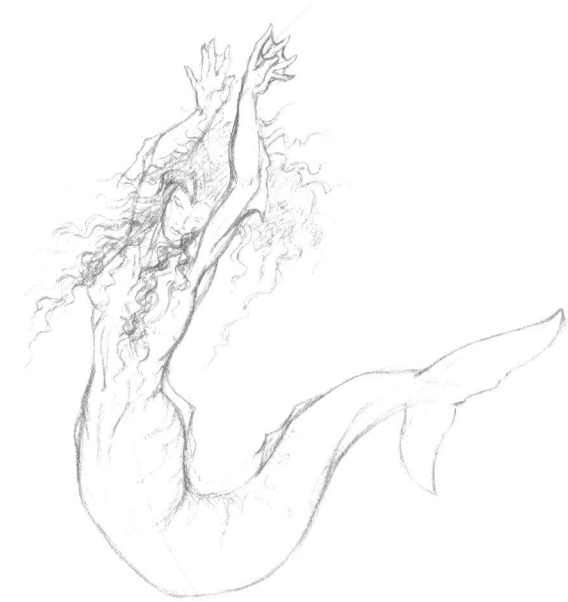

3. Once you're satisfied with the figure's overall shape, begin to define the forms by sketching specific groups of muscles and curves. Use basic marks to indicate the facial features, draw the flukes of the tail, and add details to her long fingers. Then block in the general shape of her hair. Because she's suspended in water, keep your strokes very loose and free to suggest the way the hair floats around her and defies gravity, though you draw it with somewhat of a downward sweep to show that it still has some weight and buoyancy. Draw a rough line to indicate a ridge along the base of her spine and the top of her tail.

4. Still using the HB pencil, further refine the details. Draw the eyes, eyebrows, nose, and mouth, and refine the shape of her face. Add webbing between her outstretched fingers and sketch fins on her elbows. Then add more definition to her hair, making it curly. There's a lot of hair, so add a flat layer of shading to help keep track of what's there. Lightly sketch some loose marks along her tail to suggest the markings.

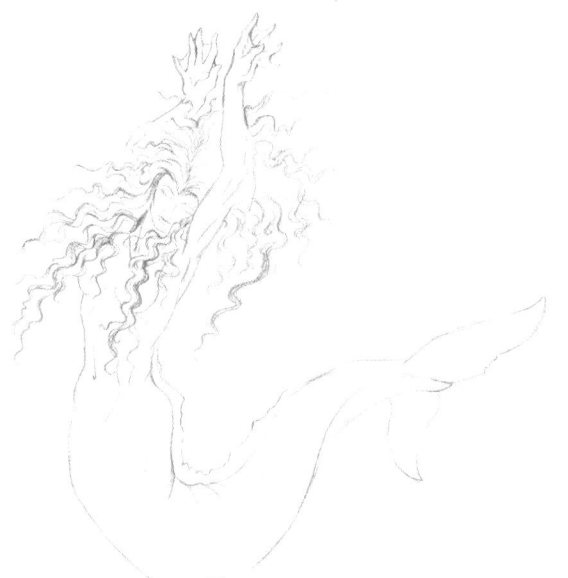

5. Once you're happy with your sketch, transfer it to a clean sheet of paper, using a light table if desired. Be especially careful when transferring the lines for the mermaid's hair. It's probably the most complex part of the image, as there are so many lines for the different bunches of hair. This requires a lot of patience, so take your time with it. Omit the markings on the tail for now so you can lay down a base of shading on the tail before rendering the details. Use the sketch from step 4 as a reference for the markings later.

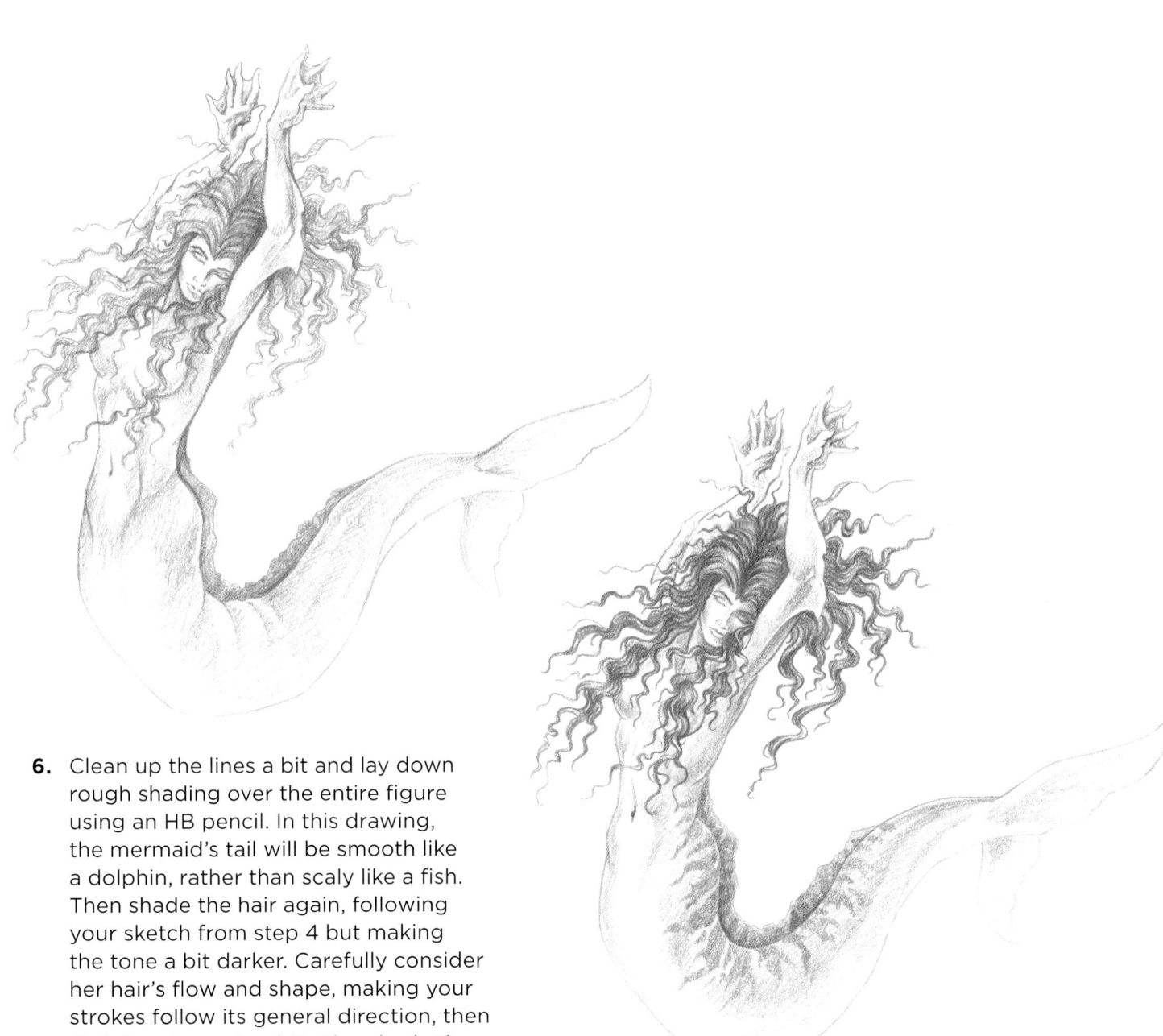

6. Clean up the lines a bit and lay down rough shading over the entire figure using an HB pencil. In this drawing, the mermaid's tail will be smooth like a dolphin, rather than scaly like a fish. Then shade the hair again, following your sketch from step 4 but making the tone a bit darker. Carefully consider her hair's flow and shape, making your strokes follow its general direction, then defining the curls a bit. Also shade the ridge on her tail so that it's darker than the rest of the tail.

7. Continue using an HB pencil to shade the figure, blending and smoothing the tone with a kneaded eraser. Use a softer 2B pencil to darken the hair further, still using strokes that follow the direction of the hair growth to keep it looking smooth. Spend a lot of time on the hair, emphasizing some curls and smoothing out others. Moving to the face, carefully shade around the features. Add long fingernails that almost look like claws, and indicate some folds in the webbing between her fingers. Refer to your sketch in step 4 and use a 2B pencil to create the markings on the torso and tail. Add some darker areas along the ridge of the tail to give it form and texture.

8. Use the HB and 2B pencils to continue refining the shading on the tail, which is darker on top and fades into white on the underside. Use a kneaded eraser and the HB pencil to shade the lightest areas, and the 2B to blend the tone into the darker shadows. Returning to the hair, use the 2B pencil and an even softer 4B pencil to make the hair even darker, deepening the shadows in the curls. Then use a kneaded eraser and a very small plastic stick eraser to lift out some highlights in the hair. Using the 2B and HB pencils, add more floating tendrils of hair, which helps make the hair look less like a solid mass. Next use the 2B pencil to darken the markings on the torso and tail, adding shadows where they follow the curve of the body. Mold a kneaded eraser into a narrow wedge shape and carefully lift out a line along the top edge of the tail to show where the light is hitting. Then use the small stick eraser to erase a very fine line where the brightest highlight hits, making the tail look slick and shiny. Finally, use the 2B pencil to create the deepest shadows on the ridge of the tail, and use an eraser to lift out some very light highlights on the ridge.

FISHY FEATURES

In addition to giving your creature a tail, it's a good idea to incorporate other fishlike features to make your drawing more believable. Perhaps your creature is naturally bald, which helps it move more easily through water. Or maybe it has fins and frills in lieu of hair, as in the example near right. You could also try making its ears finlike, as seen far right. Consider what kinds of markings your creature will have—looking at pictures of tropical fish will provide inspiration. The more you let Mother Nature's influence touch your work, the more believable and natural your creatures will seem.

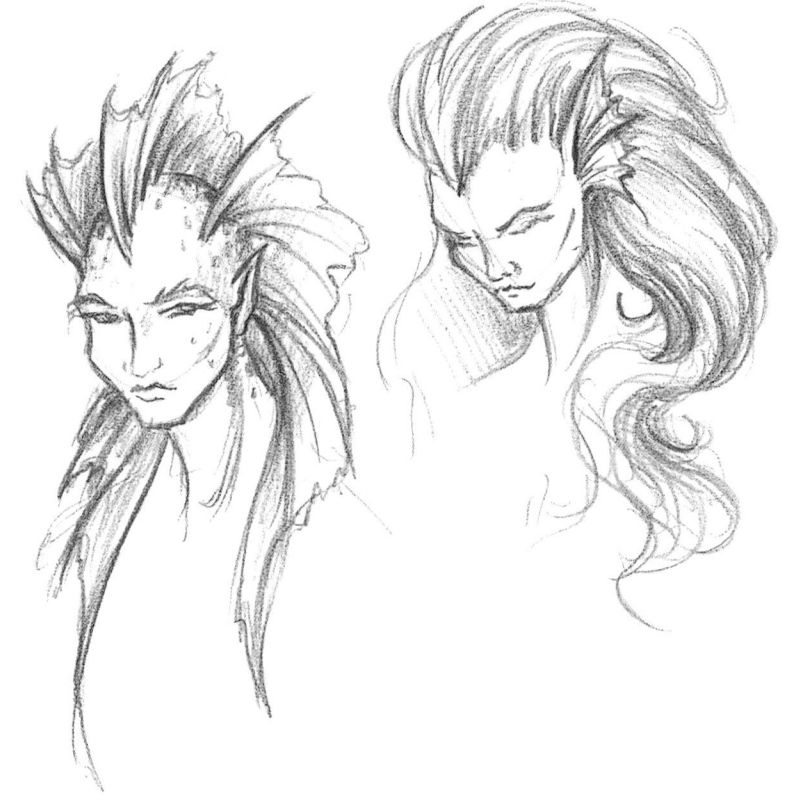

About the Artists

Michael Dobrzycki is an accomplished painter, carpenter, puppet maker, and sketch artist whose work has been featured in more than a dozen children's books and small press publications over the last few years. In 2001, Michael was inducted into the Disneyland Entertainment Hall of Fame. He received a master's degree in illustration from California State University, Fullerton, and holds bachelor's degrees in both art and history from Whittier College. He is currently a visiting professor at Whittier College. Michael lives in Whittier, California.

Kythera of Anevern is a self-taught artist who revels in the strange and unusual. She has designed a handful of logos for small businesses and contributed illustrations for various role-playing game books. She also displays her work at fantasy and animation conventions, including the annual Gathering of the Gargoyles, where she has won many awards. She received her BFA in intermedia from Arizona State University and currently lives in Los Angeles.

After earning a Bachelor of Fine Arts in Illustration from California State University, Long Beach, professional illustrator **Jacob Glaser** created storyboards, concept art, packaging, graphics, logos, animation, and illustrative art for entertainment, design, and advertising projects. Currently, he is based in Los Angeles with his wife and son and working as an art director at Park County (creators of *South Park*), painting whenever he can. He believes in aliens, ghosts, and all sorts of magical nonsense—possibly because he played Dungeons and Dragons too often in high school.

Brynn Metheney is a concept artist specializing in creature and character designs for film, games, and publishing. Her clients include Sony Pictures, Dark Horse Comics, Disney Publishing, Dreamscape Immersive, Warner Bros., and Wizards of the Coasts, and she has been involved with such projects as Luc Besson's *Valerian and the City of a Thousand Planets*, Warner Bros.'s *Scooby-Doo*, and Boots Riley's *Sorry to Bother You*. Brynn also teaches creature design at Otis College of Art and Design in Los Angeles, California, and The Animation Workshop in Viborg, Denmark. She lives in the greater Los Angeles area.

Index

Quarto.com
WalterFoster.com

Published in 2026 by Walter Foster Publishing, an imprint of The Quarto Group, 100 Cummings Center, Suite 265-D, Beverly, MA 01915, USA.
T (978) 282-9590 F (978) 283-2742

EEA Representation, WTS Tax d.o.o., Žanova ulica 3, 4000 Kranj, Slovenia.
www.wts-tax.si

Walter Foster Publishing titles are also available at discount for retail, wholesale, promotional, and bulk purchase. For details, contact the Special Sales Manager by email at specialsales@quarto.com or by mail at The Quarto Group, Attn: Special Sales Manager, 100 Cummings Center, Suite 265-D, Beverly, MA 01915, USA.

30 29 28 27 26   1 2 3 4 5

ISBN: 978-1-5771-5842-4

Digital edition published in 2026
eISBN: 978-1-5771-5843-1

Library of Congress Cataloging-in-Publication Data available

Content compiled from the following titles: *Art of Drawing Dragons* by Michael Dobrzycki (9781600580123); *The Art of Drawing Fantasy Characters* by Jacob Glaser (9781600581663); *Dragons & Fantasy* by Kythera of Anevern (9781600580680); *Draw Like an Artist: 100 Fantasy Creatures and Characters* by Brynn Metheney (9781631599644)

Design and page layout: Cindy Samargia Laun
Front cover art © Michael Dobrzycki
Back cover art © Joana Contreras (Kythera of Anevern)

Printed in Guangdong, China TT032026